The Poetry
of Charles Tomlinson

Charles Tomlinson
Photo by Joachim K. Utz

The Poetry of Charles Tomlinson
Border Lines

Judith P. Saunders

Madison • Teaneck
Fairleigh Dickinson University Press
London: Associated University Presses

© 2003 by Rosemont Publishing & Printing Corp.

All rights reserved. Authorization to photocopy items for internal or personal use, or the internal or personal use of specific clients, is granted by the copyright owner, provided that a base fee of $10.00, plus eight cents per page, per copy is paid directly to the Copyright Clearance Center, 222 Rosewood Drive, Danvers, Massachusetts 01923. [0-8386-3976-3/03 $10.00 + 8¢ pp, pc.]

Associated University Presses
2010 Eastpark Boulevard
Cranbury, NJ 08512

Associated University Presses
Unit 304
The Chandlery
50 Westminster Bridge Road
London SE1 7QY, England

Associated University Presses
P.O. Box 338, Port Credit
Mississauga, Ontario
Canada L5G 4L8

The paper used in this publication meets the requirements of the American National Standard for Permanence of Paper for Printed Library Materials Z39.48-1984.

Library of Congress Cataloging-in-Publication Data

Saunders, Judith P.
　The poetry of Charles Tomlinson : border lines / Judith P. Saunders.
　　p.　cm.
　Includes bibliographical references and index.
　ISBN 0-8386-3976-3 (alk. paper)
　1. Tomlinson, Charles, 1927—Criticism and interpretation.　I. Title.
PR6039.O349 Z84　2003
821'.914—dc21
　　　　　　　　　　　　　　　　　　　　　　　　　　　　2002151741

PRINTED IN THE UNITED STATES OF AMERICA

in memory of Robert Edward and Helen Brinkman Prichard

Contents

Acknowledgments	9
List of Abbreviations	11
Introduction	15
1. Elemental Demarcation	19
2. Cultural and Historical Boundaries	41
3. Contrapuntal Designs	69
4. Perceptual Boundaries	102
5. Graphic Framing	125
6. Contiguity and Conjunction	148
Notes	172
Works Cited	187
General Index	192
Index of Poems by Charles Tomlinson	194

Acknowledgments

THIS PROJECT WAS SUPPORTED BY A SUMMER RESEARCH GRANT AND A sabbatical leave from Marist College. Thanks are due to my colleague Louise Poresky for editorial advice concerning drafts of chapters 3 and 5. For first introducing me to the work of Charles Tomlinson I am grateful to Professor Donald Wesling of the University of California at San Diego. Thanks are also due to Charles Tomlinson himself, who has responded graciously to queries and provided useful background information.

Parts of chapter 5 of the present work appeared in a slightly different version in *Sagetrieb* 14, no. 3 (1995): 107–18, copyright 1997 by the National Poetry Foundation, under the title "Shifting Perspectives and a Moving Frame: Charles Tomlinson and the Automobile." Discussions of the poems "Byzantium" and "Crossing Brooklyn Ferry," in chapters 2 and 6, respectively, of the present work, appeared in slightly different versions in *The Arkansas Quarterly* 2, no. 1 (1993): 30–41, copyright 1993 by Epiphany Publications, in an article titled "Charles Tomlinson and the Art of Sustained Allusion."

Grateful acknowledgment is made to Charles Tomlinson and to Carcanet Press for permission to reprint and quote from copyrighted materials in the following works: *Collected Poems* (Oxford and New York: Oxford University Press, 1987); *The Return* (Oxford and New York: Oxford University Press, 1987); *Annunciations* (Oxford and New York: Oxford University Press, 1989); *The Door in the Wall* (Oxford and New York: Oxford University Press, 1992); *Jubilation* (Oxford and New York: Oxford University Press, 1995); *The Vineyard Above the Sea* (Manchester: Carcanet, 1999).

List of Abbreviations: Works by Charles Tomlinson

A   *Annunciations*. Oxford: Oxford University Press, 1989.
AS   *American Scenes and Other Poems*. 1966. In *The Collected Poems*. Rev. ed. Oxford: Oxford University Press, 1987.
DW   *The Door in the Wall*. Oxford: Oxford University Press, 1992.
F   *The Flood*. 1981. In *The Collected Poems*. Rev. ed. Oxford: Oxford University Press, 1987.
J   *Jubilation*. Oxford: Oxford University Press, 1995.
N   *The Necklace*. 1955. In *The Collected Poems*. Rev. ed. Oxford: Oxford University Press, 1987.
NNY   *Notes from New York and Other Poems*. 1984. In *The Collected Poems*. Rev. ed. Oxford: Oxford University Press, 1987.
PL   *A Peopled Landscape*. 1963. In *The Collected Poems*. Rev. ed. Oxford: Oxford University Press, 1987.
PP   "The Poet as Painter." In *Eden: Graphics and Poetry*. Bristol: Redcliffe, 1985.
R   *The Return*. Oxford: Oxford University Press, 1987.
S   *The Shaft*. 1978. In *The Collected Poems*. Rev. ed. Oxford: Oxford University Press, 1987.
SIB   *Seeing Is Believing*. 1960. In *The Collected Poems*. Rev. ed. Oxford: Oxford University Press, 1987.
VS   *The Vineyard Above the Sea*. Manchester: Carcanet, 1999.
WI   *The Way In and Other Poems*. 1974. In *The Collected Poems*. Rev. ed. Oxford: Oxford University Press, 1987.
WrW   *Written on Water*. 1972. In *The Collected Poems*. Rev. ed. Oxford: Oxford University Press, 1987.
WW   *The Way of a World*. 1969. In *The Collected Poems*. Rev. ed. Oxford: Oxford University Press, 1987.

The Poetry
of Charles Tomlinson

Introduction

Edges are centres

IN A CAREER NOW SPANNING NEARLY FIFTY YEARS, CHARLES TOMLINSON has published more than fourteen books of poetry, garnering international recognition. He has been awarded prizes and honors both at home in the United Kingdom and internationally, particularly in the United States and in Italy. Widely travelled and widely read, he is in every sense a citizen of the world. History, mythology, literature, music, and the visual arts all provide impetus for his poetry, as does the physical world itself in both its human and nonhuman aspects. Equally passionate in his exploration of landscapes without and landscapes within, Tomlinson organizes his poems persistently around lines of demarcation: boundaries, frontiers, thresholds, frames.[1] In any scene he likes to draw readers' attention to the point at which two realms, literal or metaphoric, intersect. His poems define what lies on either side, investigating the implications of that contiguity and inviting a back-and-forth process of comparison and contrast. Thus a preoccupation with borders unifies his poetry both methodologically and thematically.

His chosen focus reflects his conviction that we live in a highly differentiated world, teeming with "variegated excess" ("Northern Spring" SIB).[2] He is endlessly fascinated by the boundaries upon which discrete identity depends, the interrelationships they necessarily define. "At one level, the issue is an ecological one," he comments; "at another level, it means chastening yourself by realizing your relationship to all that surrounds you."[3] His poems demonstrate, as Richard Swigg has noted, that "connections and relations . . . become most clearly visible when one also respects the separateness of things," i.e., "all that we must negotiate with and not assume."[4] Tomlinson recognizes that any line of convergence is simultaneously one of divergence, a place where two territories separate as well as the place where they come together. A border defines alien country, promising yet forbidding a view into something strange and new; it both inhibits and promotes acquaintanceship. Resonant with "the fascination of inside and outside," borders provide good opportunity to ponder resemblance and difference, meetings and partings, amity and enmity, in a cosmos characterized by spectacular diversity (PP 20).

Tomlinson offers explicit description of the possibilities and the paradox inherent in borders in a poem entitled "At the Edge." He writes:

> Edges are centres: once you have found
>   Their lines of force, the least of gossamers
> Leads and frees you, nets you a universe
>   Whose iridescent weave shines true
> Because you see it, but whose centre is not you:

(F)

Standing on the boundary line between two distinctly defined areas, we find ourselves at the outermost perimeter, or edge, of each, while at the same time we are centrally located, i.e., standing precisely in the middle of the two. Every edge is in fact the central point for viewing a landscape much larger than the area it bounds; and by opening up this larger perspective, it "frees" us from a stifling parochialism. Tomlinson rejoices in the multiple views of the world made possible by exploration of successive boundary lines. "He is intent," as Michael Hennessey puts it, "on recognizing the complexity of man's perceptual relationship with the world."[5] As each new edge becomes central in its turn, a whole new vision of the world emerges, "iridescent" with possibility. Tomlinson is concerned with more than sensory perception in the physical universe; his conclusions extend themselves without fanfare to the less concrete realm of psychologically or culturally induced boundaries. He is endorsing a spirit of perpetual open-mindedness, an ongoing quest to transcend the outermost limits of our experience, both literal and figurative. Not by ignoring these limits, but by savoring the particularities, the otherness, that they define and contain, can we best appreciate the complexity and variety of the world we inhabit.[6] Borders force us to see a different side to things. They prevent us from perceiving the world as undifferentiated sameness, and thus they rescue us from the monotony of egocentrism or "stale assumptions."[7]

"Hedgerows," a short poem set in Suffolk, England, invokes praise for borders with a blending of passion and whimsy characteristic of Tomlinson's poetic voice.

Hedgerows
for Peter Porter

In Suffolk they are no longer there:
    The post-modern landscape has gone medieval:
The stuff for the staff of life you townsmen
    Still lean on, Peter, flows up to the tarmac
An inland sea. Once they begin to disappear
    You see what an urbanity hedgerows are:
Feeling their way across the featureless land,
    Shutting out swamp and gripping the soil together,
They contain, compel as civilly as stanzas
    In the cultivator's poem of earth and sun
Where harvests fatten to be freighted up for London.

(NNY)

This poem bemoans the disappearance of the high hedges which for so long closely lined mile after mile of British countryside and roadways. Twentieth-century demands for faster, more efficient production and transport of goods have caused roads to be widened and re-routed, fields reconfigured, with consequent destruction of the lines of trees formerly bounding them. Tomlinson laments this "post-modern landscape," so obviously dedicated to the material comforts of an increasingly urban population. But he has more in mind than simple displacement of the old by the new. The hedgerows point to other kinds of meanings—aesthetic, philosophical, and moral—meanings that emerge clearly now in the hedges' absence. Hedgerows provide, for example, arrangement and design in an otherwise "featureless" landscape; they define the perimeters of tillable land, "shutting out swamp." They further embody "urbanity," the "civil" and civilizing concept of "contain[ment]." Here Tomlinson associates the hedgerows (and tolerance for slow, narrow roads) with virtues of politeness and self-control, e.g., the ability to wait one's turn or to abide convention—in short, a willingness to accept boundaries.[8] Modern priorities of speed and convenience appear mannerless in contrast, deriving from an undifferentiating spirit of consumption.

The analogy between hedgerows and poetic stanzas enables Tomlinson to enlarge the statement in his poem dramatically. Both hedgerows and stanzas "contain" and "compel": they arrange experience into patterns arbitrarily delimited; they form boundaries excluding many other ways of journeying, or ways of saying. Both these instances of patterned enclosure yield aesthetic pleasure, Tomlinson asserts, by imposing form.[9] No matter how much inconvenience is caused by working with the compulsions inherent in poem or hedgerow, enjoyment of the aesthetic pleasures they create is part of what makes us human. Their strictures may even be regarded as life-affirming acts of nourishment. "Gripping the soil together," hedgerows play a useful role in growing "the stuff for the staff of life." Tomlinson subtly suggests that the limits implicit in poetic form similarly act as a creative, cohesive force with respect to language, making possible the artfully compact utterance that is poetry. The nostalgia for hedgerows expressed in this brief poem bears witness wonderfully to the far-ranging import of border lines, illustrating their power to lend defining significance to interior as well as exterior space.

Because borders serve Tomlinson as formal and thematic principle throughout his career, the discussion that follows addresses the whole body of his work with little emphasis on chronology. As Michael Kirkham states, readers encounter "a tight web of intricate interconnections," a "continuous process of thought": "the poems speak to each other, and each poem means more by its relation to the whole."[10] Investigation of the profusion of boundaries to be found in the poems is organized according to type and function (e.g., spatial, temporal, ideological, perceptual, metaphysical) rather than year by year, or book by book.

1
Elemental Demarcation

The visible sea / Remains a sullen frontier to / Its unimaginable fathoms.

THE LANDSCAPE OF TOMLINSON'S POETRY IS DOMINATED BY SEAMS, MARgins, furrows, edges, frontiers, rims, cracks, limits, brinks, bounds, rents, rifts, and barriers. And of the innumerable border markers commanding his attention, those in the physical universe assume primacy; they underlie the countless demarcations—concrete and abstract, literal and metaphoric—that impart to his vision of the world much of its special character. He grounds his perceptions of the phenomenal world in an intense appreciation of elemental force and mass: fire, water, air, and earth, in their myriad manifestations.[1] He declares the central importance to his poetry of 'The Four Elements' in his essay "The Poet as Painter," discovering in the Midlands landscape of his childhood the origins of this preoccupation (PP 10).[2] As he traces visible margins in the world around him, he is drawn repeatedly to lines marking instances of elemental divergence and convergence. His poems take us to "the glacier's edge, eating at the track / That faltered past it . . . that faint line" ("The Glacier" NNY), or to "the tide-edge," "just where the bedrock forces water / To an instant of definition" ("Morwenna's Cliff" NNY). We watch "first light . . . / . . . among shadows / As the seam splits / At sky-level" ("Cloud Change" PL), see how "light's guarded frontier / Is glittering everywhere" ("In March" WI); we stand where "cliffs come sheering down into woodland" ("Casarola" S); we examine "the seam that runs sinewing England" ("Near Bickering" J) or "sudden / Fissuring along the mountain side" ("In Abruzzo" VS); we marvel at "a moonshell that . . . / . . . hangs / Fragile at the edge of visibility" ("After a Death" WI), a "skyline saw-toothed to raw angles" ("Legend" WrW). Often verb choice emphasizes the dramatic character of these powerful elemental conjunctions, e.g., *eating, forcing, splitting, sheering, sinewing, fissuring, saw-toothing*.

Such borders are charged with aesthetic excitement. In "Autumn" Tomlinson describes the skyline with a metaphor drawn from music, noting "a change of key where a hill / meets heaven" (J). Likening the pleasure we take in observing such a line of demarcation to the pleasure evoked by a shift in tone from one range of sounds to another, he reminds us that variety in sensory stimulation is a virtue in itself. We delight in experiencing difference, in recognizing distinctions. Thus his poems draw attention to junctions that bring into relief the aesthetic appeal of snow, rock, sun, wind, stream, or wave, as well as the strength. As the sky changes color at sunset, for example, vivid hues at the horizon provide a contrasting rim for the landscape: "This green twilight has violet borders" ("The Art of Poetry" N). Ordinary reeds growing in a pond command special attention when outlined simultaneously by water and sky, each green stem, or "blade," standing out against the two blue backgrounds. To describe the plants thus framed, Tomlinson chooses a metaphor emphasizing keenness of delineation: "blue double-whets them" ("Reeds" SIB). The long stems become knives, their edges honed on both sides by force of contrast. Using the same analogy, Tomlinson depicts the lustrous outlining effect of morning frost. The suddenly "bladed atmosphere" is one of renewal, in which objects take on an intensified identity: "where you discern once more / oak-leaf by hawthorn, for the frost / rewhets their edges" ("Winter-Piece" PL). In another poem about frost he chooses similarly crisp, cutting imagery to describe "trees ranked in white, / Their detail microscopically incised" ("December" J). Such examples stress the connection between nature's fierce extremities and its loveliness: edges are beautiful, often, precisely because they are sharply etched.

A large number of poems focuses on bodies of water and the various kinds of borders they create, e.g., between water and shore, between upper air and underwater depths. Whether great or small in volume, whether moving or still, waters necessarily define themselves against sky and against land: "bay / And sky, contrary in motion, swerve / Against each other's patternings" ("The Return" R). The "surf-line" itself is, inevitably, a point of forceful conjunction: "a whitening line," the "tide-edge" compels a critical "instant of definition" as one element crashes into another ("Icos" SIB, "The Atlantic" SIB, "Morwenna's Cliff" NNY). Force confronts mass. The "severing sea" is "muscular"; it possesses "an inexhaustible physicality" ("Porto Venere" DW). In "Marine," the current-driven water is compared to an animal, lifelike in its mobility and strength, as it drives itself into a rocky outcropping: "its flank / Grazes against rock" (WI). In a similar example, "the sea is bristling up" to "granular rocks" ("San Fruttuoso" F). Tomlinson draws on the drama of the sea-edge metaphorically to describe another elemental confrontation, the meeting of water with fire in the furnace of a steel factory. "Fire [is] fiercest at the frontier where / an arm of water doubles / and disjoints it," he explains ("Steel" PL). The meeting of "these molten and metallic contraries" results in "successive, sea-on-shore / concussive bursts" of sound. Supporting the "sea-on-shore" analogy, the powerful modifier "concussive" captures perfectly the hard-hitting character of these particular kinds of convergence.

In addition to the boundaries formed where waters meet the banks or channels containing them, the surface of a lake, sea, stream, or pond functions as another type of demarcation; it is a line that separates the realm of air above from the depths below. "The visible sea / Remains a sullen frontier to / Its unimaginable fathoms," he declares ("Mackinnon's Boat" WrW). This "visible . . . frontier" separates two utterly distinct realms; in the course of the fishing expedition, "flailing / Seashapes" are hauled up into "an atmosphere they had not known existed." Hardly able to breathe in this alien environment ("their breath all at once grown rare"), lobsters, crabs, and other creatures of the deep struggle futilely to escape back into their own domain. Michael Kirkham justly notes that in emphasizing "the absolute discreteness of the two realities and in particular the impenetrable otherness, inconceivable to the human mind, of the sea-world," Tomlinson implies the larger "*wholeness* of this human-inhuman world," which encompasses both sides of the boundary line: an "interdependence" of realities that are unassailably separate.[3]

The diametric opposition between upper-air and underwater worlds is reiterated more quietly in "September Swamp," a poem set in Pennsylvania on the Susquehanna River. Above the water's algae-coated surface is a world of air, light, wings, and music.

September Swamp

The name of the bird that punctuates this swamp
    With its swamp-bird cries

I do not know: that it belongs here
    With that songless song—one
Unhurried, repeated note—is clear
    From the cicadas' dense, unchanging raga,
From the way the water, that scarcely stirs,
    Is seeping invisibly beneath the green
That mantles a slow and certain course
    To the Susquehanna. The leaves that fall
On to this surface will never flow so far:
    All movement is below, save for the blue
Crackle of the dragonflies through static air,
    And turtles like the resurrecting dead, that raise
A serpentine neck and head, and then
    Ease free the whole armoured body,
Sloughing the weed aside, to climb
    A half-sunken log and taste
The luxury of light. They
    Are the consciousness of this place, its satisfaction,
Between the dragonflies' swift, aerial transaction
    And the unsunned fecundity that first gave rise
To swampsong, turtle and to dragonflies;
    That, under the weight of the September heat,
Is urging its furtive current towards open sea.

(DW)

The cicadas' "dense, unchanging raga" is "punctuat[ed]" by "swamp-bird cries" and the "crackle" of dragonflies' whizzing flight. Below the surface is a concealing darkness; even the "furtive current" of the water itself is hidden from view. Only turtles emerge from the subaqueous dark, venturing across a line of demarcation rendered even more distinct by the layer of vegetation sealing off any possible glimpse of the depths below.

The metaphoric equation of turtles with "the consciousness of this place" imparts a suggestively Freudian cast to the scene. As "consciousness," or ego, the turtles negotiate connections between id-like primal depths and the "aerial" heights of super-ego: "the luxury of light." The primacy of the hidden life below the surface is incontrovertible, i.e., it "first gave rise" to the whole. The internal triple rhyme in the phrase "unsunned fecundity" further highlights the primitive fertility of what lies deep and dark and hidden on the nether side of the border. The striking analogy between the emerging turtles and "the resurrecting dead" also hints at the paradoxical character of the swamp's "depths": this region of dark concealment initially appears to be lifeless, its invisible creative activity becoming only gradually apparent. The confrontation depicted here between water and air is less "concussive" than that of ocean water crashing against land, but equivalent in intensity, the contrast between the two converging elements just as complete.

The structure of this short poem echoes its tripartite imagery. The first six lines describe the upper region, including the bird and cicadas that dominate it. The next five lines describe the water, concentrating on its green "mantl[ed]" surface (which forms the principal border line in the scene). In line twelve, midway through the poem, the poet abruptly announces that "all movement is below," shifting his attention to the underwater portion of the scene. The last thirteen lines focus on the turtles and their role in navigating two disparate realms. The poem concludes with a reminder that this "swamp" is actually a river, moving imperceptibly "towards open sea," thus reinforcing the idea that all the important action here truly does take place "below" and out of sight. Insofar as the poem subtly invites comparison between this natural scene and the human psyche, the slow but definitive journeying toward "open sea" again asserts the preeminence of forces or processes hidden from conscious awareness. The force of what lies in the "unsunned" depths of self propels us through life, evidently, more than does deliberate intent.

Even more prominent in Tomlinson's poetry than liquid boundaries are the less palpable lines demarcated by light. "Light touches the senses awake," he declares ("At a Glance" NNY). It is a first cause, in that perception depends upon it absolutely; "primeval light," he names it in "The Flood" (F). Its absence or presence dictates, for instance, whether distant mountains will be "there of a morning"— seemingly so close "you could almost rest your hand upon / Their bulky ripple"—or "only a void and formlessness" ("At a Glance"). This phrasing equates the power of light to *bring the mountains into view* with the power to *bring them into being*. Indeed, the convergence of light with earth's surface creates the most prominent natural boundary of any, "the sky-line limit," or horizon ("At a Glance"). Wherever we stand, the horizon represents "the edge of visibility," a "sudden frontier" that limits and frames what we see of the world ("After a Death" WI). "Darkening the edges of the land," the light of sunset meets powerfully, sometimes harshly, with the rim of earth it bounds, e.g., "sunset light is singeing the horizon" ("Suggestions for the Improvement of a Sunset" N, "The Trees" DW). The choice of the verb "singe" reminds us that light is essentially an emanation of fire, heightening appreciation of its immense, at times almost menacing, might. There is majesty, too, and often beauty, in the very intensity of these collision-like encounters, as many of Tomlinson's descriptions reveal: "Sunset lies along the edge of our cloud horizon, flushing it a deeper royal purple, holding to the west in an orange stripe just ahead of the darkening cloud-edge" ("Sight and Flight" NNY).

Where light meets objects (as when the sun shines at an angle against the immense mass of earth or some portion of earth), it creates a dark reflection, or shadow. Each line of shadow, or silhouette, represents an intangible but nonetheless impact-rich border along which objects take form through force of contrast, e.g., "hard dark . . . buttressed by hard glare" ("Black Nude" PL). Thus the glow of "unyielding" afternoon sun causes the recesses in an old wall to fill with shade. As a result, each stone stand outs with separate clarity against its own dark-rimmed outline: "the shadowed space / Divides walls / Into friable pink blocks" ("Stone Walls: at Chew Magna" SIB). The effect is one of "dislocation"; one notices individual stones instead of the wall itself. The observer's attention is irresistibly drawn to "the filaments of all these / Sagging networks" of shade fragmenting the whole into myriad component parts. Perception of the wall is altered because of these shaded borders with their temporarily dismantling effect; they are examples of the "edges" Tomlinson treasures on account of the new perspectives they offer on the ordinary ("At the Edge" F). To become conscious of the distinct identity and position of each individual stone composing a wall is to see that wall in a new way, and such new perception is, the poem's concluding lines assert, a gift to be gratefully seized: "who would unmake / This dislocation where / Each [stone] is located?"

In "Head Hewn with an Axe" Tomlinson admires the artistry with which a sculpture of "whittled crystal" has been shaped to take maximum advantage of the defining contrast between light and shade, "fissured / For the invasion of shadows" (PL). The success of this three-dimensional work of art depends crucially upon "the enrichment of the alignment" of one element against the other:

> Sun against shade against sun:
> That daily food, which
> Were it not for such importunities
> Would go untasted:

> The suave block, desecrated
> In six strokes. The light
> Is staunching its wounds.

The poem balances cutting, warlike imagery ("invasion," "hacked," "desecrated," "wounds") with claims of healing ("staunching") and nourishment ("daily food"). Achingly stark contrasts between light and dark are essential to the aesthetic delight this sculpture delivers to the beholder. Its beauty almost hurts. To achieve the desired aesthetic effects, the artist must possess courage to "hack," to "wound," the crystalline rock that is his medium. A gently worked, smoothly surfaced piece would not please in equal measure, for the sharply shadowed lines necessary to highlight depths and to realize shape would be missing. "The facets of the crystal represent different ways of seeing and seeing through," he observes; it provides "a multifaceted way of looking at things."[4] As he concludes in another poem, "light . . . must . . . feed its opposite" ("Fire" DW).

In the absence of light, moreover, there are no shadows; the darkness of shade paradoxically is dependent upon brightness. "The sun flung out at the foot of the tree / A perfect shadow on snow," one poem begins, identifying the sun as active agent in the formation of this "replica" of the tree's trunk and bare branches ("The Shadow" J). Pausing "among the complications of summit branches," the poet and his companions can almost imagine that they are up in the tree itself, rather than walking across its shadow. A moment later, however, the shadows look more like roots, and the speaker wonders if he might be travelling below ground rather than high above it: "Or was it roots were opening through the white / An underworld thoroughfare towards daylight?" The tree's shadow is bounded by the contrasting whiteness of light shining on a snow-covered field, which he interprets as the "daylight" at the end of the eerie, underground tunnel through which he appears to be moving. When the walkers reach "that dark frontier" where the shadow ends, they emerge into what seems like a different realm, a patternless "world of untrodden snow." The poem's conclusion echoes its opening lines, again acknowledging the sun as author of this evocative shadow-world: due to a sudden fading of light, the tree's shadow simply disappears, "the shadow all at once gone out as the sun withdrew." The creative force of sunlight here makes and then unmakes a network of shadows, visually intricate, and intricate, too, in its appeal to the observer's imagination. Once perceived as a labyrinthine "underworld," an ordinary tree's shadow assumes some of the mysterious significance associated with Greek story and myth.

Tomlinson's poems suggest other ways in which the most ordinary of shadow-lines may point beyond itself to something vaster. "In March," a poem set in the English countryside, celebrates a "dry bright" day at the turning point between winter and spring (WI):

> the shadows from the hedge
>   Ink-stain half way across
> The road to where a jagged blade
>   Of light eats into them: light's guarded frontier

The border between glossy black shadow and "glittering" light is almost painfully sharp-edged. The advancing "frontier" of light appears to be resisted, "held / Back" by the massed bulk of solid objects in the scene, e.g., hedges, walls, barn, house, and haystack. Yet scattered bits of straw catch and reflect the sun's rays, "flecks of pallid gold" that abet the conquest of shade by light, lending the transformative power of a fairy tale to the equinoctial sun. Organizing his description of the day around the "blade" or line of light dividing shadow from sunlight, Tomlinson ends his poem with a glimpse of a crow in flight, a "shining, flying shadow" echoing in the sky the line of demarcation he has traced so carefully on the ground.

"The Blade" develops the imagery from "In March" still more elaborately, taking as its title the knife-like edge dividing last light from approaching dark.

The Blade

> I looked to the west:
> I saw it thrust
> a single blade
> between the shadows:
> a lean stiletto-shard
> tapering to its tip
> yellowed along greensward,
> lit on a roof that lay
> mid-way across its path
> and then outran it:
> it was so keen,

> it seemed to go
> right through and cut
> in two the land
> it was lancing. Then
> as I stood,
> the shaft shifted,
> fading across grass,
> withdrew as visibly as the sand
> down the throat of an hour-glass:
> you could see time
> trickle out, a grainy
> lesion, and the green
> filter back to fill
> the crack in creation.
>
> (A)

The poem records the glare of light preceding sundown, the west "thrust[ing] / a single blade / between the shadows: / a lean stiletto-shard." The apparent power of this advancing line of blinding light to separate and divide is conveyed by metaphors of sharpness and slicing: "it seemed to go / right through and cut / in two the land / it was lancing." The final lines of the poem describe an ominous "lesion" in the land, a "crack in creation" re-filled gradually by the softer twilight that follows the sun's last glaring rays. All at once the central metaphor of the poem shifts, as the cutting blade is replaced by an hour-glass: the observer's renewed ability to see objects that were briefly hidden by dagger-like dazzle is compared to the movement of sand back into the lower half of the glass. The ending of day takes on quasi-apocalyptic feel in this poem where the sun wields a razor-sharp weapon and appears, momentarily at least, to cut a hole in the visible world.

Just as the "jagged" edge between sun and shade of "In March" implicitly indicates the less immediately visible border between seasons, the sharp dividing line between light and dark in "The Blade" marks the boundary between day and night. In the first poem, spring light is in process of vanquishing winter's shade; in the second, daylight is receding, giving way to dark. In both poems, obviously, borders between light and dark function as more than simple visual phenomena: they generate awareness of planetary movement, moments of astronomically significant transition. Like the "concussive" convergence of water and fire, or sea and shore, confrontations of light with shade resonate with an impact transcending the immediate occasion. Thus boundaries in space may mark boundaries in time. Repeatedly Tomlinson draws attention to this powerful overlapping effect, to the perceptible "rifts," or "displacements," temporal cycles exact ("Upstate" DW). Typically he fixes on the precise moment when one phenomenon is succeeded by another. The displacement of day by night, for example, seems to hover, poised, at a visible dividing line: "a lingering / At the edge of time, a perfect neighbouring" ("Images of Perfection" S). Caught between "apocalypse" and "revelation," time seems to pause for an instant at a finally definitive "edge" of transition. In "Varenna," the closing of day is rendered visible by "the column of sundown" reflected on the surface of a lake, a "tall encroachment" (J).

Seasonal transitions are the object of equally careful consideration in poems that take us (as does "In March") to the moment when one period of the year yields to the next. "Listening to Leaves" portrays the end of autumn when "the timbre of the leaves is changing" to a "metallic hiss" signalling the imminent arrival of winter: "we balance on a blade between the two" (VS). "In April" depicts a corresponding equinoctial moment in the other half of the year:

> and the winter that would not go
> was blocking spring
> through the upper sky piling
> ledges of cold onto
> ridges of ripening warmth
>
> (F)

The boundary between two seasons manifests itself here as an uneven but sharply drawn line where "ledges of cold" meet "ridges of . . . warmth." Tomlinson is intrigued by every instance of "this in-between of time," invariably focusing on phenomena acting as "guardians of a frontier" ("Harvest" A).[5] Thus in "October" he greets the prospect of the oncoming winter with gladness: "awaiting cold, we welcome in the frost"—with its power to "cleanse" the earth of summer's residue of decaying vegetation—"as eagerly as we shall look to spring" (S).[6] Persistently such poems highlight the outermost boundary of a season, causing us to recognize and to delight in the fulcrum of energies gathered there.

The most definitive of temporal boundaries is, of course, the "sudden frontier" dividing life from death, that almost unimaginable border "at the edge of visibility" ("After a Death" WI). In two elegiac poems Tomlinson marks that great divide with special elegance. "A Death in the Desert" mourns the death of Homer Vance, an acquaintance who died just a week before the poet arrived to visit him. Tomlinson describes "the week / that lay / uncrossably between us" with an intensity of regret, likening the border between life and death to the desert itself, an "endless / waterless sea-bed" (AS). In "Music and the Poet's Cat" he draws upon music, "the scream of the woodwind / in *Tapiola*," to represent this impenetrable barrier. Engaging the senses, even assaulting them, the notes he hears are beyond question real, yet the impalpability of music makes it an ideal vehicle for evoking a presence that is no longer physical. When the poet hears a piece that once had excited his cat's displeasure ("your ears resented the discords"), inevitably he is reminded of his lost pet (A). The music reawakens grief by emphasizing the absoluteness of the separation between living and dead:

> and my ears take in
> those selfsame notes
> across this rent
> in time and I
> resent both it and them.

Summoning memory unbidden, the music indicates a demarcation as abrupt as a rip or tear; "this rent / in time" definitely is not susceptible to trespass.[7]

Tomlinson's preoccupation with spatial and temporal boundaries includes a pronounced concern with borders setting off human from natural territories. Repeatedly his poems ask us to visualize lines defining the limits of human occupation and thereby to acknowledge regions outside human control and influence. At their simplest, such borders may function chiefly as barricades erected by humans against the assaults of nature, "fencing that fullness back" ("Reflections" SIB). He calls attention, for example, to "walls" that "defend / Hayfields against the Irish Sea" ("At the Hill Fort" NNY), and elsewhere notes: "They are fencing the upland against / the drifts this wind, those clouds / would bury it under" ("The Snow Fences" AS). In "The Cycle" he describes the "threshold line" of a house as the point where snow and floodwaters attempt to enter and overtake human space, sometimes with temporary success (A):

> The house is going under as the drift
> Climbs walls and door and, sieving through,
>   Gathers finely in a threshold line.
> It appears to mean that we—the ones who've seen
>   A flood seeping across that limit—
> Stand guarding a frontier, the incursion
>   Refusing to disband until it must . . .

The threshold here is defined as a "line," a "limit," a "frontier," where humans "guard" a domestic site from invasion by natural forces inimical to their welfare. In "Civilities of Lamplight" Tomlinson presents man-made sources of light (both literal and figurative) as a similar kind of protective border marking off a "haven" of human construction, a space defined by a "hedge-bound track" of illumination tunneling through its opposite: the lamp creates "a sealed / Furrow on dark" (SIB).

"At Delft," a tribute to Vermeer and his much admired rendering of light, reverses the terms in "Civilities of Lamplight" by depicting a natural light source shining on man-made objects. Tomlinson presents a city of geometrically defined proportions, "each street / Its neighbour's parallel, each house / A displacement in that mathematic," the tiled floors a "tessellation" (SIB). The morning sunlight that brings these details sharply into focus is itself contrastingly "diffused and indiscriminate." It forms a visible margin, bright yet amorphous, outlining the city's deliberate architecture: "All that is human here stands clarified / By all that accompanies and bounds." The natural world provides a contrapuntal "accompan[iment]" to civilized space, reinforcing the value of confrontation with otherness. Despite its ability to overwhelm and even destroy human designs, nature is much more than something to be fended off; it is a necessary presence against which we define ourselves. Typically, as J. E. Chamberlain observes, Tomlinson's poems achieve "an exquisite poise" between "the natural virtues of the forest and the sky," on the one hand, and "the human sanctities of the town and the historical moment," on the other.[8]

A group of poems recording encounters, or near encounters, between humans and various wild animals enables Tomlinson to develop this theme with special vividness. He creates a strongly realized visual boundary between human and nonhuman territories in "The Fox Gallery," for instance, a poem describing "a long house" by chance laid out directly parallel to an often used wild trail: "the fox's way" (WW). From the upper windows the poet and his companion observe wild creatures moving "the whole length of the meadow / parallel with the restraining line / of wall and pane." The house itself marks the limits of fox territory; the absoluteness of the "restraining line" becomes vividly clear when one day a fox appears heading "not from side / to side, but straight / at the house." Abruptly the animal changes direction; the human spectators "watched it sheer off deterred / by habitation, and saw / how utterly the two worlds were / disparate." Tomlinson organizes his poem around perceptions possible only at the precise point where these different worlds meet. The view from this boundary line stimulates reactions that resist easy categorizing. There is wonder as well as disquiet in the human response to the foxes, recognition of the "utterly . . . disparate" realm they represent and, on the poet's part, a keen desire to observe as much of it as possible.

In "Foxes' Moon" he again presents two distinct worlds: one ancient and "pastoral," belonging to the foxes with their "flint hearts and sharpened senses," the other contemporary and urban, overwhelmed by human encroachments of houses and automobiles, "asphalt," and "wires" (WI). The line of demarcation between the two is identified as the point "where / The last farm meets the first / Row from the approaching town." This demarcation is further emphasized by the association of rural territory with night and the more densely populated area with day. Night is the foxes' time, when they edge across the boundary line to feed on "the garbage of the yards." Scarcely disturbing human inhabitants with their "volpine" presence, the foxes are "ghosts unacknowledged in the moonlight / Of the suburb, and like ghosts they flow / Back," fleeing from the coming dawn in this "world not theirs." Only in dreams do the sleeping humans sense the nighttime intrusion by natives of another, more nearly primeval realm. Characteristically, Tomlinson invests this boundary line with special tension. "These / Are the fox hours," he declares, hours "cleansed / Of all the meanings we can use / And so refuse them." Everything in the poem leads toward this point of tension between modern civilization and raw nature, whose "meanings" lack utility when interpreted in an alien (i.e., civilized) context. "Fox hours" represent a highly charged zone right at the border, a place or time resonant with potential precisely because it is "cleansed" of the familiar. For the foxes the border is a place of literal feeding; for the humans it is a moment in which suburban life may be reinvigorated by glimpses of primal, nonhuman purpose and energy.

The fleeting instance of border violation depicted in "Foxes' Moon," when denizens of one realm surreptitiously cross over into the other, stirs awareness in us of lost connections with ancient, potentially frightening forces. "At the Autumn Equinox" narrates a similar sort of incident in which wild creatures intrude at night upon human territory, this time evoking a larger measure of alarm. Set in Italy, the poem describes wild boars crossing the border between "forests" and "orchards" in search of food, invading regions tamed by human cultivation (A). Their intrusion is more damaging, more disturbing, than the ghostly visits made by foxes to suburban yards in the earlier poem. "Tearing apart / The careful terraces," the boars display voraciously ruinous appetite; they "crunch and crush a whole harvest." Again Tomlinson emphasizes diametric distinctions between two separate realms: "They had undone and taken back again / Into their nomad scavengers' domain / All we had shaped for use, and laid it waste." The terraced vineyards aptly illustrate the realm of human design and controlled "use," standing in obvious contrast to the "domain" of the wild beasts with its ruthless hungers, its planless "squander[ing]." The boars impress the poet as alien and "strange": "A sufficiency of fear confessed their otherness." He goes on to imagine the landscape prior to human occupation, "infested" with gigantic trees, calling to mind a primitive fertility and vastness of scale. The boars are relics of this fearsome vitality.

The result of the boars' encroachment across the boundary of contemporary civilization is a twofold destruction: having razed the vineyards, the animals themselves are "machine gunned" by *Carabinieri* as they follow an asphalt road ("man-made ribbon") into town. Unlike the foxes, who flee silently back to the greenwood at dawn, the boars extend their rampaging foray past the point of retreat. "Confused," they become victims of the world they came to rob, the road "luring them on / Helpless into the shadow of habitation." The same verb used early in the poem to describe their attack on the grape harvest— "tear"—recurs in the final lines of the poem to describe the creatures' ripped flesh. Indeed, the very air of morning seems "torn" by this spectacle of incongruous brutality: a heap of wild beasts lying slaughtered in the road outside a police station. Like "Foxes' Moon" or "The Fox Gallery," this poem takes readers to the dividing line between nature in its wildest state and tamed, or civilized, space. Only at this border, impinged upon by its opposite, does the particularity of each assume full shape and meaning.

"Geese Going South" is another poem stressing how close we may be, even in a twentieth-century environment, to contact with unfettered nature. In this instance migrating geese take advantage of darkness to rest and feed on a "high ridge" just outside a town whose sleeping inhabitants "scarcely dream[] of their nocturnal presence" (DW). Unlike the foxes or boars, the birds keep sharply to their own side of a dividing line they unconsciously acknowledge as they pass by the town without entering it, firmly resisting the observing poet's attempt to approach them more closely. He remains the sole spectator of this drama of "restless moon-glossed wings" and "serpentine stirrings." Poised though they are right at a border dividing the wild from the domestic, the townspeople fail to recognize it or to take note of what lies on the other side. Here, as is frequently the case in Tomlinson's work, "nature is as alien as it is welcome."[9] The poet helps readers to appreciate something of what the unwitting townspeople have missed, suggesting the birds' mysterious beauty ("Flocks, skeining the air-lanes / In stately buoyancy even seem / To dance"), and also hinting at the irresistible impulse motivating those "wings . . . aching to be gone." Personifying the wings, attributing migratory yearning to the birds' very bodies, Tomlinson acknowledges the realm of instinctive drives, primordial territory outside the boundaries of what we like to think of as rational intention and conscious choice. The geese offer us a chance to observe and imagine that other realm more fully:

> What does a goose, I ask myself,
> Dream of among its kind, or are they all
>   Of a single mind where moonlight shows
> The flight-lanes they still strain towards
>   Even in sleep?

These encounters with wild creatures are particularly compelling because in such instances what lies just outside domesticated space is a *living* otherness. The basic premises of these poems are reiterated, moreover, in many others featuring nonsentient phenomena such as mountains, ravines, trees, ocean, or rivers. In "The Peak," for example, a mountain serves as the principal agent of the natural world. In the scene depicted, natural and human features at first appear to converge. The poet describes driving down a mountain that has been "scooped and scraped" by erosive forces of ice into the form of a human face, or profile (R). There is paradox in the fact that precisely here, where "no foot had walked," an apparently human shape should appear. As a result of accidental, or "blind[]," workings of the elements, the human and the nonhuman meet at this "mountain-head possess[ing] a face." Beyond this mountain, however, a still higher peak can be descried, "its seamed rock / Worn by no human wrinkles." In no way reminiscent of human design, that farther peak stands "at a frontier" marking the point where nature separates itself utterly and finally from all things human. Below lies the secure familiarity of human habitation. Here the dividing line is reinforced not by a contrast between night and day, but by a juxtaposition of high and low:

> But the lowlands opened to receive us,
> > Brought us the first sun free of mountain shadow
> And the demarcation of ploughland, vineyard, meadow.
> > From above the snow-line, and above the snow,
> Something was tracking us, measuring our return
> > Past the stone certitude of barn on barn.

On the human side of the "demarcation," the poet lingers on signs of agriculture such as ploughed fields, ripening crops, filled barns. Thus he emphasizes the sustenance derived from human cultivation of natural resources which in their raw state offer no such nourishment or "certitude." On the farther side of the "snow-line," nature can be felt as an almost ominous presence, a stalking "Something" that spies on the progress humans make as they move away from its "shadow." Nature is a hunter, a predator even, reluctant to allow us to escape it. Tomlinson personifies the nonhuman here in order to emphasize the alien threat it may pose to us, at the same time suggesting why, in the course of human evolution, our ancestors so assiduously sought to retreat from it, resist it, and reshape it. Sketching a view of what lies on both sides of the line dividing nature's untrammeled power from human attempts to tame it, this poem calls forth a wary awe in response to nature even as it articulates a grateful appreciation of hard-won human comforts.[10]

"Upstate" similarly draws a line separating "mountain meadow" from "downhill," where "a wandering border of small stones" indicates a site of former human habitation (DW). The higher region, penetrated only by occasional hikers, is inhospitable, chilly, full of thorny bushes: "barbed stalks / Had scored my ankles, grasses / Grudged me footroom"; the cold air is "straight from Canada." Discovering the row of headstones, the poet imagines "barns / And houses that have disappeared already / From the cleared spaces." Raw nature is already expanding across the now undefended border, replacing once carefully ploughed and planted fields with weedy brambles: "Thorn has undone endeavour." These gravestones mark temporal as well as spatial limits to human occupancy, suggesting the fragility of human efforts to carve out habitable space on the planet: "Time here / Rifts as sudden as the weather / In its displacements."

Tomlinson investigates ruins and abandoned dwellings in other poems as well; such sites are by definition points of convergence, where nature is in process of reclaiming territory once shaped to human purposes. In "Trebiano," for instance, hawks now "inhabit the gaps in castle masonry," while ivy "forces a slow and silent entry" and a fig-tree "fasten[s] itself to the threshold" (VS). Here wild creatures and uncultivated vegetation behave like an invading army, gradually but irresistibly taking possession of the deserted stronghold. In "Casarola," Tomlinson takes us to view a deserted mill and surrounding buildings. Although the stone masonry is "still-perfect," already the roofs are overgrown: "mossed tiles like a city of the dead / Grow green in the wood" (S). The scene of "desolation" inspires nostalgia. "There is a beauty / In this abandonment," the poet muses, but he goes on to conclude that "there would be more / In the slow activity of smoke / Seeping at roof and lintel." As in "Upstate," nature here is patiently regaining space temporarily lost to human enterprise: "nature / Daily takes the distinctness from that signature / Men had left there in stone and wood."

Nostalgia for lost human territory is not the only response triggered by ruins in Tomlinson's poems. Contemplating ghost towns in the American southwest, he emphasizes instead the liberating effect of reclamation or "displacement" by elemental forces ("Two Views of Two Ghost Towns" AS). A personified "mob of objects" frees itself with apparent relief from "the weight of human / meanings, human need":

> *Keep Off*
> the warning says, and all
> the mob of objects, freed

> under the brightly hard
> displacement of the desert light
> repeat it: the unaxled wheels,
> doorless doors and windowless
> regard of space. Clear
> of the weight of human
> meanings, human need,
> gradually
> houses splinter to the ground
> in white and red, two
> rotting parallels . . .

Here nature exercises its powers to open a once closed and confining human environment to "space" and "light." As the process of decay and erosion reclaims our discarded tools and dwellings, it warns us, in effect, to "keep off"; it reminds us that the phenomenal world enjoys an existence quite apart from the uses and significance we may impose upon it.[11]

In the face of nature's steady obliteration, relics of human occupation prove scarcely more enduring than footprints on a beach, where "the primeval slidings" of the tide "erase them . . . to wash the slate clean" ("Writing on Sand" F). Even when humans succeed in taming for their own use portions of a natural environment, nature is all too apt to manifest a spirit of recalcitrant independence. In rueful, semi-comic tone, Tomlinson reports an instance of nature retaining the upper hand: "After fifty years, the hawthorn hedge / That ran through the new estate / Still divides the garden ends" ("The Hawthorn in Trent Vale" R). Deliberately planted, but now unwanted, the hardy shrub "resists . . . every move to fell it or constrain." This all too visible, inconvenient natural fence once served human ends but the hawthorn, like a vegetative version of the sorcerer's apprentice, has proven stronger than its cultivator. "This ghost / From a farm now gone, remains to haunt" the present occupants, its unrelenting energy derived from primal sources: "Green fire and blossom fed / From the darkness under bed and masonry." Here nature's strength is associated with underground depths rather than with mountainous heights. Whether far above civilized space or far below it, whether illustrated by blasting temperatures or by rampant fertility, nature evinces powers finally not amenable to human harnessing. The aggravating line of shrubbery that "divides the garden ends" provides a visible reminder

1: ELEMENTAL DEMARCATION   37

of the more significant border line dividing domesticated from undomesticated nature. Despite its surface flippancy, the poem raises disquieting questions. It leaves us wondering how many other human efforts to control nature may prove ironically self-defeating and ultimately illusory.

"Weather Report" further explores the unreliable quality of barricades separating us from nature's indefatigable forces. The poem traces the advent of snow, beginning in Scandinavia and moving toward southern England as the winter season progresses. The "first snow" to be spotted in the southernmost areas arrives on vehicles travelling from farther north, "an earnest of that threat / Cromarty, Mull, Fair Isle and Fasnet / Have weathered already" (J). Initially the snow is very much elsewhere, up beyond the borders of northern counties and countries, but inexorably it approaches nearer.

> It has passed
> Down the Pennine chain and choked Shap Fell;
> The Snake is lost and every moor
> In Derbyshire under a deep, advancing pile.
> It covers the county, dwindling south,
> But the wind that carries it, overshoots
> The frontier snow has mapped. . . .

Like an army, the snow line pushes south; passing borders that one by one prove insecure, it "choke[s]" each region in turn. As the conspicuous use of place names emphasizes, the "frontier" keeps moving ever closer. Tomlinson concludes his poem with the assertion that in this confrontation between humans and nature, man-made borders are meaningless: "this turbulence that began as Swedish air / . . . has turned . . . / To the weather of the one nation we suddenly are."

If nature's powers often menace human comfort and safety, civilization likewise can endanger the natural environment. In "From the Motorway," it is human presence that appears ominous. In this poem, Tomlinson describes how roadways form a boundary line around a piece of land relegated by humans to a dumping ground. "A hump of land three roads / Have severed from all other" is approachable only by birds (NNY). The jettisoned debris of modern civilization is presented as toxic, both literally and figuratively. The poet foresees a "sodium glow" emanating from the huge mound, gradually to be shaped by processes of composting and random seeding into a hill where small vermin will feed and live. Nothing else will grow there: "it will breed no ghosts / But only . . . the bones of tiny prey." The *breeding of bones* seems ominous, macabre; the place is an ever-growing charnel-house. "No one will ever go there." The boundary line separating this place of poisonous residue from a healthy natural environment is absolute. Irretrievably isolated, the spot will remain "as inaccessible as Eden"; we shall never "have it back." The biblical analogy in the last line of the poem invites us to link the dump, and all its implications of complacent excess, with the negative connotations of Original Sin. The visible border "sever[ing]" this landfill from the unspoiled world of which it once was a part is likened to the boundary between a fallen world and paradise.[12]

Numerous poems explore the natural environment, its "fragility and value," in the context of human depredation.[13] The disillusionment with which human space is presented in "From the Motorway" is echoed more unobtrusively in "Far Point," a poem set in northern Canada. Tomlinson is visiting a small settlement marking the outermost limit of populated territory: "The road ends here. If your way / lies north, then you must take / to the forest or the bay" (A). Straddling the boundary line between civilization and nature, this outpost is inhabited by a variety of exiles. The "café / which is a poolroom which is a bar" is patronized mainly by a mixture of aging American draft-dodgers who "never went back" and "a group of Indians" alienated from their cultural heritage:

> The pool-players, backs to the light,
> stand facing away
> from centuries of clambake, potlatch
> and tribal ferocities

The waitress-*cum*-barmaid is a German immigrant, "a cheerful exile" who still counts out change in her native language. This motley assortment of people appears to lead an existence drained of purpose, characterized chiefly by listless drinking and gaming:

> The cue's click, click
> rehearses its softly merciless music
> ticking away the increment
> of unwanted time. . . .

In this deadened environment, people severed through a variety of causes from their pasts are caught in an aimless limbo, their lives reduced to "unwanted time."

What lies beyond this scene of suspended animation is nature in all its fertile grandeur. Irresistibly it reclaims what humans have abandoned, turning rotted old totem poles "back into trees," for instance, as seeds falling into the cracked wood take root and sprout. To the pool-players at the café, the totem poles represent something lost and gone, something they "stand facing away / from"; nature's energies seize on the artefacts, however, gradually transforming them into an organic part of a larger, living whole. Tomlinson ends the poem with a long look north toward the sea strait, fir trees, and distant mountains. He contrasts the lifelessness of the café crowd with apparently unquenchable sources of elemental vitality. As mist rises from the mountain peaks, details hidden in the distant view grow clearer:

> and we see it is summits
> we are peering at,
> that go on unveiling themselves
> as if they were being created.

Godlike, nature reveals itself, engaging in a process of continuous creation and re-creation. Mountains and sky seem all but sentient in this scene; personification lends it active powers and mystical beauty. The disparity between life and lifelessness in the natural and human environments portrayed in "Far Point" gives proof of nature's enormous powers of vitality and endurance. Human endeavor appears contrastingly meager and pointless: the road does end here. Viewed from this outer margin of civilization, nature's powers seem more magnificent than frightening.

"Far Point" includes details, moreover, that suggest the deleterious effect of human incursions into natural territory. An anecdote embedded in the poem records interaction between humans and a wild animal: a young deer that in a freak instance of domestication has become someone's pet. The poet spends some time watching the deer—how it swims through the waves behind its master's boat, or plays as an equal with pet dogs. This encounter with a wild animal marks the boundary line between nature and civilization: in domesticating a deer, humans have crossed that line, trespassing in alien territory and seizing spoils.

> 'You know how he found it?
> It was being born. Out in the woods.
> He couldn't resist touching the fur
> so the mother abandoned it—
> it was the smell of a man on it frightened her.'

The poet's informant emphasizes the perpetual danger to which the pet deer is exposed, how its tameness renders it too easy a target for hunters. Such an example of humans exercising control over the natural world inspires neither confidence nor admiration. This footnote to the portrait of "Far Point" adds subtly to the sense of waste and futility associated with the human realm he describes in the poem.

The lines of demarcation in the physical universe to which Tomlinson consistently directs the reader's eye are sites of profound elemental confrontation. And when elemental and domesticated spaces edge up against one another, increasingly complex, impact-rich encounters occur.[14] Both overtly and covertly, borders separating human and nonhuman territory serve as crucial foci in Tomlinson's depictions of place. In his presentation of both rural and urban environments, he brings us repeatedly to boundary lines where, as he puts it, "the civilized, discriminating faculties and the sense of the elemental, of origins, reinforce each other" (PP 20). Immediacy of juxtaposition "reinforce[s]" the distinct identity of disparate realms, defining the limits and clarifying the potential of each. Thus Tomlinson helps us to recognize that there is another world out there, older and wilder by far than the one in which we chiefly live, and his poems compel us to ponder our relationship to it, e.g., the steps by which we have distanced ourselves from it, the threats it still may pose to us, the threats we pose in turn to it, its potential as a source of vital renewal as well as of danger. Poem after poem brings readers to the edge of new awareness, pointing toward the untamed fertility located just across the borders of everyday awareness.

2
Cultural and Historical Boundaries

And so we . . . translate our worlds to one another

INVESTIGATING HOW PHYSICAL FEATURES OF THE WORLD MAY BE OVERlaid or altered by artefacts of human occupation, Tomlinson devotes significant attention to boundaries marking cultural encounters and historical transitions. Numerous poems focus on points of junction and disjunction between different times, different peoples, different customs. Frequently, too, boundaries in space dramatize boundaries in human history. In a poem like "Hedgerows," for example, visually explicit borders created by the hedges assume historical as well as spatial implications (NNY). In addition to marking the perimeters of fields and roads, the fast disappearing lines of shrubbery function metaphorically as a boundary between the old and the new, between two different sets of social, economic, and moral assumptions. Tomlinson's many poems about ruins and abandoned habitations point similarly to demarcations with strong historical significance. Nature and civilization converge around relics of human occupation like the "wandering border of small stones" in "Upstate" that differentiate what now is from what once was.

Human memory renders us acutely sensitive to the irreversible movement of time. "Poem for My Father" responds to changes in the physical features of a place, changes described as both consequence and visible sign of events in twentieth-century human history: "For everything we see / Teaches the time that we are living in" (NNY). The opening lines of the poem establish a precise context:

> I bring to countryside my father's sense
> Of an exile ended when he fished his way
> Along the stained canal and out between
> The first farms, the uninterrupted green,

> To find once more the Suffolk he had known
> Before the Somme. . . .

The point at which suburbs yield to an apparently undisturbed pastoral ("uninterrupted green") marks the shift between modern and prewar England. Nostalgia is most acute on the far side of the dividing line between suburban and rural landscapes, where the "sense / Of an exile ended" seems almost to undo the cataclysmic upheavals of World War I. The final lines of the poem indicate that such yearning to cancel the effects of time leaves us momentarily "poised between paradise and history," i.e., between time and timelessness, between the stasis of an idealized past and the flux of an always imperfect present. The power of human memory can in effect create new boundaries by conjuring up the past, a realm into which there is no longer entry.

Human desires for permanence notwithstanding, the history of the planet is in essence the record of changes over time, each change in its turn definitive. In "Near Corinium" Tomlinson observes portions of this record layered in the earth itself, "history's particles" excavated during the mundane activity of highway construction (S). He sees in "the subsoil" evidence of prehistoric life forms, "whorl-wheel fossils," and of asteroidal collisions, "shatterings / from the meteors." Atop these remnants from prehistory, the digging reveals proof not only of human civilization but of conflict between different groups, e.g., an inscription on a limestone block reading "'I, Caius Marius restored / this Jupiter column / the Christians had defaced.'" These bits and pieces left over from earlier times "inlay" the ground meaningfully, delineating beginnings and endings of epochs with "traceries / finer than the lines / of spider floss." If there is a larger "whole," as Tomlinson speculates toward the end of the poem, it will be discovered only through careful study of these individual fragments of "torn tapestry."

He presents a similarly intricate, layered arrangement of cultural and historical borders in "Along the Mohawk," set in New York state. In this poem he asks readers to visualize three parallel lines, each of which has served in its time as principal thoroughfare in the region. The Mohawk River, by far the oldest of the three, already played a role in the economy and travel of indigenous peoples; long before European settlers arrived on the scene it was the "waterway . . . of the Algonquin" (A). The railroad tracks, now fallen into disuse, are laid out parallel to the river. The third and last line is formed by the highway that has replaced both river and railway as chief transportation route. Each of the pathways, whether natural or humanly engineered, represents a period in the area's history and remains to bear testimony to a particular way of life.

The displacement at the heart of the poem is described in terms of contamination and quiescence, e.g., the river water now is "discoloured," "muddy," and "docile"; it appears to lack the vigorous majesty appropriate to the part it once played. Tomlinson attributes the successive displacements he details to successive invasions. The Algonquin use their "waterway" to attack a stockaded town of European settlers, who are themselves guilty of violating Native American lands. The question of who ultimately is "victim" and who "victor" in that encounter is blurred by Tomlinson's syntax in this poem depicting an ongoing cycle of takeovers. River traffic ceases with the advent of trains, and the railway in its turn has been "silenced" by the automobile. A small, scared rabbit hiding along the river's shore "crouches against invaders," evidently regarding all humans as dangerous. The rabbit earns two mentions in a poem of only twenty lines, a reminder that the incursion of humans into the rest of nature preceded and has outlasted all other invasive events.

The shoreline itself remains a point of convergence in the scene. In fact, the river's "muddy margins" lend consoling continuity to the scene: its waters still contain fish; a child still raises an "Indian cry" from one shore to the other; even the noise of the cars flashing past on the highway mimics with a "swish" the sound of moving waters. And the older lines of travel still attract a few wayfarers: the "fishers" drawn to the river's remaining bounty follow the "disused railroad's asphalted avenue" in their journey to the fishing grounds. Here, where a river is bordered by a railroad that is bordered by a highway, three parallel lines appear to be all but superimposed upon one another. Like layers at an archaeological dig, they constitute borders in time as well as in space, denoting a series of radical cultural shifts: encroachment and displacement, even disappearance, e.g., "Where did the Mohawks go?" Geographical conjunction serves to emphasize cultural and historical disjunctions.

Tomlinson examines instances of such cultural confrontation and transition in a variety of locales. "Jemez," a short poem set in New Mexico, again illustrates the ease with which visible or palpable boundaries can indicate others less accessible to the outward senses.

Jemez

When we were children said
Eva they told us
the trees on the skyline there
—we turned to see
the trees on the skyline there
stand staring down—
were the kachinas and we
believed them but today
if you say to children
the trees on the skyline there
—the skyline trees stand
calling up sap out of rock and sand—
are the kachinas they
reply kachinas?
they're nothing but trees

(F)

The poem first directs attention to a row of trees "on the skyline." Fourfold repetition of that phrase highlights the role of the trees in forming a visible margin just at the horizon, rising up into the sky from the brink of land. Less concretely, moreover, the trees represent another demarcation, that between traditional and contemporary belief systems. Formerly, children agreed to view the trees as a row of tall kachinas. These tribal spirits stood, as it were, on the boundary between the ordinary and the supra-ordinary, or between the natural and the supernatural. Today Hopi children resist such authoritative interpretation, insisting that the trees are "nothing but trees," whose own organic processes (the power of "calling up sap out of rock and sand") constitute the whole of their mystery. In the space of just one or two generations, Tomlinson's informant explains, belief in the immediate presence of the kachina and their powers has receded. And in the course of the poem a literally observable line of trees has come to delineate the cultural divide between old and young, between myth and mythlessness.

A poem set in Portugal depicts a similarly decisive boundary between traditional and contemporary ways of life. Inhabitants of the Rua do Carriçal live in a small pastoral oasis, on an "island street" cut off from the surrounding urban noise and "psychosis" ("Rua do Carriçal" VS). The street is marked by features of an older, simpler way of life: a woman washing her balcony floor, a man engaged in small agricultural efforts who waters "a miniature garden" of flowers and vegetables. "Jammed" as it is "between two thoroughfares," the street is hemmed in by the maddeningly noisy and ugly by-products of a technologically sophisticated metropolis:

> Besieged by pylons,
> a radio-mast, street-
> end traffic and the monomaniac note
> from a generator . . .

Discordant graffiti *("Psychotic Lesbian Nuns")* also intrude into this tiny Eden, but residents retain their "island innocence"; happily, they "cannot read this scrawl / since it is daubed in English." Although their "urban Innisfree" is experiencing encroachment, it appears reassuringly intact, as the final lines of the poem indicate:

> immune from harm
> the pre-Freudian Carriçal exudes
> into Lusitanian noon
> its convent calm.

The unexpected survival of this small fragment of an archaic world is reinforced by the poet's deliberate use of the ancient name for Portugal (Lusitania) to characterize the "island street." A peace deriving from inherited custom and faith, closeness to the earth, and personal self-sufficiency here sets itself apart, both physically and spiritually, from the hullaballoo, clutter, and self-conscious angst of the late twentieth century.

A poem set in Mexico illustrates equally striking disjunction between traditional and contemporary cultures. "Teotihuacán" focuses on an ancient religion decayed and now supplanted by commercial fervor. One of the principal holy sites of the pre-Columbian Americas, with pyramids dedicated to the Sun, to the Moon, and to Quetzatcoatl, the city of Teotihuacán presently is inhabited by street merchants rather than by acolytes in service to divinities. The incessant refrain of *"compra? compra?"* ("will you buy? will you buy?") reflects the displacement of the sacred by the mercantile (NNY). "It is the gods they are selling," the speaker marvels sardonically. These native vendors underline the erosion of their ancient faith by hawking to tourists cheap replicas of once holy icons. Tomlinson places the vocabulary of commerce and the vocabulary of worship in harsh juxtaposition to illustrate the shift in values separating this contemporary "priesthood of vendors" from the religion that once dominated the ancestral empire. The gods themselves illustrate the disturbing convergence between old and new.

While "Teotihuacán" and "Jemez" depict the collapse of traditional beliefs within the cultures inheriting them, "In Michoacán" presents a hostile encounter between two different theologies, with conquest providing the implicit background.

In Michoacán

A poor church
but an obstinate devotion
had filled it
with flowers.

What power drew
those flower-fraught Indians down
by narrow trails
no one knew

Until the earthquake:
after it, the altar
split wide open
like a hell-mouth,

And inside the wreck
there sat
its guardian idol:
squat, smiling, Aztec.

(AS)

When the site of worship, the altar itself, is physically "split wide," the irremediable dissonance between traditional and imposed beliefs becomes breathtakingly visible. Once the "smiling," hidden god has been disclosed, and the pious behavior of the supposedly faithful reinterpreted, it becomes evident that the native population did successfully defend its own metaphysical territory. An ancient faith has been preserved behind the facade of the new, the altar ironically serving as the point of convergence (and divergence) between them. Concealed loyalties, quickening behind and within the "wreck" of the established Church, have prevailed. On a further note of irony, the hell-like region associated by conquering Christians with evil proves to be the locus of the secret "power" animating the colonized and dispossessed.

Formally, the poem mimics the struggle it depicts, emphasizing the tension collecting at the point where mutually inimical energies intersect. The moment of unexpected revelation occurs exactly at the midpoint of the poem. Enjambment linking the last line of the second quatrain with the first line of the third draws out the suspense at the poem's center: "no one knew"—*pause*—"Until the earthquake." The first two stanzas are concerned with the worshippers' superficially compliant behavior, the last two with their triumphantly subversive motives. This structure, with four quatrains "split" down the middle, effectively mirrors the theme of irreconcilable conflict.

The poet's use of the same rhyme scheme in all four quatrains (not by any means a set habit of Tomlinson's) underlines the antiphonal shaping of the poem. Envelope rhyme, often slant, and displaced from end-line position, governs all four stanzas, although unpredictably placed internal rhymes tend to disguise this pattern. In the first stanza, for instance, the *poor / flower* rhyme in lines #1 and #4 encloses the *it / obstinate* rhyme in lines #2 and #3. In the third stanza, however, the extra rhymes of *until / hell* and *after / alter* almost overwhelm the enveloping *earth / mouth* (#1 and #4) and *it / split* (#2 and #3). In lines as short as these, the interpolation of additional rhymes distracts attention from what is in essence a predictable rhyme scheme, executed in highly contemporary fashion. This formal regularity works subtly to reinforce the thematic conflict between diametrically opposed forces.

"In the Emperor's Garden," also set in Mexico, again depicts subversive resistance to conquest, concentrating on the land itself as the locus of dispute. A Frenchman's dream of re-creating Versailles in colonized territory is frustrated by "tropical exuberance": plantings thrive with perverse lushness, confounding all attempts at schematic arrangement (A). The "urgent earth" itself, "Mexican at heart," buckles and shifts under the weight of vegetation that quickly "outgrew the proportions of the place." The dark overthrow of foreign schemes by indigenous forces is emphasized by the "opaque and sombre canopy" formed overhead by a roof of "interlaced" foliage: lacking in sunny, open spaces, the whole is closed in by "impermeable shade." Even more significantly, a garden that "should have been level" instead "hangs / Precipitously above a deep ravine." This gash in the earth serves as visible sign of the breach between cultures. Stone walls which were to subdivide the garden, containing it in well-defined units, are collapsing into the ever deepening "abyss":

> As the retaining walls bequeathed their symmetry
> To the volcanic, shifting soil, their masonry
> Silently easing its spoils into the abyss beneath.

The very soil of the place is in revolt against foreign control, slyly undermining imposed designs; its passionate energies constitute a literally underground resistance. This guerilla action even succeeds in wresting and secreting "spoils" from the enemy. The eruptive subterranean forces at work here are reminiscent of the buried Aztec god of "In Michoacán," whose hidden power successfully subverted efforts to suppress native religion. "You are forced to say / One thing," Tomlinson notes: "This is not French." A tangible site of convergence and confrontation, the garden shows the fastidiously geometric precision of a European sensibility insidiously overpowered by the New World's irrepressible fecundity.

"Weeper in Jalisco" shows Tomlinson meditating on antagonisms within a single doctrinal framework. Inside a Mexican church filled with representations of martyred saints, he contrasts the earthly suffering Christianity countenances with the heavenly restitution it promises. "All / hacked, mauled, bound," the saints "bleed" beneath a "dome of gold" (AS). Their torments have been recorded with a grisly detail incongruous in these otherwise "glistening" surroundings and in the face of the martyrs' own presumed "early resurrection" into glory. Their eternal peace is "blood- / bought"; the unusual enjambment at the hyphen focuses attention on this word, further suggesting the ambiguous value of a spiritual reward "bought" by physical pain. The contrast between "blood" and "gold," between human misery and heavenly splendor, is restated in slightly different terms as the martyred but now happy dead are compared to us, the living: "They / are in paradise now / and we are not—." There is absolute disparity between the eternal bliss they now enjoy and our continuing earthly trials. The saints have disappeared "up" into another sphere:

> leaving us this
> tableau of wounds, the crack

>   in the universe sealed
>   behind their flying backs.

The phrase "tableau of wounds" assumes double resonance, describing the human condition *per se* as well as the frieze of "hacked" saints decorating this house of God.

The difference between "here" and "there" is strongly iterated as Tomlinson introduces the "weeper" of the poem's title, a woman who "sprawls and wails" to saints who are located definitively elsewhere, on the other side of that "sealed" "crack / in the universe." Her unidentified griefs are said to replicate those of the saints to whom she prays: "she is the voice / those wounds cry through / unappeasably bleeding." It is now she who "shoulders / the price and weight" exacted of Christians for their paradise. Separated utterly and entirely from the "keening" worshipper, the saints appear to offer no effectual comfort, a hint that the hope of ultimate redemption may not invariably assuage earthly woes. The poem thus concentrates on the unbreachable gulf between material problems and immaterial solutions, between human need and institutionalized doctrinal response. Here, as with "In Michoacán," socially and theologically based boundaries are emphatically lines of division: a "split" in the earth or a "crack" in the cosmos. Antagonistic relationships between or within culturally defined value systems can best be understood, such metaphors suggest, in terms of an abruptly opening space, an absolute cut-off point.

The emphasis on "gold" decorations in the Jalisco church hints at socioeconomic disparity too, that between individual poverty and institutional affluence. Tomlinson addresses disturbing dichotomies between rich and poor in a number of other poems as well, often identifying the church as a locus of dissonance between avowed ideals and social realities. "Los Pobrecitos" takes as its title a street beggar's description of herself and her cohorts: *"Caridad para los pobrecitos"*: charity for *the little poor ones* (NNY). The poet interprets this choice of words as a "courteous" and "cunning" attempt to make the act of giving psychologically more comfortable. The recipients' self-declared smallness seems to endow the donors with a corresponding largeness—in size, in status, and in moral worth. If the poor are small and powerless, moreover, they represent no threat to the socioeconomic *status quo;* thus the rich are invited to assume a comfortably nurturing, quasi-parental role. As Tomlinson drily suggests, "diminutives sweeten / between beggar and giver / the injustices of living."

These mendicant "sitters in shadows" form the dark underside of a society characterized by enormous disparities between rich and poor. Haunting church vestibules and the "porches" of public buildings, "los pobrecitos" provide, with their presence, "both prologue and epilogue / to each gold interior," an ironic framing of Christian values and institutions. Drawn from the literary realm, Tomlinson's *prologue-epilogue* metaphor demonstrates how poverty surrounds and emphasizes the prosperity—the "gold interior" or central drama—of the lives of the wealthy. Just as visitors are compelled to encounter members of the underclass every time they enter or leave a public building, so the reality of poverty serves as visible premise and consequence of unequal distribution of resources in this society.

In another poem set in Mexico, Tomlinson juxtaposes religious responses to social and economic inequities with political solutions. While a public celebration of Constitution Day is under way, the "proletariat" is "going the wrong way," i.e., turning to prayer and "the Dark Virgin of Tepeyac hill" for redress of its problems ("Constitution Day" AS):

> penitents come pouring in
> to the gold interior and effigy,
> deaf to the Day and seeking
> the promise of a more than human mercy.

Their need for assistance beyond any offered by government or other "human" agencies is understandable in light of the description of the "committee" in power:

> quite the best-
> dressed Mexicans I have seen,
> perched there beyond the doom
> of the ragged rest . . .

Governmental authority merely seals the already existing economic gap between haves and have-nots. The physical separation of the two groups, one "perched . . . beyond" the other, is echoed in "The Bootblack," which depicts another scene from the same day's celebration. The shiner of shoes is located "down there," invisible except for glimpses of hair, hands, back, and shoulder blades (AS). His apparent acquiescence to his own socially and economically depressed position reminds Tomlinson of rationalizations typically offered in Judeo-Christian doctrine for social stratification and its accompanying evils:

> I say: 'The shoes
> are fit for a king.' And he smiles.
> Will he be
> angry or mirthful when he
> inherits the earth?

Scriptural allusion emphasizes the enormous hierarchical shift necessary for this literally low-placed individual to succeed to the kingly inheritance promised him—conveniently—in another world (Matthew 5:5). The ironic tone of the concluding speculation raises questions about repressed resentments, forcing recognition of the instability inherent in any system predicated upon disparate opportunity. Inevitably the boundaries between rich and poor are fraught with such tensions, Tomlinson asserts, even in the absence of immediate physical reminders of those on the other side of the economic divide. When Manhattan is buried in mist, still "the unseen" makes itself felt: "the homelessness beyond the mist-lopped towers— / Presses upon us" ("On Madison" NNY).

Not all social differences rub against one another with such abrasiveness; elsewhere Tomlinson addresses disjunctions in custom or belief marked by less disturbing implications. In addition to poems portraying radical inter- and intra-cultural conflict, the reader finds others in which the poet discovers elements of two or more cultural legacies co-existing relatively benignly in the same place. Because the individual character and historical roots of each tradition remain recognizable, the result is an intriguing cultural riprap, a loosely constructed assemblage of recognizable, discrete parts. In the American southwest, for example, near San Antonio, New Mexico, Tomlinson finds himself spectator at a native dance layered with multiple meanings. "All ranged / in a double line," the dancers enact a "dual betrayal": the conquest of the Moors in Spain simultaneously becomes the story of the triumph of Cortez over the Aztecs in Mexico ("The Matachines" WW). The female traitor-collaborator figures in the two historical narratives (the Moroccan emperor's daughter and Cortez's "Indian mistress") "meet / in the white / minute girl / dancing in her / communion dress" who plays the oddly co-mingled part. This "Moorish dance" overlaid with a Native American plot is further complicated by the introduction of a seemingly extraneous bullfighting motif:

> and where the bull
> came from
> nobody says
> or why she
> must betray
> him too . . .

The celebration of the feast day of St. Antonio of Padua is thus a "dance of / multiform confusions":

> whatever we
> do or
> mean in this
> dance
> of the bull
> and the betrayal:
> whatever we
> do we mean
> as praise, praise
> to the saint
> and the occasion . . .

Incongruity is Tomlinson's theme here, an incongruity created by the juxtaposing of different cultural traditions rather than by hostile confrontation between them.[1] Their boundaries remain discernible, even as the history of one culture is superimposed upon that of the other. Just as the river, railroad tracks, and highway in "Along the Mohawk" provide visible record of cultural-historical changes, so the line of dancers in this poem—imitated pictorially by the elongated shape of the poem on the page—serves as the point of convergence between incompletely blended cultural histories.

"The Mediterranean" takes readers to a different part of the world but focuses on similar kinds of visible incongruities. Remnants of Italy's past, in the shape of traditionally cultivated vineyards and old architectural masterpieces, survive into the present but sit cheek-by-jowl with products of modern technology: "This country of grapes / Is a country, also, of trains, planes and gasworks," the poet announces (SIB). The proximity of mundane, homely conveniences to relics of a seemingly more exotic or romantic past triggers startled resentment in the beholder. "'Tramway and palace' rankles," he acknowledges, reading aloud from a guidebook that refers to both in the same breath.

Is the splendor of the palace not diminished, even mocked, by such even-handed mention? The imagination, Tomlinson avers, is reluctant to embrace such a grotesque combination. By the end of the poem he concludes, however, that the imagination demands truth more urgently than anything else, that it ultimately rejects the "half lies" of "advertisements" or "politics." "This country" is, in fact, an intersection of old and new, of nature and artifice, of beauty and utility. "The sea laps by the railroad tracks," Tomlinson muses, implying that an unsullied ocean view might be aesthetically more satisfying, but quickly he adds that "to have admitted this [contiguity of the railway] also defines the sea." Again, as is evident in numerous poems discussed in chapter 1, territories natural and human, ancient and modern, gain clarity of definition as they press against one another's boundaries. Ultimately the imagination profits from such clarifying "lines of force" ("At the Edge" F).

In a poem set in New York City, Tomlinson salutes the cultural plurality of the U.S.A., rescuing the old *melting pot* cliché from triteness. Many of the employees and patrons he observes in a busy mid-town bar and grill are "actors between shows" ("At Hanratty's" DW). There is disparity, therefore, between what they are and what they seem to be: are the waiters *acting*, he wonders, as they take orders and bring food? His musings on role-playing are complicated by the discovery that many of the servers are first- or second-generation immigrants. "Whirling past / like a small dervish," one waitress proves to be "Turkish by descent," though she has rejected traditional clothing and is uncertain of her parents' precise cultural identity ("'Kurdies'"? or "'Kirghiz'"?). "She acts like an American," Tomlinson declares, and with the double entendre on the word "act" he introduces the idea that playing a role may be the first step toward assuming a new identity in earnest. Perhaps the waiters and waitresses "grow into a patience they begin / by merely feigning," just as new immigrants may acquire a genuinely American identity that they first can only play-act. New York City itself, port of entry for so many aspiring new citizens, is swarming with inhabitants in various stages of assimilation:

> of nationalities learning parts
> that are new to them—of Juans
> who would prefer
> to be called John.

Even though any one individual may achieve perfect or near perfect assimilation, the continuous arrival of newcomers effectively prevents the place from becoming culturally homogeneous. Tomlinson's focus is on the process itself, never-to-be-completed, of multicultural mixing. Discrete identities and backgrounds jostle continuously against one another, confirming the heterogeneous character of the whole.

In Puerto Rico Tomlinson contemplates another variation on the sociohistorical potpourri of the Americas. He describes the mixed European influence on architecture in the city of San Juan, for instance: "coming here is like returning to Europe" ("San Juan" DW). He finds, moreover, as he did in Italy, uneasy juxtaposition of old and new: a majestic cathedral sits "marooned among the parked cars," seemingly cut off from its origins and out of place in its modernized surroundings ("San Juan"). The small town of Aguadilla provides an even more amazing collage of impressions. There is an immediate contrast between the hot, crowded roadway, clogged with "stalled" traffic, and refreshing glimpses of a pastoral setting, e.g., "feather dusters of the sugar-cane blossoms / wave to us from beyond the houses in open country" ("Crossing Aguadilla" DW). Crowded with inhabitants who appear both "excitable" and "patient" as they wait for a procession to pass, the main intersection hums with a plethora of unrelated activities. Cars pass by a girl with a microphone reading "passages of scriptural exhortation" to responsive pedestrians. This intersection doubling as an open-air church is at the same time an amusement park; "a tiny train" filled with children circles around a "patch of park," and "salsa music" fills the air. Tomlinson's descriptions emphasize ironic or amusing juxtapositions in the busy hodgepodge, e.g., "the Charismatic Church" next door to "the Miracle Pharmacy"; a street named "Absence" near another called "Happy Days"; a sign announcing "Jesus is Coming / Prepare yourself" beside a McDonald's fast-food restaurant. Penitents are "falling on their knees in the dust of the roadway" even as "imperturbably intent" shoppers go about their business. All these beneficiaries of mixed historical legacies and cultural influences continue moving, like "el tren infantil," along their own particular tracks ("as if forever") in this small place riddled with divergent impulses.

Sometimes Tomlinson presents intercultural encounters that are more personal, more hypothetical, than those in the preceding examples: they occur in the arena of mind, when the poet-visitor confronts one place with mental images of another. Assisted by memory and imagination, he brings two or more places, together with their accumulated histories, into abrupt adjacency. Thus he writes a friend that since his return home from a visit to Japan, "the trees have a Japanese look / . . . bare in their wintry sinuousness" ("Letter to Uehata" A). The scene immediately before him, with branches bereft of foliage during an English winter, is overlaid with vivid impressions of the stylized, carefully wrought appearance of trees in an oriental garden. The actual does not merge completely with the remembered, but rather co-exists with it: "I can read / In the bareness of the trees a double scene— / Where I am now and where we both were then." Regarding English trees from a point of view that now includes Japanese trees, Tomlinson allows acquaintance with something previously alien to challenge and revitalize his perception of the familiar.

"A Sense of Distance" explains how the mind brings about such a meeting between geographically distinct places. Home in England, he recalls a sojourn in the American southwest. The intensity of the remembered landscape renders it as real in his consciousness as the place where he now stands:

> For I am in England,
> and the mind's embrace
> catches-up this English
> and that horizonless desert space
> into its own . . .
>
> (WW)

The mind creates "a single sphere" encompassing perceptions both of "space" here and now and of "space" remembered, dramatically expanding the range of sensory experience: "all / the kingdoms of possibilities shone / like sandgrains crystalline in the mind's own sun." Each separate "grain" of reality preserves its own "crystalline" distinctness in this mental universe, which becomes a worthy equivalent to the physical world. Effecting a convergence between noncontiguous places or times, the mind thus extends indefinitely the benefits associated with a border view.[2] These meetings in "the mind's embrace" function as more than simply strong comparisons, although they naturally lend themselves to such purpose. In "Letter to Uehata" Tomlinson is not merely comparing English trees to Japanese trees, for instance, but viewing English trees from a new perspective, appreciating two points of view simultaneously. Thus he stands poised perfectly on a boundary line laid out in imaginative "space."

In fact, it is not absolutely necessary that perception of a place be based upon personal familiarity in order for it to be juxtaposed in the mind with some other locality. A "world imagined that is really there / ... reaches for our thoughts across ... space"; landscapes never seen thus can be "stored within the mind's bright satellite" ("Here and There" A). The imagination may be stimulated by mental images derived from reports or pictures, as in a poem titled "Macchu Picchu" which actually is set in Gloucestershire, England. Standing at his own front door, watching an awesome display of cloud formations in the darkening sky of an impending storm, the poet imposes upon the scene a mental picture of a place he has never visited in person.[3] His memory of photographs supplies him with vivid images of "a whole high geography" of "piling crag" and "mountain ... across the view of empty upper-sky" (R). He describes an English sky as if it were in the immediate vicinity of the Andes, so close that a bird "astray from there" easily makes the trip from Macchu Picchu to Ozleworth, Gloucestershire, with apocalyptic news. Nothing less than the geography of the world's most gorgeously inaccessible mountaintop fortress—last retreat of a people facing imminent conquest—will serve to convey the hugely threatening potency of the Gloucestershire storm. Again Tomlinson conveys "doubleness" in a scene, portraying each of the two places in terms of the other. Storm clouds in England resemble a famous site in the Andes, a site which itself becomes seemingly vulnerable to a tempest originating on another continent. The poem salutes the raw power of natural forces threatening to "dispossess[]" and "efface" every last refuge on earth.

One of the most spectacular examples of the mind's power to contain and juxtapose different places and times can be found in "Byzantium," a poem recording an incident from an extended visit to New York City.

Byzantium

In that 'corridor of garments'
Orchard Street the cry
of a gigantic nightingale or thrush
drops out of the sky.

Out of the sky?
Out of the water-whistle

> of a vendor of plastic birds—
> and with so much of pastoral artifice
>
> that the Sundaying Jews
> in their cars on
> Delancey Street might be
> tourists along the Vale of Hebron.
>
> I choose a bird all green
> for the colour that is not here
> to testify to the birds of Gloucestershire
> where it is I have been.
>
> For, once I have gone
> back, such a roulade
> and cataract will never come
> to the ear as on the sidewalks of Byzantium.
>
> (NNY)

Visiting New York City, Tomlinson not only observes it from an English perspective, he anticipates in advance how his perception of his English home later will be affected by the New York sojourn ("once I have gone / back . . ."), peering back and forth at the two places from both directions. The encounter between New York City and Gloucestershire is rendered still more elaborate by the extended allusion operating throughout the poem to juxtapose New York City with the semihistorical, semi-imaginary "holy city" of Yeats's "Sailing to Byzantium."[4] Holding all three places at once in his mental universe, the poet focuses on birds as the center of this three-way cultural intersection. He examines the "plastic birds" for sale on the streets of the garment district in light of both the real "birds of Gloucestershire" and the idealized golden bird in Yeats's poem.

The sheer number and noise of the "gigantic" creatures that "drop[] out of the sky" on Delancey Street momentarily deceive him into thinking they are real, lending New York a larger-than-life, science fiction-like vitality. The plastic flock takes over the street, commanding attention by creating a fantastical display—"a roulade / and cataract" of sound unlike anything the visitor ever before has heard. Picking up on the music motif prominent in Yeats's poem, Tomlinson describes sounds that resemble neither the "sensual music" which prevails in the beginning of "Sailing to Byzantium," nor the more spiritualized, highly crafted "sing[ing]" which Yeats's poet-speaker achieves in his mythically transformed state at the poem's conclusion. The noises emitted by the water-whistles clearly are not "sensual," not natural at all. Just as clearly, these plastic cries dispense no consoling or prophetic wisdom, even though they are the product of considerable art. Interestingly, Tomlinson does not suggest that the odd hootings are ugly; rather, they constitute a surprising kind of music, an overwhelming rush of sound (a veritable "cataract") that seems to sweep the listener up, willy-nilly.

Evidently the toys possess some power to move him, to capture his fancy. In selecting one to take home as a souvenir, he implies that this particular piece of whimsy—well crafted, noisy, nonbiodegradable, useless, and amazing—sums up for him the essence of New York. This toy bird will "testify to the birds of Gloucestershire / where it is [he has] been." With these lines, the speaker articulates the dramatic antithesis between home, where birds are real, and New York, where the only birds in sight are products of eccentric artifice. These will serve as mementos of a place that has devoted its ingenuity (undeniable), its craftsmanship (exquisite), and its technology (the best) not to create art which can speak of eternal verities, à la Yeats, but to manufacture mass-market plastic playthings.

Choosing a green bird, "for the colour that is not here," the British visitor further emphasizes differences between "here" and the country from which he has come. He echoes Yeats's phrasing ("Once out of nature I shall never take / My bodily form from any natural thing") in reverse, noting that "once [he has] gone / back," the very idea of a place like New York City will seem nearly unimaginable. A wildly, weirdly unique place, this city is "out of nature" like no place else on earth. Tone in the poem is ambivalent as Tomlinson confirms the remarkable qualities of "the sidewalks of Byzantium." The tip of the hat to James W. Blake's popular song, "The Sidewalks of New York," appropriately calls to mind the whole line from which the song's title is taken, along with its embedded allusion to Milton's "L'Allegro" ("Girls and boys together . . . tripped the light fantastic on the sidewalks of New York"). The speaker is by no means wholly approving of New York and its commitment to fantastic "artifice." He is visiting an astounding place, so one-of-a-kind that he needs tangible evidence of its highly developed peculiarities to display to unbelieving natives back home. In the final lines of the poem he expresses some sadness as he acknowledges that "once . . . back" he will hear nothing like the strange "music" of New York. But return home he will, and with some relief, to a greener, more natural way of life that boasts real, if less exceptional, birds.

Ignoring the thematic conflict between aging and immortality which is central to Yeats's poem, Tomlinson focuses instead on the polarity between "nature" and "artifice" in the special context of New York City, which is presented as an ironic version of Yeats's Byzantium. Full of artful invention, but lacking well-defined spiritual dimensions, this modern Byzantium inspires disquiet as much as awe. Tomlinson's response to it is both playful and alarmed; he seems pleased that such a place exists and at the same time glad not to remain in it permanently. Yeats seeks deliberate refuge in a city desirable precisely *because* it is "out of nature"; Tomlinson implies, in contrast, that while occasional excursions outside the confines of a natural environment can be exhilarating, life in a place devoid of "green" is unthinkable in the long run. A glance at the conclusions of the two poems shows that Tomlinson's speaker and Yeats's speaker are journeying toward destinations diametrically opposed.

New York City thus serves as the pivot point in a three-way intercultural confrontation. The poet distinguishes the exuberant "artifice" of New York from the natural "green" of England, using Yeats's Byzantium, with its mythic stature, to refine his impressions of New York's particular aura of unreality. The American city defines itself in terms of the other two places that bound it in the universe of Tomlinson's poem. As traveller and observer, Tomlinson might almost be likened to Melville's sperm whale, whose widely separated eyes enable it to sustain a divided and hence perpetually doubled view of the world: "he can at the same moment attentively examine two distinct prospects."[5] The fascination with historical and cultural encounters—boundaries in space and time, whether closely or loosely guarded, hostile or friendly—is amplified by the tendency to facilitate still more such intriguing and enriching meeting points in the interior terrain of mind.

Unsurprisingly, Tomlinson's life and career reflect the same energetic interest in cross-cultural convergence that infuses his poetry. Travel and residence abroad have played a major role in his development as a poet. His first extended foreign stay coincides, as he explains, with "the experience of beginning to write poems (my first real poems) in Italy in 1950–1951."[6] His sojourn in the region of Liguria acquainted him with the young Italian poet Paolo Bertolani, and the ensuing literary friendship provided Tomlinson with some useful points of comparison and contrast at various stages of their subsequent lives and careers. In particular, Tomlinson notes how he himself continued to seek and assimilate international influences, in contrast to his Italian friend's exclusive residence in his native place and concentrated focus on its landscapes, heritage, and politics: "He dug down and in and I reached out as far afield as America and Mexico."[7] The Italian experience was followed by a travelling fellowship to the United States (1959–60): "so . . . began a long and fruitful relationship with America."[8] A visiting professorship at the University of New Mexico (1962–63) resulted in an enduring engagement with the landscape and people of the American southwest, illustrated by numerous poems. A series of visits in ensuing years, including another academic appointment (this time at Colgate University), further extended his acquaintanceship with the New World, eventually embracing Canada and Mexico as well as many parts of the U.S.A.[9] Poems set in a variety of European countries testify to his explorations on the Continent (e.g., "Netherlands," "In Abruzzo," "Portuguese Pieces," "Paris in Sixty-Nine," "Tübingen"). Travel in Japan is marked by the "Zipangu" sequence and other poems. Tomlinson's résumé is liberally and consistently punctuated by lecture and reading tours abroad; he revisits known territory as well as breaking new ground, maintaining an extensive global network of literary contacts and friendships. When asked to identify contemporaries exercising special influence on his work, he named an international trio: Donald Davie from England, George Oppen from the U.S., and Octavio Paz from Mexico.[10]

Poems contemplating locales directly or obliquely identified as not native to him account for a significant proportion of his work. Early in his career he jokes about this propensity even as he defends it, in a poem called "More Foreign Cities" (SIB). He takes as epigraph a comment from a contemporary poet-critic: "'Nobody wants any more poems about foreign cities . . .'"[11] The poem offers a quiet rebuttal of this irritated pronouncement, illustrating how an outsider's perceptions of a place can transcend the triteness of description based on mere novelty, instead stimulating unexpected insights. His interest in unfamiliar and exotic locations co-exists, moreover, with an abiding concern for customs and landscapes close at hand. His books tend to bring together poems inspired by a variety of places. In his 1984 collection *Notes from New York and Other Poems*, for instance, he begins with a number of poems dedicated to impressions gathered from a visit to Manhattan, e.g., "At the Trade Center," "On Madison," "Lament for Doormen," and "Hero Sandwiches." This group of poems is followed without pause or explanation by others set definitively in England, in Tomlinson's native territory, e.g., "To Ivor Gurney," "Poem for My Father," "Near Hartland," "Morwenna's Cliff." Toward the end of the collection he positions a few poems set in Mexico, e.g., "Valle de Oaxaco," "At Trotsky's House." *The Return* (1987) similarly begins with a number of poems set in Italy, commemorating the poet's revisiting of scenes from his earlier sojourn there. The collection also contains poems set in Germany and the Netherlands, however, and others depicting scenes in Oklahoma, New Mexico, and England. Such easy movement from one part of the world to another, along with the clear conviction that one book can contain them all, accentuates the Whitmanesque exuberance in Tomlinson's embrace of diverse places, his unfeigned delight in the unique heritage belonging to each. His poems are rooted in impressively detailed historical and cultural awareness. He writes of the places he has visited, not like a tourist, but like a citizen of the world determined to see and understand as much of his birthright as possible.

The strength of Tomlinson's American connections has lent an international flavor to his reputation, as well as to his poetry and to his sense of himself as global citizen.[12] The U.S. has been a source of publishing opportunities throughout his career, and he has had an American audience consistently receptive to his work. He acknowledges the American critic Hugh Kenner as one of the first to promote his work: Kenner found an American publisher for Tomlinson's second book, *Seeing Is Believing* (New York: McDowell, 1958). Over the years, Tomlinson's work has appeared regularly in American periodicals (including, among others, *Poetry, Partisan Review, Antaeus,* and *Ploughshares*) and with especial frequency in *The Hudson Review*, which presented him with the Bennett Award for literary achievement in 1993. Travel and residence in the United States early in his career resulted in personal contacts with writers and artists such as William Carlos Williams, Marianne Moore, Yvor Winters, Louis Zukovsky, George Oppen, Georgia O'Keeffe, Robert Duncan, Robert Creeley, Wallace Stevens, and others.[13] Such acquaintanceships proved all the more valuable in that they provided a personal context for some important literary influences. Consistently Tomlinson names Stevens, Williams, and Moore as significant literary forebears,[14] and he has paid substantial tribute to their importance to him through projects such as his editions of Williams's *Selected Poems* (1976 and 1985) and anthology of criticism, *William Carlos Williams: A Critical Anthology* (1972), his literary memoir, *Some Americans: A Personal Record* (1981) (focusing on Pound, Oppen, Williams, and O'Keeffe), and numerous lectures and essays. Critical comment on Tomlinson has addressed both formal and thematic aspects of his American legacy, investigating, for instance, his adaptation of Williams's triadic line and his indebtedness to Stevens and Moore for "the voicing of nature's textures, contours, and many-faceted surfaces."[15] He has managed, moreover, "to assimilate his modern masters without becoming imitative just as he has been able to write persuasively about so many foreign landscapes without seeming touristic."[16]

The obvious and often acknowledged American side to Tomlinson—his easy familiarity with the United States, his large American audience, the strongly American strain in his literary sources and models—is counterbalanced by his active engagement with literatures and cultures outside the English-speaking world. It was the study of foreign languages, he reports, that triggered his sense of belonging to a world much larger and more diverse than his native Stoke-on-Trent: "I escaped through schooling. . . . and simply reveled in learning languages: languages meant another world out there."[17] His energetic pursuit of the riches to be gleaned in that "world out there" makes itself manifest in many aspects of his career, including a working knowledge of several languages besides his native English, e.g., Latin, Spanish, Italian, French, German.[18] A glance at some of his lecture topics discloses his broad-based commitment to a multinational framework for literature, e.g., "Ovid in Augustan Translation" (Albuquerque, 1981), "Shelley in Italia" (Terenzo, 1986). A deeply held conviction that literary works from many cultures should be accessible to a general audience of readers, coupled with his passion for languages, has led him to undertake substantial translation projects. Editor of *The Oxford Book of Verse in English Translation* (1980), he has translated the work of Giuseppe Ungaretti, Antonio Machado, César Vallejo, Octavio Paz, and others. He credits the task of translation with influencing and enriching his own development as a poet: it offers "insights into ways of broadening one's own scope," often leading to valuable experimentation with new topics, forms, and tones.[19] The challenge of working with another language furthermore provides the poet-translator with "something to bounce off, something to direct his inwardness at"; the foreign words themselves function like "pebbles and grit that can't be immediately ingested and subdued to one's own will." He adds: "In a curious way the business of translation and my fascination with translating re-duplicates or rather puts in a different manner this whole question of inwardness and outwardness, the self and the other. Your inner man . . . needs the challenge of other ways of doing things, of the other possibilities, of more comprehensive and perhaps definitive standards arrived at by previous poets."[20]

While his commitment to a multilingual literary world ("something bigger than myself") has led Tomlinson to become a translator of considerable stature, it has also caused him to embark upon more unusual literary enterprises.[21] To produce *Renga* (1971), a chain of poems in four languages, he collaborated with three other poets: Octavio Paz from Mexico, Jacques Roubaud from France, and Edoardo Sanguineti from Italy. The international dimensions of the project extend beyond Europe and the Americas, moreover, since the four contributors to *Renga* sought to create a Western equivalent for Japanese *kusari-renga*.[22] This ancient Japanese form consists of a series of three- and two-line segments of prescribed syllable count, corresponding to the 5–7–5 and 7–7 pattern of a tanka; contributing poets (usually four) take turns composing one segment at a time, so that the poem's evolution cannot be foreseen or controlled by its authors, either individually or collectively. "The completed text," as Michael Edwards explains, "was therefore not one but many poems, and was susceptible of a plurality of readings."[23]

Tomlinson and his collaborators sought to westernize the Japanese form by creating a sequence of sonnets, "the sole traditional form which has remained alive up to our own times . . . composed, like the tanka of semi-independent and separable entities."[24] They employed different sonnet types in the four series comprising their "chain," but introduced a contemporary flavor by discarding traditional metrical and rhyme schemes and by sometimes inverting the order of quatrains, tercets, and couplets. Every sonnet (except for the last in each of the four series) is composed in four languages; the four poets took turns composing either a quatrain or half of a sestet. The potential for multiple readings inherent in this multilingual experiment is further complicated by the poets' plan to create both sequential and crosswise coherence, i.e., in addition to reading the sonnets in sequential, or linear, order, one may read the first poems in each series as a group, followed by the second poems in each series, and so on.

The object of the collaboration was not to submerge the four poets' individual identities in an undifferentiated communal voice, but rather to preserve these in the process of conjoining them: "To see if four voices from the four corners could find a basic harmony. To see if each could remain *I* and *you* while at the same time becoming *us*."[25] The project thus preserves boundaries, between different languages and between individual poets, even as it forges a larger, collective whole to contain them. Paz, principal instigator of the *Renga* project, sees it as a natural extension of the preoccupation with translation ("not only of texts but of customs . . . all kinds of usages and practices") characterizing the twentieth century.[26] In Paz's view, this contemporary international "renga" proved to be less linear than its Japanese progenitor, not "a river which glides on," but rather "a place of meeting and opposition of different voices," i.e., "we had replaced the linear, melodic order by counterpoint and polyphony: four verbal currents which flowed simultaneously and which wove between them a network of allusions."[27] Composing this sequence of sonnets in which Italian, French, English, and Spanish shuttle back and forth, the four poets found each linguistic junction, or switch in language, a source of new impetus and inspiration. As Tomlinson puts it, in contributing to a "mutual structure," "one's self was discovered by the juxtapositions and the confrontations that met it."[28] The reader, faced with a "vertiginous language-leap" every few lines, is likewise compelled to spend time at the boundaries between one language and another in this poem which intensifies "the diverse resources of each national speech."[29] Like a similar bilingual project Tomlinson undertook later with Paz (*Airborn / Hijos del Aire* 1979 and 1981), the *Renga* venture illustrates in its radical conjunctions the passionate interest in border experiences that pervades Tomlinson's life and art. The innovative sonnet chain bristles with sharp, clear lines of cultural and linguistic demarcation as one language intersects with another, again and again, and the four poets visibly gather energy at these highly charged points of conjunction.

Even when working alone, Tomlinson frequently employs two or more languages within a single poem, drawing on his linguistic versatility to incorporate an apt word, or phrase, or line into a text composed principally in English. In exploring the possibilities of such simultaneous convergence and disjunction in his poetry, he is of course carrying on a tradition begun by early modernists like Pound and Eliot. That generation of poets often produced mosaic-like effects, confronting readers with little islands of foreign text stuck in amongst the English: one need think only of Pound's *Cantos* or Eliot's *Waste*

Land. Unlike such predecessors, however, Tomlinson tends to weave foreign words and phrases into his poems with un-self-conscious seamlessness, linking them closely by means of metre, rhyme, or syntax into the fabric of the poem. Despite the obvious demands the inclusion of foreign vocabulary makes on a reader, there is nothing elitist or flaunting in his approach, but simple delight in exercising multiple options for the expression of meaning.

Often the introduction of a phrase from a second language reinforces a poem's setting or adds background texture, as when bits of Spanish sprinkled in poems set in Mexico serve to intensify the reader's experience of being taken somewhere new and immersed in a different culture. Sometimes, however, Tomlinson draws on foreign languages for less obvious purposes. He incorporates German phrases into a poem describing the small highway town of Barstow, California, for example, for reasons a reader could not anticipate. Likening the wire-fenced yards to "tiny Belsens," he first makes a connection between this "placeless place" and the no-man's land of a concentration camp ("At Barstow" AS). He proceeds to lighten the mood of the poem immediately, however, by introducing an absurdly incommensurate, and hence humorous, comparison with Wagnerian opera: he mocks the spiritual deadness emanating from this particular fork in the highway with the wry observation that "the Götterdämmerung / would be like this":

> No funeral pyres, no choirs
> of lost trombones. An Untergang
> without a clang, without
> a glimmer of gone glory
> however dimmed. . . .

The complete absence of grandeur in this desolate "conjunction / of gasoline and desert air" renders it unsuitable for operatic treatment; no orchestra will accompany or commemorate its emptiness, for it fails to achieve tragic stature. As Tomlinson directs a touch of satire toward Wagnerian excess (those "choirs / of lost trombones"), he softens at the same time the harshness of his judgment on Barstow. It is a place to mock more than to condemn; criticism of its deficiencies is as much a sport as a moral exercise.

His play on the German word "Untergang" contributes importantly to the spirit of whimsical derision in the poem. The cultural void that

Barstow exemplifies is all the more humorous in the face of the implied comparison with Wagner's opera plots, and by rhyming the English word "clang" on the last syllable of "Untergang" Tomlinson intensifies the comic effect. The rhyme is full if "Untergang" is pronounced in anglicized fashion, slant if it is pronounced correctly (UntergAHng); a reader also might be tempted to slide into full rhyme by pronouncing "clang" as the German "Klang" (clAHng). Pedestrian associations with the noise of a "clang" effectively undercut the potential gravity inherent in the idea of an "Untergang." And the dual-language rhyme (with its invitation to multiple pronunciations), sandwiched in close sequence with *pyre / choir* and *glimmer / dimmed*, wittily underscores the deflating disjunctions inherent in the operatic comparison Tomlinson has invoked.

A poem set in Mexico exemplifies Tomlinson's equal facility in playing with English-Spanish combinations. Watching the funeral of a local civil servant, he describes the strangely waltz-like music a church organist inserts into the program of funeral music:

>   The waltz
>   seemed right as did
>   the deathmarch, the woe
>   of the inconsolable brass
>   preceding to the *campo santo*
>   the corpse, the women
>   and the *compañeros*
>   who sweated from street to street
>   under the bier,
>   swaying it like a boat.
>   ("The Tax Inspector" R)

Rhymes on the long *o* sound, beginning with "w*o*e" and "ins*o*nsolable," easily pick up and include the final syllables of "campo," "santo," and "boat"; "compañeros" forms part of this long, echoing sequence, and also produces an unusual slant rhyme with "corpse." The Spanish phrases are not set apart in terms of grammar and syntax, but integrated without break or awkwardness into the structure of an English sentence. Whether musing on a line from Rilke or reading posters in a Mexican bus, Tomlinson laces non-English vocabulary into his poems with a light and dextrous hand. In so doing, he pulls the reader more completely into the immediate environment of the poem, making powerful acknowledgement of another culture as he renders it alive and present.

In a poem dedicated to Octavio Paz, published in *The Door in the Wall* (1992), Tomlinson ponders the strong pull foreign places have exerted on him. "Twenty years ago," he reminds Paz, they both confronted opportunities to turn foreign sojourns into long-term residence, Paz considering England as a possible new home, and Tomlinson the U.S.A. ("In a Cambridge Garden"):

> Had you stayed on
> Twenty years ago, had I gone
>   To live in the house at Nine Mile Swamp,
> My children would have been Americans, and you
>   An exotic in this Cambridge garden. . . .

Tempting as these options once seemed, Tomlinson concludes that both of them were wise in choosing finally to remain in their native lands:

> These inquests on past possibilities
>   Serve merely to say that we
> Were right to choose the differing parsimonies
>   Of the places we belonged to. . . .

The substitution of the word "parsimonies" for the expected "patrimonies" suggests the richness of possibility that both rejected, yet Tomlinson seems certain that the apparent limitations of "the places we belonged to" ultimately provide the right foundation for a life—a spot to occupy with confidence while probing other parts of the world.[30] As men and as poets, the two in no way abandoned their keen interest in wider frontiers, but both continued to cherish the "belong[ing]" that is birthright rather than choice. Meeting his old friend now for a brief visit in this English garden, Tomlinson thinks about what each might have gained—and lost—had they, in effect, switched places, trading Europe for America and America for Europe. Twenty years ago their lives intersected at the brink of that possible exchange, and now they rehearse the consequences of their decisions, imagining, too, the hypothetical consequences of different ones: "And so we coincide / Against distance, wind and tide, meet / And translate our worlds to one another." To "translate . . . worlds" presupposes a distinction between the native and the foreign, the conviction that there is some portion of the earth to which an individual feels inextricably tied.

Even while Tomlinson's powerful sense of inhabiting a world much larger than any single nation has made him a traveller and won him highly developed familiarity with many far-flung parts of the globe, he has retained a deeply rooted English identity. His Englishness defines itself against his internationalism; hence, as Michael Edwards avers, "his strengths are both cosmopolitan and local."[31] Just as the four languages of the collaborative *Renga* preserve their individual integrity even while pressing repeatedly against one another's boundaries, so Tomlinson's engagement with English places, themes, and history is as pronounced as is his passion for investigating foreign terrain. His career has been "an exercise in the creative effects of cultural hybridization."[32] His poetry accordingly illustrates a continuous systole and diastole, exploration of the new—the other—alternating with intense concentration on the familiar. Reminiscing in a poem to one of his daughters about some of their early experiences in the United States, he comments: "How far we (a wandering family) have come / Since that day I backpacked you down / Into an Arizona canyon" ("To My Daughter" J). "Wandering" has enriched their lives, honed their identities by bringing them to the verge of new ones, while "the ties of blood / Root[] us in place, not like the unmoving trees / And yet, as subject to earth, water, time / As they."

3
Contrapuntal Designs

And the innumerable views
Kept troubling him, until
He granted them. Amen.

BORDERS DEFINE BY DIFFERENTIATING; THEY ENFORCE DISTINCTIONS. Because they mark the point at which adjacent regions or phenomena assume separate identities, inevitably they invite a mode of comprehension based on comparison and contrast, parallels and antitheses. Implicit throughout discussion thus far of the accumulating examples of Tomlinson's intense interest in boundaries is the preeminence of the principle of juxtaposition. Focusing from the beginning of his career on "relations and contraries" (the title of his first book), he shows tide set against shore, glacier against rock, earth against sky, sun against cloud; he juxtaposes Spanish and English, poverty and wealth, woodslope and cornland, old gods and new. Encompassing historical, economic, and sociopolitical polarities as well as the elemental, Tomlinson's preoccupation with "poised contraries" is neither static nor reductive.[1] Boundary lines may change position, even while remaining precisely denoted, as witness the framing window of a moving vehicle, or the "blade" of sunset repeatedly reconfiguring a landscape into areas of light and shadow. Alterations in political, intellectual, spiritual, or aesthetic allegiances likewise compel a re-charting of existing boundaries. Still more critical is the propulsive effect of borders on an observer's attention, which necessarily shifts back and forth along any defining edge, taking in first what lies on one side and noting then what lies on the other. Borders thus invite endlessly alternating points of view, a zigzaging pattern of shifting perspectives.

The habit of laying one idea or thing against another in order to explore the interplay between them is as central to Tomlinson's poetics as to his personal philosophy. He lingers along the crisp boundaries his poems present, savoring the distinctions they forge. The dynamics of counterpoint drive his work both thematically and technically, encompassing virtually all the elements of lyric poetry that lend themselves to the demonstration of antiphonal relationships. Diction, syntax, rhyme, stanza, line, and figurative usage, for instance, are influenced by this persistent interest, as are larger decisions concerning structure and content.

Throughout Tomlinson's poetry, the convergence of disparate phenomena is charged with activity and movement, juxtaposition serving to unleash "the energies pouring through space and time" ("Chance" A). In the evocation of these "energies," verbs play an insistent role. Tomlinson chooses and deploys action words with lavish inventiveness, favoring a vocabulary that seethes with motion and power. The verbs that dominate his dramatic renderings of "relations and contraries" often do double-duty, moreover, by lending the force of personification to the activity of inanimate or abstract phenomena and thereby investing it with quasi-human volition. "All moves / towards encounter," he muses; "the roof greets the cloud," and "lengthened shadows" are "intersecting" ("Winter Encounters" SIB).[2] Moving cloud formations create the appearance of "a vast / opposition throughout the sky," so that "the still / seems also on the move / the other way" ("Into Distance" S). Nothing is too inert to participate in the universal movement toward defining edges and the "shifting ties" thus forged: "inanimate or human, / The distinction fails in these brisk exchanges."

Tomlinson emphasizes the vitality of engagements between such personified energies repeatedly, as in Italy, when he admires an ocean view by night:

> The adagio of lights is gathering
> Across the sway and counter-lines as bay
> And sky, contrary in motion, swerve
> Against each other's patternings . . .
>
> ("The Return" R)

He perceives the juxtaposition of bay and sky not as a set pattern, but as mobile "pattern*ings*," formed by action and counteraction whose elements "swerve / Against" one another with decisive strength—almost, it would seem, with intention (emphasis added). Elsewhere, viewing the paralleled precision of a freshly plowed field, he admires the finished design less than "all the insatiable / activity towards it" ("Lines" PL). He personifies the tractor, which "hesitates" at each "reversal," then "turns and drags" its blade around to plow in the opposite direction. The machine, as he portrays it, "breeds" furrows, "line on line / until they fill a field"; in its "concerted / on-rush," it displays what looks like organic will and "aggression."

Personification plays an equally decisive role in his vehement depiction of a tree-lined avenue in the throes of a windstorm:

> At the wind's invasion
>   The greenness teeters till the indented parallels
> Lunge to a restive halt, defying still
>   The patient geometry that planted them
>   ("The Chestnut Avenue: at Alton House" PL)

"Assail[ed]" by fierce wind, the trees do not merely "sway"; they "lunge" and "defy." Such activity belies the precision, or "geometry," that guided the planting of them, investing them with a higher level of animation than any normally associated with vegetation. In the frenzy of their motions, they seem, human-like, to "deny" the design imposed on them by human cultivators. The trees' struggle takes place at the "frontier" between nature and "civility," a boundary to which Tomlinson's poetry takes us repeatedly, as discussion in chapter 1 already has indicated. Here powerful verbs anthropomorphize an aggressive confrontation between human "order" and an "incalculable" natural counterforce. Subjected to equal and opposite pressures, the trees respond to each in turn, "teeter[ing]" between them.

The back-and-forth movement of ocean against shore functions similarly as an image embodying the head-on meeting of oppositional forces. The unremitting struggle is described in detail in "The Atlantic," where the contents of an entire ocean appear to be "launched into an opposing wind" (SIB). The enormous, watery mass "hangs / Grappled beneath the onrush," and finally "drops from that hold / Over and shoreward" (SIB). Both sea and land are heavily personified, the incoming surf inevitably "collapsing" on the beach that "receives it," finally "relinquishing its power" and reversing itself, "unravelled," its force temporarily "spent." In the prose poem "A Process," a "whole moving belt" of water "swallows itself," only "to be regurgitated as combed-over foam," then "flung in reverse against the onrush that immediately pushes it forward" ("A Process" WW).

Verbs like "swallow," "regurgitate," "flung," and "push" epitomize the passionate, almost human intensity of that "encounter." In another description of surf, the alternating colors of sea water and foam appear to be the result of calculated violence: the "machine of nature" keeps on "crushing white from blue" ("Up at La Serra" PL). In "Cronkhite Beach" breaking waves appear to be "moving mountains / which as they sailed-in threw / the surf backwards from their peaks" with explosive force, "each like a separate volcano" (F). "On the Dunes" shows how "omnivorous water" has "pulverized" everything in its path, "washed [it] down with its midnight feast," for "there is sand in the teeth of the wave" (VS).

Equally assertive personification characterizes confrontations at seasonal boundaries, e.g., "the winter that would not go" is "blocking spring," deliberately "pushing sun / back" ("In April" F). "Orion Over Farne" presents the transition from autumn to winter as a flesh-rending battle between constellations: "the Scorpion tears / Orion" (A). The sounds of November storms are described in terms of a predator's attack, as "constellation / On hunted constellation grinds and growls." The sudden cold of winter's onset emerges as a "rawness menacing" ("In the Balance" S). Frost decorates window panes with "embattled sprays," and "gates snap like gunshot"; the atmosphere is "bladed," a "white resistance" ("Winter-Piece" PL). "The lengthening light" of early spring struggles against "the obduracy of March" ("Hawks" WrW); cold overwhelms "a reluctant April" ("Hill Walk" WI). New vegetation does not emerge in passive contrast to the gloomy barrenness of winter, but actively flares up in opposition to it: "this sodden, variable green / Igniting against the grey" ("Letter from Costa Brava" PL). Elsewhere "sun is *tautening* the field's edge shadow-line," and "haze *beats back* the summer sheen" ("In Arden" S, emphasis added).

This heavy reliance on verbs signifying antagonistic interaction, the forcefulness they express often enhanced by their personifying effect, is central to Tomlinson's presentation of converging antitheses. Things resist, refuse, deny, withstand, tug free. They churn; they push; they press; they surge; they quench; they drag; they hew; they clash; they eat; they cut. They threaten, divide, assault, and ink-out. This is the language of struggle and altercation. The "energies pouring through space and time" so often figure as sets of actively wrestling opponents because, in "bringing . . . sharp disparities to bear," juxtaposition accentuates differences and frequently appears to intensify them ("At

Holwell Farm" SIB). When the sun shines full on a tumbledown house, for example, "the sunburst / Serves only to darken its crevices, / To bring out the blackness in its window eye" ("History of a House" VS). Similarly, when contemplating the contrast between dazzling sunlight and heavily canopied rainforest in Puerto Rico ("flame" versus "shade"), Tomlinson writes: "light / That is the servant of surfaces, must filter / To feed its opposite—dark soil" ("Fire" DW). The necessary biological relationship between unremitting sunlight and luxuriant plant growth points to the equally inevitable, if more abstract, relationship between dichotomous phenomena in general. Opposites do "feed," and feed off, each other. Each "complements" the other "in opposition," defining by way of contradiction ("At Holwell Farm").

Thus, even as he highlights the antagonism inherent in relationships based on antithesis, Tomlinson claims they are mutually fructifying. The prose poem "Oppositions" presents an illustrative meeting between earth and air; these elements seem clearly contrary in nature, the solidity of the one contrasting with the insubstantiality of the other. Tomlinson asks readers to picture layers of mist sinking into low-lying bits of land, to envision how the contours of a landscape become more pronounced when moisture-packed air renders the boundary between earth and its enveloping atmosphere temporarily visible: "mistlines flow slowly in, filling the land's declivity that lay unseen until that indistinctness had acknowledged them" (WW). Paradoxically, the very "indistinctness" of mist brings topography more clearly into relief; the fog-filled air traces the solid shape of the earth with new precision. An ordinarily invisible borderline, briefly highlighted by a special atmospheric occurrence, causes us to perceive our immediate environment more accurately, to gain knowledge about it that will outlast the occasion. Tomlinson's choice of the verb "acknowledge," one thing *acknowledging* its opposite, indicates by means of personification his sense of a vital relationship between converging, juxtaposed elements. Opposites serve to challenge, to defy, or to question one another; and in so doing, they nourish, they clarify, they redefine.

Deftly pressing action words into service of his designs, Tomlinson extends his attention to microscopic linguistic levels: patterns of verb formation, complementing patterns of verb selection, contribute significantly to the dynamic thrust of his preoccupation with antithesis. He demonstrates a persistent affinity for verbs formed by means of affixation, often inventing novel usages and employing them for maximum impact. Two kinds of verb prefix exercise special appeal for him: those that cancel or reverse the action expressed by a verb (particularly *un* and *dis*), and those that repeat or reinstate it (particularly *re*). Verbs with such prefixes are conspicuous in his poetry, e.g., "re-murmur," "uncreate," "remeasure," "unwindowed," "recompose," "unblinded," "re-rhymed," "rebegotten." Often, too, they appear in combinations that emphasize a process of alternating action, e.g., "resolve . . . dissolving," "told . . . re-told," "shaping . . . unshaping," "disintegrating . . . reassembling," "redefined . . . reachieved," "disrupt . . . restore . . . disperse." Both singly and in sequences, such prefixed verbs enact a fugue-like rebounding of energies.

Not infrequently Tomlinson inserts a hyphen between prefix and stem, thus calling attention to the effect of the prefix on the action of the verb, e.g., "re-touching," "re-open," "un-made," "re-tongue," "re-told," "re-joining." Such hyphenation can be explained in some instances as a simple expedient to prevent awkwardness or misreading. A hyphen may separate two vowels, as in "re-establish" or "re-ascend." A more interesting necessity compels the insertion of other hyphens: when Tomlinson builds a verb by affixing a prefix to a stem, the resulting word may already exist in the English lexicon but with a meaning different from that which he intends. In "Crossing the Moor," for example, he employs the term "re-forming" to describe the "face [of the] universe" being *formed anew* by "weather, space, and time" (J). To omit the hyphen might cause a reader to stumble, to substitute the usual meaning of the word *reform* (the notion of amendment or rehabilitation) for the intended idea, i.e., a process of reshaping. In a case like this, the hyphen accentuates the prefix and the reconstructive force of its meaning: *re*-form. In "The Chances of Rhyme" Tomlinson similarly chooses to hyphenate the word "re-lease," noting immediately that he wishes readers to understand the word "in both / Senses," i.e., to juxtapose the ordinary meaning (to let loose) with something like its opposite (WW): to renew a contract or connection. The hyphen emphasizes provocatively contrapuntal implications of the homonym he has invented.

At the same time that hyphens highlight the meanings imposed by prefixes on the action of verbs, they suggest the provisional nature of the combinations thus formed—and hence of the actions denoted. Hyphenating "re-told" or "re-join," for example, when he might have omitted the hyphens with no fear of misapprehension, Tomlinson deftly points out that the particular focus of meaning invoked by a prefix is not an inextricable or permanent property of the verb. Hyphenation draws attention to the susceptibility of an action to redirection. In this "world-in-making," actions are subject to varied, often contrary, influences ("Macchu Picchu" R): *con*structive, *de*constructive, *re*constructive.

Sometimes Tomlinson further heightens the effect of affixation by forcing a line break at the hyphen. The severed prefix wraps around the end of one line and envelops the beginning of the next, forcing the reader to wait in suspense for the meaning-bearing portion of the verb to appear. Such instances of enjambment effectively stretch the claim of a prefix on the reader's attention. In "The Discovery" the break in the middle of the word "re-echoed" also serves to position the stem directly beneath the verb with which it is paired (DW):

> echoed and re-
> echoed chambered
> in earth and leaves:

The contrast between the action (echoing) and the action as modified (echoing *again*) is enhanced by this deliberate placement, which creates the visual equivalent of an echo. Calling attention to the separable nature of the prefix, the poet successfully mimics the sustained reverberation of sound waves. In another example, "Misprint," he describes the disconcerting effect of a typographical error, a single wrong letter derailing the sense of a whole manuscript:

> instead, one
> single letter has un-
> made, punned
> meaning away . . .
>
> (S)

Here, too, enjambment heightens the effect of both hyphen and prefix; *un*-making is the crux of the poem. The verb, separated at its hinge between the deconstructive force of *un* and the constructive act of *making*, sums up the essence of the poet's rueful meditation. Attempting to make meaning, he has instead watched its collapse. The broken verb, bumping down the stairway of a seemingly awkward line break, points perfectly toward the interruption of a line of communication.

When Tomlinson applies prefixes to build unaccustomed or novel terms (e.g., "uncreate," "unskein," "rebegotten"), he is, like any ordinary speaker, enjoying the linguistic flexibility of rules of affixation. No reader will fail to recognize his meaning when he writes, for example, of "undoubling" or "unpicking"; the power of the prefix "un" to cancel the named action renders his meaning readily comprehensible, even if the form it takes is unexpected. Like all novelties, moreover, these creations fitted to particular contexts attract special notice. They serve a purpose beyond their immediate usefulness in expressing meaning because a never-before-heard term tends to jump out at a reader. An odd or unexpected use of affixation, invoked to reverse or reinstate an action, demands a moment of reflection. The prefix in its role as radical modifier of action pushes itself into the foreground of awareness.

The emphatic effect of even a single instance of such inventive affixation may be observed in "Swimming Chenango Lake." Focusing on the changing surface of a body of water, Tomlinson notes how "a wind is unscaping all images" and creating "a mere mosaic of tiny shatterings" (WW). "Unscaping" describes the wind's destructive effect on the pattern of reflections visible on the lake; wind ripples the water and thus shreds the "waterscape." The deceptively solid appearance of the water (compared by Tomlinson to "flowing obsidian") is emphasized by the novel term "unscaping," which suggests a vigorous physical dismantling. The term also appears to personify the wind, enhancing its action by implying purposefulness. The reader thinks, perhaps, of a landscaper, someone who makes things (e.g., flower beds, fish ponds) to create a deliberately planned environment. The activities of an *un*scaper, contrastingly, would comprise deliberate obliteration and deconstruction. Even as wind-driven undulations pull apart the surface designs on the water, however, they are simultaneously engaged in "incessant[] shaping" of new ones. *Unscaping* and *shaping*, two distinctly opposing forces at work on the same medium, create a "mosaic" undergoing perpetual rearrangement.

Tomlinson's manipulation of prefixed verbs achieves its most potent effects when he presents them in pairs and longer series. He employs iterative stacking of a prefix upon itself, in tandem with different verbs (unblinded / unbounded, redefined / reachieved). He arranges alternation of different prefixes in combination with the same verb (resolve / dissolve, shaping / unshaping), as well as alternation of prefixed and unprefixed forms of the same verb (making / unmaking). All such sequencings highlight the contrapuntal energies latent in the action named, i.e., its susceptibility to drastic shifts in the direction of its energy. "In the Estuary," for instance, depicts in detail the movement of the tide, concentrating on the continuously changing features of the rivermouth: "an archipelago / Of islets" rises up before a "continental mass" (F). The poem portrays a place in flux, "neither sea nor land," governed by "an unseen moon." The poet's pivotal observation is that "you could not map / This making and unmaking." Here the insertion and deletion of a prefix imitates the back-and-forth movement that is his central recognition. *Making* and *unmaking*: "You end in contraries like the bight itself," he concludes. "Rolling and unrolling," the sea provides ideal illustration of contrarily acting forces; "lifting" "on its way in, and, on its way out . . . dropping" ("Fiascherino" N). "Morwenna's Cliff" portrays a particularly arresting phenomenon governed by the predictable actions of ocean water. The "tide-edge" rushing up to the base of the cliff forms what looks like "a human face," but this illusion is discernible only at the "instant of definition" when the cliff is outlined by the breaking of an incoming wave (NNY). "The face comes imaging up from chaos," "printing and reprinting itself" at the exact boundary between water and land. In "Shorelines" the ocean likewise "writes and rewrites its margins" (VS).

The whole of "MacKinnon's Boat," a poem ostensibly narrating a fishing expedition, concerns an "alternation" of energies, characteristically accentuated by the generous deployment of prefixed verbs (WrW). The poet-speaker's initial observation is that conditions are not right for creating the reflections so often visible on the sea water: "today / The waters will have nothing to do with the shaping / Or unshaping of human things." Focus shifts quickly to the rapid actions of the fishermen, which constitute a human sequence of repetition and reversal, or "shaping" and "unshaping": casting out creels and dragging them in; loosening and then tightening cage-nets; securing the catch and discarding waste. More prefixed verbs, "undo," "re-thread," and "re-tie," emerge prominently in this description of "the disparate links of [a] concerted action." The activity as a whole (i.e., fishing) is "one," but comprises distinct and antithetical units of action. Counterpoint is also evident in the pacing of the day's work. Breaking for cigarettes, the fishermen are "sharing the rest that comes of labour." Immediately, however, we are forced to perceive this moment of relaxation as the flip side of its necessary opposite: "But labour must come of rest: and already / They are set towards it." Syntactic inversion ("the rest that comes of labour" / "labour must come of rest") reinforces an already well established pattern of action. The poem piles example upon example to illustrate the successive propulsion of energies, both human and natural, in opposite directions: a "drawing in" and a "let[-ting] down," whether of fishing equipment or of ocean tide, "in the alternation of the forgetful waters."

"Ode to Arnold Schoenberg" similarly represents processes oscillating between opposite ends of a continuum, this time in the realm of music. Subtitled "on a performance of his concerto for violin," the poem presents pairs and sequences of prefixed verbs throughout its twenty-two triadic lines. Schoenberg's music is described in terms of the images it awakens in the listener's imagination. First one pictures a "double willow," a tree seemingly connected to its own reflection at the "margin" of a river (PL). Wind "variously / disrupts, effaces / and then restores" the reflected tree "in shivering planes." The auditory source for this image also undergoes a doubling, or echoing: "the twelve notes . . . and their reflection." Like the double tree, the notes nonetheless form a "unity," a single entity composed of mirroring parts. A pun on "winds" indicates that the woodwinds "rout" and "disperse[]" this musical unity, just as the elemental "wind" erases the reflected image of the willow. The result is "dissonance"; half of the unified whole is temporarily threatened.

> in the liberation of the dissonance
>   beauty would seem discredited
>   and yet is not:
> redefined
>   it may be reachieved,
>   thus to proceed
> through discontinuities
>   to the whole in which
>   discontinuities are held

The heaping up of words prefixed by "re" and "dis" enacts the movement of the concerto, including the to-and-fro effect of its music on the listener. This pattern of movement is reinforced unobtrusively by the triadic line structure.[3] "I'd discovered Webern and Schoenberg just when I started fragmenting my lines," Tomlinson notes, "spacing them out with breath-pauses and hesitations, caught up very consciously into the fabric of the whole."[4] Things fall apart; things come back together. There is progressive dissolution and resolution of a melodic statement. What is "reflected" in Schoenberg's music is "disrupt[ed]" . . . "dispers[ed]" . . . "discredited" . . . "restor[ed]" . . . "redefined" . . . "reachieved," overcoming "discontinuities" not by escaping but by acknowledging and containing them.

The concluding triads of the poem sum up this fine balance between discord and consonance:

> For what is sound
> > made reintelligible
> > > but the unfolded word
> > branched and budded,
> > > the wintered tree
> > > > creating, cradling space
> > and then
> > > filling it with verdure?

Dismantled sense is rendered finally "reintelligible," just as the "unfolded word" expands to realize, or revitalize, its meaning. Like the bare branches of a tree in winter, "dissonance" and "discontinuities" are "creating" the "space" needed to express something new. In a time of apparent barrenness, paradoxically, latent energies are "cradl[ed]," preparing to be born. This image beautifully illustrates the "liberation" accomplished by "dissonance," i.e., the importance of seemingly destructive forces to the larger, double-threaded "whole" they help to compose.[5]

Examples like these last begin to illustrate how a wide range of technical elements, from word placement and line structure to analogy and metaphor, builds upon effects achieved by Tomlinson's conspicuous verbs. Dramatic "encounters" and "exchanges" between juxtaposed, antithetical entities take shape linguistically, realized by precisely chosen, vigorously wielded action words, to be elaborated in larger structural and thematic contexts. Poems enact on many levels a process of building, unbuilding, and rebuilding, creating a "weave" or "cross-ply meshing" ("Listening to Leaves" VS). Such "confluence of two [or more] ways" gives rise to a "cross-hatching . . . dance," a "crossing" and "interlacing" or "interplay" of disparate elements ("Movements" WrW, "Logic" WW, "Fiascherino" N). A sequence of "chime and counterchime," an "answering of part / By part," weaves together parallel strands of perception ("Words for the

Madrigalist" WW, "Movements" WrW). It is essential that the contributing components of such a "polyphony" or "fugue"—to name two more of Tomlinson's favorite images for contrapuntal design—remain distinctly individuated. A "mosaic which dances," for instance, relies for its composition on numerous individual pieces; the ordering of these in relation to one another will change, but their separate shapes remain constant ("Dialogue" N). Always Tomlinson resists reduction of a lively complexity to blandly textured and inert generalizations.[6] Each defining border, literal or figurative, functions as an "outline separating brilliances / That would otherwise fuse" ("Dialogue"). "So many shades" of significance stimulate the mind and senses that "no single reading renders up complete / Their shifting text" ("Nature Poem" S).

One of Tomlinson's most spectacular experiments with "cross-ply meshing" is his so-named three-way poem, "On the Principle of Blowclocks." Its innovative structure is designed to express dynamic relationships between two antithetical sets of ideas, responses, phenomena, or situations while preserving the distinct identity of each.[7] Typographically, the three-way poem alternates between two different typefaces, odd-numbered lines presented in one style, even-numbered lines in another. Lines 1,3,5,7,9,11,13,15,17,19 introduce a topic, offering an angle of approach, a context for understanding, and illuminating imagery. The reader is instructed to read these lines first, ignoring the even-numbered lines with which they alternate. A second reading addresses only lines 2,4,6,8,10,12,14,16,18, which present a contrasting perspective on the same topic and develop a radically different context of imagery and understanding. Each of these first two readings is syntactically complete, moreover, and offers a coherent view of the topic. The surprise and suspense inevitably generated by the second strand of the two interwoven sets of lines culminate in the third and final reading, when the reader is instructed to read all the lines of the poem together in their proper order. Despite the alternating typefaces and ping pong-like movement between two different sets of ideas and images, this reading provides an unexpected degree of semantic and syntactic coherency. The final reading neither merges the two discrete presentations of the topic, nor dilutes the effect of carefully established visual and thematic juxtapositionings, but rather creates a framework large and flexible enough to encompass both.

On the Principle of Blowclocks
Three-way Poem[8]

The static forces
not a ball of silver
of a solid body
but a ball of air
and its material strength
whose globed sheernesses
derive from
shine with a twofold glitter:
not the quantity of mass:
once with the dew and once
an engineer would instance
with the constituent bright threads
rails or T beams, say
of all its spokes
four planes constructed to
in a tense surface
contain the same volume as
in a solid cloud of stars
four tons of mass

(WW)

The poem braids together two different descriptions of a dandelion seedpod. The first strand of the braid considers the physics of the plant's internal structure, while the second strand offers aesthetic appreciation of it. Consequently the first strand emphasizes the plant's strength, comparing it to that derived from T-beam building construction, and drawing on vocabulary such as "mass," "force," "volume," and "quantity." The second strand focuses on the airy weightlessness, the silvery sheen of the seedhead: it is a "ball of air," a "cloud of stars." This second description may make more initial sense to the reader, who doubtless remembers seedpods floating in the air, driven by the breeze. Close examination of the object, moreover, will reveal star-like structures spaced at even intervals throughout the globe-like ball. The spiky stars are, in fact, tiny T-shapes holding together the whitish fibres of the seedhead—which suggests how the poet came to compare them to the T-beams that support vast structures of metal and concrete.

On a more mundane level, the "static forces" and "material strength" Tomlinson attributes to the dandelion pod form the basis of the children's game in which a seedpod is held in front of a child's mouth and the question posed, "what time is it?" The child blows at the seedpod, trying to disperse it with a stream of forcefully expelled breath. As bits of it fall away, a partner in the game chants, "one o'clock, two o'clock," and so on, until the entire pod has disintegrated. Clock time is discovered, or measured, by the number of attempts required to reduce the seedpod to an empty stem, e.g., "it's four o'clock." The apparently fragile organic structure, or "cloud of stars," generally withstands several all-out efforts by the child to demolish it, demonstrating a more powerfully cohering "material strength" than its airy appearance might seem to imply.

Neither approach to understanding the blowclock provides a complete picture of it, as we realize clearly in the third reading of the poem, which weaves the two descriptions, or "constituent bright threads," around one another as in a Maypole dance. The T-beam comparison, exploited so unexpectedly to portray the architecture of a small plant, is useful, too, in appreciating the economy of the three-way form Tomlinson has invented. Just as a T-beam uses a compact mass to support vast weights, here the reader gets three poems in the space of one. And since each line must be read twice, in different contexts, the 19-line poem is effectively doubled in size.

The workings of the three-way poem illustrate Tomlinson's passion for principles of contrapuntal design with graphic clarity. The strictness of its demands sufficiently indicates, however, why he has not seen fit to employ this innovative verse type again. As an experiment it is dazzling; as a repeated pattern it might risk becoming formulaic. To accomplish the interlacing of dichotomous points of view that serves so persistently as his goal, Tomlinson typically makes use of flexible and open verse forms. In so doing, moreover, he draws eclectically but knowledgeably upon a variety of inherited devices and techniques. Operating "at the fine 'edge' between fixity and fluidity," he prefers to allow structure to emerge organically and individually in each poem.[9] In consequence, he demonstrates little interest in the comprehensive and intricate restrictions of traditional verse forms such as the sestina or villanelle. His forays into the sonnet form, as in *Renga* or *Airborn,* for instance, are so radically experimental as scarcely to prove an exception. Typically his selections from the legacy of poetic tradition favor relatively small and discrete formal elements. Triadic lines prove useful to him in creating a loose to-and-fro rhythm, for instance, as discussion of "Ode to Arnold Schoenberg" already has indicated. He makes frequent use of simple stanzaic patterns (e.g., couplets, tercets, quatrains), which he can position as parts of larger, antiphonally functioning segments in a poem (see, for instance, discussion of "In Michoacán" in chapter 2). More often than not, he opens up his stanzas in highly contemporary fashion, varying prescribed rhyme type and placement, as well as roughening, or abandoning, regular metrical patterns. He speaks, for instance, of "a pentameter suppled up, perhaps, by my work in so-called free verse. . . . I want all possible worlds and I want enough metrical variety—traditional and otherwise—to capture them."[10] In this as in so many other ways, his poetry stands poised at a threshold, offering "the interfused pleasure of measured verse *and* technical surprise."[11]

The device of rhyme, which features prominently in much of Tomlinson's work, assists him significantly in devising a loosely coherent structural framework for many poems. Unpredictably placed rhymes—a mixture of internal and end rhyme, slant and full—lead the reader through his poems in casually defined rhythms of progression. Because rhymes embody literally the principle of "chime and counterchime," they communicate the " 'passion for balance and antithesis' " central to his poetic vision ("Words for the Madrigalist" WW, "Like Greek Prose" VS). By unlocking the fixed predetermination of rhyme schemes, however, and at the same time mining the almost endless possibilities of consonance, assonance, and other post-Dickinsonian rhyme, Tomlinson skews the symmetry inherent in the device even as he exploits it. In his sequences of slant rhymes, both the type and the pace of echoing sounds are subject to frequent, seemingly spontaneous, shifting: one word bounces surprisingly off another, edging slyly toward the next in a vaguely seesawing design. The oblique tilt of the rhyming sounds, combined with the unexpectedness of their emergence, fosters an effect of movement far more dynamic than that achieved by traditional usage:

> the kind of poetry
> that runs the spoken word
> hard into the foreseeable and the unforeseen,
> into patterns that lie
> at the edges of what is stated, rhyme
> suddenly knotted and related

> to what was apparently done and gone,
> and now, in perfected balance, moves
> however unsymmetrically, with the dance
> of forces, on and below those surfaces
> which are the poem. . . .
>
> ("Like Greek Prose" VS)

Here he articulates his vision of rhyme as a device that twists patterns into the crewel-work of a poem, generating movement in varied directions within it. Yet "all patterns lie," or deceive, as the pun resulting from a carefully chosen line break indicates, because no single ordering of ideas and things discloses the whole truth of them. Thus Tomlinson seeks to compose patterns of rhyme that contain within them the suggestion of perpetual rearrangement. He balances the "foreseeable" with the "unforeseen," and "perfected" with "unsymmetrically" achieved balance. In the resulting "dance / of forces," rhyme functions as a critical source of propulsion "on and below those surfaces / which are the poem." Operating "at the edges of what is stated," rhyme necessarily affects readers on a level deeper than that of semantics alone.

The final lines of "Like Greek Prose" expand the image of a tilted symmetry by introducing the visual arts into a consideration of "balance" already including the literary and the musical:

> And take this scene.
> A Lapith is overcoming a Centaur:
> with effort and yet balletic ease it bends
> and accommodates it to this frieze, a half-
> rhyme in the question and answer of their posture.
> That, too, is poetry, that, too, is Greek.

The yin-yang positioning of the two combatants (representing the legendary battle at the marriage-feast of Hippodamia in Thessaly) captures visually the principle of rhyme: a balancing of oppositional forces. The symmetry of the pose is undermined, however, by an imbalance inherent in the different body shapes of the Lapith and Centaur. Thus the portrait vividly illustrates the auditory phenomenon of "half- / rhyme," the partial rupture in harmony emphasized by a line break at the hyphen.

The workings of Tomlinson's "unsymmetrically" balanced rhyme sequences can be observed in any number of poems. "Los Pobrecitos"

3: CONTRAPUNTAL DESIGNS 85

(already considered in a different context in chapter 2) will serve as a case in point.

Los Pobrecitos

> *Caridad para los pobrecitos*
> she is saying, her hand
> outstretched as she
> sways towards me:
> diminutives sweeten
> between beggar and giver
> the injustices of living:
> hers is a courteous race
> accustomed to endure:
> gentle and cunning is what they are
> these sitters in shadows,
> dogging the porches where
> they are both prologue and epilogue
> to each gold interior.
>
> (NNY)

This short poem is bristling with rhyme, beginning with internal rhyme in line one: *"los"* / *"pobrecitos."* Instances of end rhyme (e.g., "she" / "me," "giver" / "living") are augmented and indeed overwhelmed by an extravagant strewing of irregularly placed slant rhyme. The initial tendency for rhymes to occur in irregularly positioned pairs (e.g., "saying" / "sways," "sweeten" / "between") yields to longer sequences, beginning in line five. The triple rhyming sequence of "diminutives" / "giver" / "living," for instance, links lines five, six, and seven. Another sequence ("injustices" / "courteous" / "race" / "accustomed") links seven, eight, and nine, but the first syllable of "courteous" also forms part of a different sequence embracing lines eight, nine, ten, twelve, thirteen, and fourteen: "hers" / "courteous" / "endure" / "are" / "porches" / "where" / "are" / "interior." A subtle chain of sound based on the long "o" sound in "shadows" / "both" / "prologue" / "gold" (lines eleven, thirteen, and fourteen) similarly intersects with another chain linking the last syllable of "prologue" with "dogging" and "epilogue" (lines twelve and thirteen), just as "porches" also rhymes obliquely with "each," linking lines twelve and fourteen.

The poem is strung together into a loose webwork of asymmetrically placed and variously realized slant rhymes. Chains of three and more rhymes move the reader along through the poem, occasionally intertwining to form "knots" of images and ideas. Characteristically, here, rhyme provides both forward-pressing impetus and casual cohesiveness. The juxtapositioning of poverty and wealth, interior and exterior, creed and practice that forms the thematic heart of the poem gains unobtrusive vitality from the tension inherent in its patterning of sound. "Los Pobrecitos" also illustrates how rhyming activity intensifies in the concluding lines of Tomlinson's poems, highlighting closure. Typically his final rhymes win special prominence by means of end-line positioning (e.g., "where" / "interior"), supported by judicious application of full rhyme and by the cumulative effect of rhyme sequences. He closes his poems with an emphatic push in the direction of symmetry, gathering together his strands of subtly musical echoes.

Improvisational deployment of rhyme is a principal feature in Tomlinson's dynamic designs; its effect is distinctly lyrical and irrefutably contemporary.[12] In fact, his fascination with rhyme stimulates him on a variety of occasions to employ it as topic or defining metaphor.[13] In "The Chances of Rhyme," his best known, most often quoted poem, he offers an extended meditation on the subject, identifying rhyme as a touchstone in his poetics.[14]

The Chances of Rhyme

The chances of rhyme are like the chances of meeting—
    In the finding fortuitous, but once found, binding:
They say, they signify and they succeed, where to succeed
    Means not success, but a way forward
If unmapped, a literal, not a royal succession;
    Though royal (it may be) is the adjective or region
That we, nature's royalty, are led into.
    Yes. We are led, though we seem to lead
Through a fair forest, an Arden (a rhyme
    For Eden)—breeding ground for beasts
Not bestial, but loyal and legendary, which is more
    Than nature's are. Yet why should we speak
Of art, of life, as if the one were all form
    And the other all Sturm-und-Drang? And I think
Too, we should confine to Crewe or to Mow
    Cop, all those who confuse the fortuitousness

> Of art with something to be met with only
>   At extremity's brink, reducing thus
> Rhyme to a kind of rope's end, a glimpsed grass
>   To be snatched at as we plunge past it—
> Nostalgic, after all, for a hope deferred.
>   To take chances, as to make rhymes
> Is human, but between chance and impenitence
>   (A half-rhyme) come dance, vigilance
> And circumstance (meaning all that is there
>   Besides you, when you are there). And between
> Rest-in-peace and precipice,
>   Inertia and perversion, come the varieties
> Increase, lease, re-lease (in both
>   Senses); and immersion, conversion—of inert
> Mass, that is, into energies to combat confusion.
>   Let rhyme be my conclusion.
>
>   (WW)

The initial observations in this poem hold good for the most traditional of rhyming (full rhymes in end-line position, arranged in prescribed schemes) as well as for variations introduced into that tradition by contemporary poets. In all instances a "fortuitous" echoing of sounds forges prelogical and even contralogical connections between the concepts and phenomena named by the like-sounding words. Creating "binding" yet nonrational conjunctions, rhyme is therefore in its very essence paradoxical: it simultaneously serves and subverts principles of order. By facilitating "chances of meeting," moreover, rhyme lends a poem its forward-moving impetus; each connecting link of echoing sound provides "a way forward" in the linear "succession" of words and images. And since these connections based on sound defy ordinary logic, the progressions they inspire are "unmapped," even in poems governed by the most intricate of rhyme schemes: a prescribed pattern of sounds may be predictable, but the mental associations conjured up by specific rhymes surely are not. Rhyme is thus identified as an essential element—and epitomizing example—in the subliminal process by which poems take readers to unforeseen places and conclusions. Even the poets making rhymes are "led," however much they may "seem to lead," since the fertile suggestiveness of rhyme introduces an element of chance into the process of making art. In "The Poet as Painter" Tomlinson draws on organic metaphors to describe this effect: "your recurrences are never so pat as to seem simply mechanical, your outgrowths never so rambling or brambled as to spread to mere vegetation"; the result is a pattern of cohesion "surrounded by surprises" (PP 17). Consideration of this one poetic device leads inescapably to the insight that the control exercised by a poet never can be absolute.

In the second half of the poem, Tomlinson hints that the fruitful paradox inherent in rhyme can be intensified by liberating the device from traditional definitions and strictures. End rhyme, he mockingly points out, is all too often regarded as "a kind of rope's end . . . / To be snatched at as we plunge past it," and he is suspicious of such last-ditch shaping efforts. "To take chances" with the positioning of rhyme within a line means adapting freely to changing "circumstance," responding unhampered to each new opportunity. At the same time that he indirectly advocates liberty in rhyme placement, Tomlinson makes the case for "half-rhyme," lacing the last ten lines of his poem with chains of verbal echoes. He demonstrates the increased subtlety and variety of connections that can be made by way of slant rhyme, proposing wittily suggestive sequences to illustrate gradations of sound and sense "between / Rest-in-peace and precipice," or between "chance and impenitence." Slant rhyme thus becomes an antidote to stasis and absolutism: generating "energies to combat confusion," it stimulates a richly provocative process of "conversion," or reconfiguration and re-imagining. Such activity constitutes the chief end of art, as Tomlinson conceives of it. He is committed, as Donald Wesling observes, to "verbal art as process as well as product," to "a structure of relations, a formal-semantic entanglement."[15]

The metaphoric implications of his claims for rhyme clearly extend beyond the device itself and even beyond poetics. He is making an argument against simplistically polarized formulations, against the tendency to divide experience, whether in art or in life, into permanently separate categories: one "all form / And the other all Sturm-und-Drang." Rhyme provides the necessary corrective to such all-or-nothing views in its demonstrated interlacing of intention and serendipity. "The Chances of Rhyme" elevates rhyme to a cosmic principle, a resonant boundary line where forces of defining order converge with forces of spontaneous fecundity. "Chance occurrences, chance meetings invade what we do every day and yet they are drawn into a sort of pattern, as they criss-cross with our feeling of what we are, as they remind us of other happenings, or strengthen our sense of future possibility" (PP 17). The operations of natural cycles likewise serve as a paradigm for the primally embedded patterns of movement that Tomlinson describes and mimics in his poetry. The balance struck at each point in any cyclical progression must inevitably be upset and undone by forces moving that cycle forward, as, for instance, a waning moon "must pull awry the brilliant symmetry of day / On freezing day" ("February" R). "Tomlinson seems to imply that contrary relationships are at the heart of natural law," Robert J. Stanton remarks in this context; "in order to move forward, we must first stop, must first deny our motion in order to gain the necessary tension to move forward once more."[16]

Frequently the "cross-ply meshing" of rhymes in Tomlinson's poems supports thematically delineated patterns of alternation, or comparison and contrast.[17] This is the case, obviously, in the three poems just discussed: "The Chances of Rhyme," "Los Pobrecitos," and "Like Greek Prose." Invariably in Tomlinson's work the interplay between dichotomous perceptions is more than a technical preoccupation; in one form or another, it constitutes his chief subject matter. To avoid static representation of "contrary motion" on the macroscopic level of topic and theme ("Roman Fugue" J), he devises rhetorical situations enabling him to render his readings of the "shifting text" of experience as dynamic as possible. He seeks to present parallels and antitheses dramatically, to take readers through an active process of consideration rather than to foregone conclusions. Frequently he stimulates such a process by taking the position of devil's advocate. By introducing a neglected, unpopular, or seemingly wrongheaded viewpoint, he expands the reader's understanding of a topic in unanticipated ways.[18] In such cases, it is the very unexpectedness of the second strand of his "interlacing" presentation that gives a poem much of its punch. He utilizes this strategy, a kind of reverse psychology, in "History of a Malady," a poem addressing the subject of his own migraine attacks. He opens with a line from Catullus to evoke the relentless throbbing characteristic of migraine, "'others beat timbrels with uplifted hands'" (NNY), but immediately he juxtaposes that pounding pain with the intriguing visual disturbances that precede it.

Surprisingly, he devotes more than half of the 89-line poem to explaining the "gift" of heightened, wonderfully distorted, perception that heralds a migraine attack: "the whole field of sight / Blossomed corollas of disintegrating rays" (NNY). In this "superabundance of the senses" that combines exquisite agony with exquisite beauty ("neon gleams" and "patterned flashes"), there is, oddly enough, much to appreciate. The world appears scoured gorgeously clean: "finding all colours prime," "the eye exults." Even as he ruefully wonders why he does not learn to "[take] . . . warning" from such visual symptoms and come to regard them with dread, the poet-sufferer argues that the benefit inherent in the experience ("the gift / I did not bargain for") is worth exactly what it costs. Perhaps "one should have entered / Suspiciously this Eden of the sight," yet the special perceptions it offers prove revelatory, comprehending "so much that is new." "Sharpness" of pain and "sharpness" of visual acuity are inextricably united. Appropriately, Tomlinson concludes his two-pronged presentation of migraine with the image of a "double-bladed word" or "sword" that cuts both ways.

The effectiveness of the poem depends in large part upon the apparent perverseness of Tomlinson's pro-and-con approach to his topic. A reader typically does not expect to find the miseries of a painful illness perfectly counterbalanced by the advantages peculiar to it. The interplay of contraries here stands out all the more because the poem weaves together two different viewpoints on a topic that commonly admits only of one. Tomlinson assumes the role of devil's advocate on many occasions with such "careful playing against expectation"; as a result, "definition [of one object] is gained through perception of its negative."[19] Frequently, as here, he introduces an unusual perspective that "complements / In opposition" a more ordinary one ("At Holwell Farm" SIB). In "Consolations for Double Bass" he does so with wit and elegance, encouraging the reader to celebrate contributions of an often overlooked, seemingly uninspiring orchestral instrument. Like "On the Principle of Blowclocks," but in a structurally less obtrusive fashion, the poem offers contrasting views on a topic; like "History of a Malady," it highlights a viewpoint that is clearly atypical.

Consolations for Double Bass

You lament your lot at the bottom of an abyss
    Of moonlight. And yet you would not
Change it for all that bland redundance
    Overhead, the great theme leaping
Chromatic steeps in savage ease.
    The trumpets on their fugal stair
Climb each other's summits pair by pair:
    A memorial of remissive drums. The hero falls.

> A race of disappointed generals, we mourn him
>   *Nobilmente.* Confluence of a hundred streams
> In one lambency of sound, our grief
>   Beckons the full orchestra, 'Come on—
> Crash in like a house collapsing
>   On top of its hardware.' And you?
> All that you can do is state, repeat,
>   For repetition is the condition for remembering
> What must come—the moment
>   For the return to earth, to blood-beat.
> Good gut, resonant belly,
>   You are the foot a hundred others
> Tread by, the bound of their flying islands
>   And their utopias of sound. Tristan is being sung to
> Like a drowsy suckling: you
>   Are sanchoing still: that, I know,
> Is the story of another hero—but you have ridden
>   With them all to their distress, and lived
> To punctuate it, unastounded in your endless
>   Unthanked *Hundesleben,* nose to ground.
>
>   (WI)

The poem is built around extended juxtaposition; it asks us to consider the double bass in contrast to orchestral instruments that normally carry the more interesting and memorable melodic lines—particularly the attention-catching high brass. The difference in pitch between the double bass and instruments playing in higher ranges is converted metaphorically into physical location, with the double bass occupying the very "bottom" and the trumpets the "summits." All the dramatic action takes place up above on the heights, while the "you" of the poem—the personified bass instrument—remains down low, close "to earth" and "nose to ground." The Sturm-und-Drang of the story line is far removed from the repetitive, beat-marking part of the double bass. Battle imagery contrasts those instruments portraying the hero's glorious rise and tragic fall with the more mundane role of the double bass: it is the "belly" on which the army marches, "the foot a hundred others / Tread by." It provides necessary anchorage and limits ("bound") for the "flying islands," or ambitious schemes of those musically and politically at the top. The allusion to Book III of *Gulliver's Travels* further underlines the satiric mockery directed here toward the drama-packed arena of violins and horns.

Their sphere of action is utopian, fantastical, romantic; the double bass, in contrast, is associated with Sancho Panza, the dogged realist and survivor. Assigned no dazzling or heroic role, it *states*, *repeats*, and *punctuates* the dramatic stories in which others star: it fosters coherence, making sense of incipient chaos. The melodic lines and impressive ornamentation delivered by other instruments would be so much disorganized sound without the steadying effect of the double bass and its "blood-beat."

The playful spirit of the poem does not prevent it from making a serious case for the significance of a literally lowly member of the orchestra. The double bass becomes associated with virtues like persistence, industry, fidelity, dependability, and efficacy, while the high brass and similarly assertive instruments evidently are given to romantic excess, short-lived passion, and self-destructive high drama. Patterns of metaphor and allusion in the poem, all dependent upon persistent personification of the musical instruments, point clearly to implications of the central contrast outside the realm of music. The elaborate and witty juxtapositioning which is the heart of the poem rescues a hitherto "unthanked" and humble anti-hero from obscurity. The tit-for-tat contrasting of its role with that of the foregrounded instruments, in which the patently unglamorous double bass is repositioned as the focus of reader attention, establishes its indispensable function as part of a larger whole.

Tomlinson's practice of pushing unexpected points of view into prominence intensifies the contrapuntal impulse in his poems. The persuasive presentation of unusual alternatives causes readers to recognize the inadequacy of a single view, to question the completeness even of apparently self-evident conclusions unless they are derived from multifaceted consideration. Either directly or indirectly Tomlinson usually suggests a moral dimension to the insufficiency of a single point of view. This is particularly evident in the many poems addressing cultural and political conflict or socioeconomic disparities. Understanding of any place is radically deficient, ethically as well as intellectually, unless it includes groups, practices, and beliefs that have been dispossessed, supplanted, or suppressed. It is not enough to admire the beautiful "gold interior" of a cathedral; one must also notice the beggars lingering at its entrance and consider the significance of that juxtaposition ("Los Pobrecitos"). Interpretation of the pious behavior of converts will be erroneous so long as important evidence, like the Aztec idol buried beneath a Christian altar, is hidden from view. Full appreciation of such diverse, often conflicting perspectives further requires that moral sensibility be buttressed by familiarity with historical facts. To define a place, or seek to comprehend it, in terms only of the people presently populating it means overlooking the never entirely eradicated contributions of prior occupants to its institutions, its customs, its architecture, its collective identity. Tomlinson repeatedly draws attention to plural and competing cultural legacies (e.g., relics of Roman occupation in England, or of aboriginal peoples in the Americas), demonstrating that adequate perception of place necessarily embraces the rich complexities of history. Intellectual stagnation goes hand-in-hand with moral complacency: the multi-layered awareness toward which the poems urge us is incompatible with ignorance.

One of Tomlinson's favorite rhetorical methods for lending weight to alternative viewpoints, a variation on his role as devil's advocate, is to discover, in the course of a poem, that an important point of view is missing and then conspicuously to supply it. By drawing attention to what has been omitted, he highlights the necessity for including it. Examination of a pre-existing argument or object often provides occasion for the introduction of a counterbalancing perception or idea, as in the poem "On a Landscape by Li Ch'eng." The scene is dominated by a harsh, bare, natural environment; it is a seascape with snow, "grey" and "unvaried" in color. The human figures depicted appear tiny and vulnerable against this vast and cheerless natural backdrop. As they "skirt between snow and sea," they are "minute, furtive and exposed" (SIB). Unexpectedly, however, the contrast between human insignificance and natural forces is developed in the second half of the poem in a direction not envisioned by the artist Li Ch'eng. Tomlinson imagines the end of the journey, a room warmed by fire and enlivened by companionship. There a humanly created environment prevails over the natural one, and the travellers will enjoy conversation "seasoned by these extremes." Warmth, company, and security take on new meaning to those who have been subject to cold, exposure, and a "solitude . . . unchosen." Their "talk," along with the thoughts and feelings behind it, will be enriched by the contrasts coloring their experience.[20] Creating yet another image to highlight the potency of juxtaposition (the power of "extremes" to *season*), Tomlinson adds that the travellers' talk "will recall stored fruit / Bitten by a winter fire."

The poem is an illuminating example of Tomlinson's propensity for urging readers back and forth between differing points of view because in this instance we see him inventing a viewpoint not present in the inspiring occasion. Li Ch'eng's picture offers only one interpretation of the confrontation between the human and the natural, i.e., humans are small and vulnerable in the face of nature's enormous power. Tomlinson augments this perspective by presenting its antithesis, pointing toward humans' success in creating zones of comfort and security for themselves, in staving off or repelling natural hardships and dangers. By introducing this second viewpoint, Tomlinson compels readers to engage in active inner debate, to consider opposing ideas in turn rather than resting in one. The process of such debate in fact becomes the real subject of Tomlinson's poem, as well as the central value it affirms. Contemplation of "extremes" fosters a maturation, a *seasoning*, of human understanding.

"Netherlands" is another poem deriving inspiration from the visual arts, and again Tomlinson discovers that a painter's presentation of a topic appears to ignore a significant alternative view. Journeying by train through the Netherlands, the poet observes "the lines / Of dyke and drain, the glinting parallels / And the right-angles of a land handmade" (R). These features remind him irresistibly of the Dutch painter Piet Mondrian, and he imagines that he is travelling into a real-life version of what art historians describe as the "primarily linear structures" and "rhythmical network of lines" characteristic of that painter's work.[21] "The train is taking us through a Mondrian," Tomlinson declares, "the one he failed to paint." Art critics generally posit a cause-and-effect relationship between prominent traits of Mondrian's homeland and those of his artwork: "the landscape of Holland inspired him to accentuate verticals and horizontals."[22] Clearly Tomlinson is familiar with this explanation, but he finds it insufficient. It is, after all, principally the human additions to the Dutch environment that consist of vertical and horizontal lines. Though the land itself is flat, which emphasizes the linearity of the human designs imposed upon it, the sky overhead offers an immense and obvious contrast to the flat angularities lying beneath it:

> True: curvature is no feature of this view,
> Yet why did the sky never cause him to digress
> With its mile-high cloud mountains
> Pillowed and piled over hill-lessness?

Tomlinson loads these lines with alliteration and slant rhyme, thereby imparting extra lushness to the enormous softness of those "mile-high cloud mountains / Pillowed and piled" on high. Again, as in the poem based on Li Ch'eng's picture, he supplies a perspective missing from the original work of art. Here he voices explicit criticism of the painter whose views he enlarges, although his choice of the verb "digress" lends a teasing note to his judgment. Struck by the contrast in configuration between land and sky, he questions Mondrian's failure to perceive and render that contrast in his paintings. Without the antithesis between angles and curves, the vision Mondrian offers of his world is incomplete.

The strategy of discovering and remedying dialectical omissions proves especially disarming when the speaker of a poem claims responsibility for an initial lopsidedness in perception. In "Tiger Skull," for example, the poet-speaker corrects a "half truth" articulated in the first of three quatrains. Movement in the poem hinges on the admission in the second stanza that impressions and assertions offered in the first are partial, and consequently false. The poem seeks to define what it means "to be tiger," but in fact the process of defining upstages definition, assuming thematic centrality (WI).

Tiger Skull

> Frozen in a grimace, all cavernous threat,
> onslaught remains its sole end still:
> handle it, and you are taught the weight
> such a thrust to kill would carry.
>
> The mind too eagerly marries a half truth. This carapace
> lies emptied of the memory of its own sated peace,
> its bestial repose and untensed pride
> under the equanimity of sun and leaf,
>
> where to be tiger is
> to move through the uncertain terrain supple-paced:
> how little this stark and armoured mouth can say
> of the living beast.

Examination of the skeletal structure of the tiger proves deceptive because it emphasizes ferocity at the expense of all other characteristics. Without the softening effects of flesh and fur, the powerful jaw and huge teeth dominate the speaker's impression of the dead carnivore. The "stark and armoured mouth" suggests only "threat"; the "sole end" of the beast's existence appears to be "onslaught." Only when he imagines the spirit and "memory" once contained in this empty "carapace" does the speaker appreciate that a living tiger possesses qualities not traceable in its skeletal remains. "To be tiger" includes times of "sated peace" (since even the fiercest predator stops killing when its hunger has been satisfied), experiences of "repose" and "pride" and "suppled-paced" movement, or pleasure in the warmth of sun and cool of shade. Without sentimentalizing the tiger, Tomlinson's speaker pays tribute to the physical, mental, and emotional complexity that makes "the living beast" more than a mere killing machine.

The declaration in line five that "the mind too eagerly marries a half truth" constitutes the speaker's major recognition. He includes himself in his judgment concerning human thought processes: in our yearning for speedy resolution of uncertainties, we rush to limited, and limiting, conclusions. Choice of the word "marry" further indicates the passionate tenacity with which humans cling to partial truths. The poem recounts a process of discovery, as the speaker corrects his initially insufficient understanding. By force of example, clearly, he hopes to alert readers to faulty tendencies of "the mind" and encourage a patient widening of perspective.

One of those guilty of "marr[ying] a half truth" would seem to be William Blake, whose "Tyger" surely hovers in the background of Tomlinson's poem.[23] Even in the absence of any explicit borrowings, "Tiger Skull" must for any English-language reader conjure up memories of Blake's famous inquiry into the nature and origin of the great carnivore: "What immortal hand or eye, / Dare frame thy fearful symmetry?"[24] In Blake's poem the tiger is perceived solely as ferocious and frightening, the author of "deadly terrors"—an interpretation resembling that initially proposed by Tomlinson's speaker. Indeed, Blake's metaphors invest the tiger with sinister powers, causing it to loom larger than life; the beast seems to represent every cruel danger threatening mortal existence. The rhetorical question, "did he who made the Lamb make thee?" suggests that only a sadistic creator would pit weakness and naiveté against strength and treachery. The unequal contest between lamb and tiger illustrates the pitiless dichotomy between "innocence" and "experience" that defines Blake's perception of the universe. Tomlinson's poem hints that Blake's view of the tiger is overly simple, the schema behind it static. If the tiger must be perceived as a mixture of antithetical traits, so too must the world in which the tiger lives. Based on a more intricate treatment of contraries, Tomlinson's poem requires us to question and periodically revise our judgments and, more important, to welcome dualities rather than fearing or rejecting them.[25] "The mind" prospers in exploring with gusto the full, rich range of a stubbornly differentiated reality, a reality bristling with "things that we must include" precisely "because we do not understand them" ("The Impalpabilities" PL).

Because he treasures the insight to be garnered from the "counterpoise" achieved between different, even contradictory, stimuli, Tomlinson values "a changed mind," a vitally evolving, multifaceted consciousness ("The Way of a World" WW). Drawing on familiar as well as more unusual experiences, he seeks to persuade readers that continually emerging contrasts infuse perceptions with much of their significance.[26] In "The Perfection" he points to the changing colors of a sunset sky to illustrate how the apex of an experience can be recognized only in retrospect, when it becomes possible to measure a moment of peak beauty or intensity against the "lost pitch" of a falling off (S). Taking in the changing display overhead, "we never know" the point of maximum magnificence "for the moment it is" "until it has been." Or, similarly, the "colour of fallen leaves" ("neither pink nor brown") appears to alter with changing patterns of light ("Autumn" J):

> and all the degrees
> Of autumn on ground, slope, trees
> Clash suddenly with—no adjective
> Can define the blue that brightens
> Through the whole sky and, in the chemistry of sight,
> Changes this glow that crackles at our feet
> By being its antithesis:

In a world of variegated and fluctuating inter-relationships, every such "clash" represents an opportunity for sharpening, renewing, and extending comprehension.

In keeping with his predilection for situations that provoke an active process of reconsideration and discovery, one of Tomlinson's favorite vehicles for expressing dialectical tension is that of argument, debate, dialogue. Opponents confront each other directly and articulate their positions by turns, maintaining individual integrity. Dialogue is, above all else, a continuously evolving exchange: "To define the sea— / We change our opinions / With the changing light" ("Sea Change" N). Its hues and textures shift at "the insistence of wind."

The exchanges—between wind and sea, between human observer and natural environment—continue indefinitely because no single perception of the sea (e.g., "opal threatened by emeralds," "uneasy marble," "green silk") can be final. Each new defining image is, in itself alone, "a static instance" and "therefore untrue."

In "Logic" the pattern of argument and counterargument serves as metaphoric representation of intersecting "ripple-wrinkles" on the surface of a large body of water (WW). Its current drives the water in one direction, but various obstacles (e.g., grasses, stones) interrupt its flow, bisecting the lines that mark its progress: "a clear / Cross-hatching in the dance of wrinkles that / Re-patterns wherever it strikes." Like a member of a debate team, the current "must / Account for its opposite and yet remain / Itself," yielding to the force of contrary pressure while still pursuing its own ends. "Water is like logic," Tomlinson concludes, "for it flows / Meeting resistance arguing as it goes." In this persuasive metaphoric blending, the physics governing water movement help to illustrate the benefits of vigorous dialogue. To encounter contradiction is to gain "irrefutable strength" from the alternating process of accommodating and resisting opposing energies.

In "Cloud Change" Tomlinson applies the metaphor of debate to a different natural phenomenon, this time in the upper reaches of sky. Elements overhead are strenuously active in what looks like a battle, as sunlight keeps trying and failing to break up a thick cloud cover:

Cloud Change

First light—call it
First doubt among shadows
As the seam splits
At sky-level. The dark
Scarcely disperses.
The partial light
Drifts into it from beneath,
Flushes the atmosphere
Transparent. Call it
Dismissal, elemental
Reprimand to reluctance:
The dark is losing
In the day-long sway
That neither can win. Call it—
Defeat into dialogue.

(PL)

Light and dark, or sun and cloud, are the two contending elements. Sun gradually forces its way through the clouds, but cannot clear them away entirely. The result is a "day-long" toggling between "scarcely disperse[d]" darkness and emerging "partial light." The attempted displacement of clouds by sunlight is personified as a process of intellectual yielding and renewed resistance: "doubt" following by "reluctance," which calls forth a "reprimand." One side "is losing," yet "neither can win" the seesawing debate. The lively struggle between light and dark is portrayed as "dialogue," an interchange in which each participant preserves its own character and purpose. In terms of the interwoven battle imagery, the meaning of "defeat" is revised: one-time resolution, in which a single combatant cedes the field finally to the other, is replaced by the perpetual push and pull of ongoing struggle.

"Comedy" develops the image of argumentation with exhilarating wit, underscoring Tomlinson's conviction that there is a unique prospect from each new vantage point, another side to every story. In this poem the poet-speaker notices the furrows of a freshly plowed field running in the opposite direction from its fence, and he imagines these bisecting lines as a debate: thesis and antithesis, argument and rebuttal:

> It was when he began to see fields
> As arguments, the ribbed ploughland
> Contending with the direction of its fence:
> If you went with the furrows, the view
> From the fence disputed with you
>
> (WrW)

No logical synthesis of these comically contrasting elements is possible. Each invites the beholder to follow it, calling him back from pursuit of the other:

> If you sat still
> The horizontals plainly said
> You ought to be walking, and when you did
> All you were leaving behind you proved
> That you were missing the point. . . .

"The point," he avers, is to rejoice in both sides of the argument, making every effort to see each clearly and to cherish its indisputable distinctness: "And the innumerable views / Kept troubling him, until / He granted them. Amen." The playful prayerfulness of the final "amen," like the apparently lighthearted suggestion that the ability to "grant" multiple viewpoints is godlike, offers subtle testimony to the value of a dynamically receptive approach to comprehension.

Tomlinson's investigation of contending points of view, his insistent noticing of what lies just beyond the boundaries of ordinary awareness or majority opinion, lends his work much of its combined intellectual, aesthetic, and moral excitement. Repeatedly his poems invite readers to consider the world around them from unexpected angles, to revisit preconceptions or unexamined assumptions. The tiger has peaceful moments as well as fierce ones; a dandelion seedpod is characterized by strong interior structure as well as by delicate airiness. Piet Mondrian should perhaps have noticed and included in his paintings the prominent curves of the Dutch sky, along with the angularities of the landscape below. The monotonous and apparently uninteresting contributions of the double bass prove not only essential to the orchestral enterprise but illustrative of a whole range of under-appreciated, quietly heroic virtues. Possibly we should interpret the frenzied swirls and thickly swaying lines of Van Gogh's artwork not as visible symptoms of his madness, but rather as "a love of substance," a desperate reaching out toward "solidities" and "sanity" ("Van Gogh" NNY). Tomlinson's gift for injecting a speculative or sometimes teasing note into serious inquiry relieves such exploration of alternative views from any burden of portentousness. There is fun as well as profit in considering the novel vantage points toward which he steers us. Who but he would press us to consider the motives of the infamous person from Porlock whose inopportune business visit supposedly robbed Coleridge of the concluding portion of "Kubla Khan"? "He has the dream by the root, he has it out, / Has now what, unknowing, he came for" ("From Porlock" R).

Tomlinson's poems move us by taking us to places we never otherwise would think to go. These excursions beyond the limits of the mundane evoke reactions as multifarious as their subject matter. They provoke perturbing questions about the narrowness of our own interpretive tendencies even in the face of the often heartening reassessments they initiate. To acknowledge and include "innumerable views" clearly constitutes one of Tomlinson's principal poetic aims.[27] And since neither the world of things nor the world of ideas is static, perception is process rather than conclusion. Lively interactions between opposing forces, whether elemental, abstract, or sociopolitical, occur with inevitable persistence along the border lines that claim his attention. His propensity for seizing on unusual viewpoints and making these appear plausible, indeed, necessary, steers readers toward profoundly provocative reflection, at the same time underlining the inexhaustible variety inherent in the interplay of shifting identities and relationships. Deftly exploiting the contributory power of even the smallest linguistic and technical details, Tomlinson engages topic and structure, style and device, to evoke the contrapuntal energies animating the universe of his poetry.

4
Perceptual Boundaries

Waste / None of the sleights of seeing

THE BORDER LINE BETWEEN ILLUSION AND REALITY OR, BETTER PUT, BEtween alternative versions of reality, exerts special fascination for Tomlinson. It is a boundary to which he returns time and again, with unabated gusto, devoting more than sixty individual poems to its exploration. From the beginning of his career he presents himself as a poet preoccupied with perception—its processes and meanings—committed to precise, richly detailed rendering of observable reality.[1] The title of his first major collection, *Seeing Is Believing* (1958), sets the stage for poetry which, as he affirms, "usually arises directly from something seen. I want to register *that* in all its clarity or in all its implications."[2] Intriguingly, the "something seen" that inspires him includes a remarkable variety of optical misapprehensions.[3] His poems record these with the same enthusiastic fidelity to detail he dedicates to the most rigorously observed and accurate facts. Unfailingly, too, he presents illusion in counterpoint with the reality it distorts and displaces. Juxtaposing two radically different perceptions of a single phenomenon or situation, he guides readers to the exact point at which one differentiates itself from the other. Such juxtaposition encourages comparative investigation, provoking questions about the interrelationship of imagination and reality, artifice and truth, error and insight.[4] Causes of the anomalous yet enriching misperceptions Tomlinson evokes in his poems are various, his purposes in recording them invariably celebratory. Consistently he argues that perceptual illusions constitute a valuable complement to more strictly accurate apprehensions of the world, an important voice among "the several voices / That double a strength, diversify a truth" ("Fountain" R).

He never invites readers to lose themselves in illusion, which interests him solely in the context of the actual. Invariably his poems offer explanations for the misapprehensions they record and explore, enabling readers to stand with full awareness at the boundary line between what is and what seems to be. Reflections of various kinds promote many optical illusions, including the interplay of light and shadow on opaque objects and landscapes, or on translucent surfaces such as water or glass. The potentially misleading effects of reflection frequently are heightened by motion of some sort, as with wind, rain, or snow, or by movement on the part of the observer. Unusual perspectives and unexpected shifts in perspective account for a number of odd visual experiences, as does simple failure of the human eye—along with the human consciousness behind the eye—to take in the whole of a scene accurately, as in transposition or omission of letters when reading a printed text, for example. Occasionally, too, the observer's own memory or imagination may introduce images into a scene, distorting what is there by superimposing upon it the remembered or the fantasized. In one way or another, the world offers ample opportunity for perceptual errors, and Tomlinson encourages us by his example to make the most of them. Whether attributable to everyday happenstance or to highly unusual conditions, they make rightful claims on our attention. Indeed, they provide some of the most compelling, as well as the most surprising, of the "innumerable views" with which experience presents us ("Comedy" WrW).

Even though instances of misapprehension provide us with false information, they nevertheless increase our understanding, rather than reducing it. They may in some instances enhance our knowledge of an environment by showing what is missing from it: "all that was not / There, told us what was" ("Night Transfigured" WW). With his penchant for examining things the wrong way around, or from seemingly perverse points of view, Tomlinson asks, for example, whether technologically sophisticated aids to human vision ought perhaps to be understood as distortions of it, rather than as improvements. In "Through Binoculars" he points out that magnification compels an observer to focus on smaller areas, with consequent loss of ability to judge overall proportions and connections between parts. Insofar as ordinary human perceptual abilities must be our standard for correct, or accurate, vision, the views binoculars offer are "false," even "starkly mad," and surely "not mortal" (N). The principal benefit they confer, he contends, is paradoxical, for they engender appreciation of the unassisted vision they displace:

> This fictive extension into madness
> Has a kind of bracing effect:
> That normality is, after all, desirable
> One can no longer doubt having experienced its opposite.

So long as the user of binoculars remains aware that the views thus obtained are in some sense "fictive," the contrast between ordinary and magnified vision is "bracing" rather than alarming. Certainly the spirit of the poem is more playful than dire; the final effect of such small excursions into grotesque versions of reality proves both exhilarating and instructive.

In another perceptually deranging intrusion of technology into nature, a white van travelling "through the brightness of / late autumn weather" disrupts a beholder's view of colorful foliage by interposing a black and white version of the scene onto the "moving screen" of its flat, pale surface ("The White Van" WrW). As the vehicle moves through the landscape, "a shadow show" of branches and leaves is projected continuously onto the rectangular "screen" of its profile, drawing the human observer's gaze, but this cinematic sequence of moving forms lacks the crucial element of color:

> this is all shape
> and surface, you might say,
> this black and white
> abstraction of a coloured
> day . . .

Just as the bizarrely magnified world seen through binoculars stimulates the user to re-affirm the primacy of ordinary, unassisted vision, here a black and white reimaging of the natural world underlines its actual "glow / and urgency" by force of contrast: "the paint of autumn / showing the more intense" against the two-toned, two-dimensional, abstract alternative journeying through the foreground. In the wake of that "moving screen," autumn's own multifaceted beauty unrolls spectacularly, its power to move us reinforced and renewed as it "re-opens its density / of gold, green, amethyst."

The most banal mischance may deepen awareness of the actual by offering glimpses of illusional alternatives. In the poem "Hyphens" a fantastical new view of the world is triggered by a simple oversight in reading the text of an advertisement:

Hyphens

'The country's love-
liness', it said:
what I read was
'the country's love-
lines'—the unnec-
essary 's'
passed over by
the mind's blind-
ly discriminating eye:
but what I saw
was a whole scene
restored: the love-
lines drawing
together the list
'loveliness' capped
and yet left
vague, unloved:
lawns, gardens, houses,
the encircling trees.

(WI)

Instead of chiding himself for careless reading, the poet rejoices in the happy results of his substitution of the novel term "lovelines" for the overused "loveliness." In his imagination, lines of "love" radiate out across the suburban landscape, "drawing / together" its disparate elements and revitalizing the whole. The error caused by the "blind" yet "discriminating" mind's eye is serendipitous, life-affirming. It causes him to recognize the inadequacy of the picture evoked by the text he has misread, at the same time building a positive alternative: "a whole scene / restored."[5] Clever and generous deployment of hyphens throughout the sharply short lines of the poem helps readers to grasp how the mistake came to be made, to experience on their own its potent effects.

A similarly beneficent restorative process occurs in "The Tree," a poem set in an urban environment ugly with filth from factory and "mill chimney":

The Tree

This child, shovelling away
what remains of snow—

> a batter of ash and crystals—
> knows nothing of the pattern
> his bent back lifts
> above his own reflection:
> it climbs the street-lamp's stem
> and cross-bar, branching
> to take in all the lines
> from gutter, gable, slates
> and chimney-crowns to the high
> pillar of a mill chimney
> on a colourless damp sky:
> there in its topmost air
> and eyrie rears that tree
> his bending sends up
> from a treeless street, its roots
> in the eye and in the net the shining
> flagstones spread at his feet.
>
> (WI)

The "tree" of the poem's title is an optical illusion, a pattern of shadows created by a street-lamp beaming on the child with his snow shovel. The motions of his bending and lifting lend the silhouetted tree the appearance of organic growth: like Jack's magical bean plant, it grows larger and larger before the poet-observer's astonished gaze. "It climbs" from street to skyline, "branching" ever higher "to take in all the lines" of the cityscape. The scene is dominated by the presence of this huge and wholly illusionary tree. The fact that the child himself cannot see what the observing poet describes, i.e., "knows nothing" of the shadow-silhouette rising behind and above him, lends a note of poignancy to the urban ugliness the poem portrays, but does not destroy the value of the unexpected boon the illusion offers. An unreal but welcome instance of natural beauty, the "tree" supplies to a "treeless street" precisely what it otherwise lacks.[6] As in "Hyphens," a deficiency in the environment is identified by the very image correcting it, so that the poem evokes a mixture of gladness and dismay. The actual city remains unchanged, yet the poem closes by paying tribute to the "shining" image ("its roots / in the eye") that contradicts and temporarily overwhelms urban sterility.

Illusion offers simultaneous critique and completion of a scene again in the poem "In the Ward." The "ward" is a nursing home where "old women come . . . to die" (WI). Nurses serve them with a "youthful patience" tinged with "callous zest," refusing to identify with this glance into their own futures ("all they do not wish to be"). The patients' enforced isolation, their "lost connection" with the world of the living, mockingly is "rectif[ied]" by a picture on the wall of a "woodland scene." The glass covering this portrait of nature's "unkillable seasons" serves as a reflecting mirror; in strong sunlight it captures and superimposes upon "the twines of trees" the outlines of the healthy young nurses and their dying charges. Temporarily the glass brings together disparate elements, encompassing youth and age, vigor and infirmity, hospital and forest, in a reassuring coherence. Like the presence of an outsize shadow-tree on a city sidewalk, this unifying image proves bittersweet in its make-believe augmentation of the actual and in its indirect identification of a constellation of social and moral issues.[7]

In "Tyrrenhean: From the Train" Tomlinson emphasizes the potency of illusions such as those depicted in the poems just discussed: "something seen" constitutes a reality of its own in the consciousness of the perceiver. Here he glimpses from the train what looks like "a luminous steppe, a plain of blue" (R). What is actually before him is ocean, but, "not recognizing the thing it was," he sees "for a moment an elsewhere in the view." Misreading the visual cues confronting him, he superimposes a remembered "elsewhere" onto the Italian seascape. Quickly he recognizes this mirage for what it is, a "sheer impossibility." Even though "this Blue Grass was a country of the mind," however, it represents "a crop" ready for his harvesting. He garners nourishment, profit, from what he sees, despite its lack of congruence with external facts. The very "impossibility" of his momentary misapprehension invests it with extra piquancy.

The potency of the "mind's eye" is substantiated in slightly different fashion in "The Morning Moon," where the poet-speaker reports what might be called second-hand perception (DW). His imagination seizes and works upon a description given him by someone else ("you tell me") of a moon that remained clearly visible into daylight hours. He himself has "failed to see" this remarkable sight, but the details provided by his informant enable him to construct a strongly etched picture of it in his mind. What he experiences in this instance is not precisely an optical illusion or misapprehension; the moon was really there, clearly visible "above the house-top" in broad daylight. Since he did not see it for himself, however, his perception of it is essentially invention. Derived as it is from reported reality, the image in his mind almost certainly does not correspond fully with what was there to be seen. He acknowledges, for example, that in his imaginative reconstruction the moon takes on exaggerated size and importance, so that it eclipses the sun:

> in my picture of the scene
> the sun is lost to me,
> with this high visitant
> in the zenith of the mind's eye.
>
> Mapped, without motion,
> so starkly near, so far,
> that which I never saw hangs
> as still as the pole star.

Grammar and syntax in the closing lines suggest several dimensions to the analogy between pole star and "that which I never saw." The moon itself, which seems fixed in the morning sky directly above his house, obviously functions here like a pole star. At the same time, however, it is the speaker's ability to conjure up in his own imagination what he "never saw" that "hangs / as still as the pole star." The "mind's eye," with its perceptual power, assumes the role of an unwavering guide, looming hugely at the center of things; its power is more significant than any specific images it may build. What the pole star/moon in this instance points toward, moreover, is the speaker's own home, so that he also pays tribute to the domestic life he shares with the unnamed "you" of the poem, clearly a member of his household. Thus he links the shaping properties of perception—its power to move by no means limited to actual visual events—with the ability of human beings to transmit to one another the gift of "something seen," suggesting that such mutual vision and revisioning form a vital part of enduring human bonds.

Deliberately courted or accidentally discovered, illusional experiences offer manifold unsought benefits. Repeatedly they provide respite from the humdrum by contradicting it. Tomlinson finds compensation for the mundane dreariness of a rainy day, for example, in the beautifully distorted views he obtains of a familiar room when he gazes at it through rain-streaked windows:

> through the wet panes
> Objects arrange themselves,

> Blue tessellations, faintly irised
> Dividing the room
> Into an observed music.
>
> As one approaches the windows
> Fugues of colour
> May be derived from a familiar interior,
> A chair may be segmented and reassembled
> ("Variant on a Scrap of Conversation" SIB)

A formerly immobile scene is reinvigorated by the appearance of movement lent by water cascading down glass, a well-known arrangement of objects reorganized into new patterns of colors and shapes. This illusion of rearrangement, shimmering with "blue tessellations" and "fugues of colour," is as psychologically refreshing as it is aesthetically pleasing.

The poem's origin, like its title, is explained by an epigraph: "'There's nothing at all to be said for the day. . . .'" The poet refutes this negative comment decisively, portraying the rain as a revitalizing agent. "To challenge the accepted vision" is in itself valuable, as he explains in the third and final stanza of the poem. He concludes by mentioning, with apparent off-handedness, another easily visualized example of splendidly flawed perception:

> To challenge the accepted vision
> A further instance would be the wine-stopper,
> Its head (cut into facets)
> An eye for the cubist.

The prismatic effects of a many-faceted, cut-glass object induce a "segmented and reassembled" vision of things much like that produced by the wet window panes. A cubist's "eye" similarly perceives the world as a mosaic of planes susceptible to reshuffling: each new combination of its components offers different insight into the whole. In comparing his rainy-day optical effects with those cultivated intentionally by cubist painters, Tomlinson suggests that perceptual accident and artistic creation have much in common.[8] Based on compelling illusion, both modify reality as we ordinarily know it. And in so doing, by turns they please, they stimulate, they liberate, they signify.

To emphasize that optical illusions arising from the interplay of natural elements like rain, sun, and wind can affect us in much the same way a painting or a piece of sculpture might, Tomlinson frequently personifies the causative agency. In a poem set in Manhattan, he details the effect of late afternoon shadows on architecturally crammed streets as if it were a continuously evolving work-in-progress: "the shadows have been building / A city of their own within the streets" ("All Afternoon" NNY). The shadows are presented as active, shaping agents, "carefully correcting the perspectives / With dark diagonals, and paring back / Sidewalks," constructing, in short, a "counter-city." Creators of illusion, they behave like artists with conscious designs, availing themselves of techniques such as perspective, revising their work, concerned with meaning, e.g., they "confound" the "fire-escapes already meshed / In slatted ambiguities." To build such an alternative reality requires strength and force, as a second pattern of imagery indicates: the city is a battleground as well as a canvas. "Like ladders for assault," shadows lay siege to New York City; like a successful invading army, they "scale the façades," then "tie them to the earth." The border between actual and illusory is disputed with military determination, even as it is drawn and redrawn with artistic authority. To distinguish one realm from the other, tactile testing is necessary: "you touch / The sliding shapes to find which place is which."

A mirror initiates artful and astonishing rearrangement of a city street in another Manhattan poem. A scattered array of household furniture incongruously lines the street, presumably awaiting pick-up by either a moving van or a garbage truck. Propped together with the rest, a large mirror reflects passing vehicles and pedestrians, creating a "multiplicity" of partial and oddly configured images ("The Mirror in the Roadway" NNY). Suspending chairs in the air, or "hoisting the image / of a stopped truck / on to a dresser top," the mirror assumes, like the shadows in "All Afternoon," an actively directive role in the scene. Strong enough to heave a large, heavy object into the air, the mirror is also capable, magician-like, of balancing it on top of something much smaller and lighter. The resulting picture of a cumbersome vehicle perched delicately upon an article of bedroom furniture is reminiscent of surrealist art, or of photomontage. Using its frame like a cutting edge, the mirror "has sheered away" fragments of the actual, only to recombine them, every "piece / to be inserted elsewhere / in the jigsaw." The kaleidoscopically changing reflections provide an amusing sequence of visual puzzles, the mirror's frame precisely delineating the boundary between fantastical and mundane. The observer's grip on reality is never seriously compromised while the circus of images in the mirror charms the eye and revives the spirit.

Tomlinson reports numerous instances of perceptual misdirection in this same spirit of lighthearted appreciation. He is drawn to reflecting surfaces of various kinds, such as glass, water, and mirrors, because they multiply opportunities for observing familiar images comically contorted and scrambled. Movement further assists the process of distortion, e.g., a brook "travels / With the hillside in it—an upside-down / Horizon" ("Black Brook" NNY). By attributing active volition to the elements composing such misleading reflections, moreover, he emphasizes the persuasive robustness of the perceptual experiences they mediate. To watch "half a man / Float by" in a puddle of water stirred by plopping raindrops is, certainly, to be deceived ("Parking Lot" A). For one enchanting moment, however, the deception constitutes a perceptual reality in its own right: "I *see* half a man / Float by," the poet-observer declares (emphasis added). Thus he validates what the senses communicate, even as he explains the mechanisms of error inspiring them.

In "9 A.M.," a poem focusing on the shadowed reflections of early morning light in an urban setting, he is confronted with a variety of grotesque and amusing sights:

> I see a running man, dwarfed
> By his shadow-legs; a man whose shadow-stick
>   Trails a long stilt to far-off shadow-feet;
> A pigeon flies down to land
>   On its inverted cut-out, and the cars
> Carry for a moment the shadow-shaft
>   Of the lamps they are passing under. . . .
>
> (J)

The source of the optical illusions is clear, as is the reason for reporting them with such accuracy: they divert us "for a moment" by reconfiguring the world, injecting it with breathtaking novelty. The poem closes by directing attention to a flag whipping in the wind or, rather, to the moving "shadow-flag" projected on the side of a tall building:

> Screened far above me on a single
>   Facet of sky-high wall, I see

> The shadow-flag an hour will efface,
>   Passing its serpentine black rag
> From side to side across a surface
>   Of resplendent concrete it is energetically cleansing.

The pointlessness of the shadow-flag's apparent activity is wittily underscored by the vigorous purpose ascribed to it. It does not merely appear to be engaged in unnecessary housekeeping activity; it "is," in fact, "energetically" so occupied. Its motives equally opaque, the pigeon lands with deliberate precision on its own inverted "cut-out" shadow. Inexplicably, the body of the man with a "long stilt" for legs, his feet "far-off" from his trunk, has undergone actual elongation. Here, as is often the case, Tomlinson heightens the whimsy inherent in reported misperceptions by framing them ironically, in terms that demand credulity. The commonplace causes typically assigned to them underscore the frequency with which such perceptual mix-ups may surprise and delight. Ordinary operations of sun, shadow, wind, rain, or snow stimulate creative misapprehension on every side, offering temporary visual entrée into "a place always just out of reach" that lies just across the threshold of everyday sensory experience ("The Stair" DW). As Ruth Grogan notes, Tomlinson positions his meditations with special gusto precisely "on the border" between "what the eye possesses" and "what the eye cannot possess."[9]

The poem "Before the Concert" explores one of these favorite, unreachable places, presenting a world reflected in a glass of water. The "transparency of its contents" serves to "contain" the objects around it (DW). To see the "image" of the table "on which [the glass] stands," along with "a draped, red cloth" and two "foreshortened lutes / waiting to make music there" is to yearn to "possess" them; they sit suspended in a perfect, miniature "universe." When a musician reaches out and lifts the glass to drink, however, that wholly desirable, all-but-graspable little world must inevitably "disappear":

> those minute instruments,
> their world quicksilvering into water
> under a melting window—
> that is a room I shall never enter.

The music those "foreshortened" lutes might have made within the world of the water glass never will be heard, any more than the beholder can "enter" the "room" containing the alternative concert. Deftly evoking Keats's famously "unheard" melodies, Tomlinson underlines the idea that this artful, if accidental, reconfiguration of reality is inherently "sweeter" than the mundane version of things it momentarily replaces.

Over and over the poems demonstrate how easily explainable combinations of lighting and perspective enable us to see the commonplace playfully or gorgeously "replenished" ("To Modulate" VS). Ordinary homes become tree houses, their stolid usefulness converted Swiss Family Robinson-style into childlike fantasies of escape. Viewed on a rising slope "through the boughs of an oak," for example, an old country mansion "appears / to be suspended, all / one hundred tons of stone," from the branches through which the poet glimpses it ("The Tree House" VS). As the observer continues walking, the oak appears to be engaged in the act of lifting the house into "its royal embrace," so as to "raise it—a tree house— / up into the air," at the same time raising it from the realm of the mundane to that of the extraordinary. On another occasion Tomlinson observes how the limbs of a spruce tree leaning against his own home have formed "a kind of stair, a walk-way" used by squirrels ("The Stair" DW). The whole appearance of the place is altered by this new route of access, serving to "teach / These wooden walls that this house is a tree house." The illusion casts a spell on "the real by way of the imaginary," lending an aura of otherworldly adventure to his everyday surroundings. "We live in a place always just out of reach," he concludes; however well we may think we know our world, experiences such as this prove that it is always possible to see things in a different light. Our perception of "the real" undergoes perpetual renewal, taking us repeatedly to the brink of the mysterious.

Familiar surroundings are similarly revitalized by illusions projecting exteriors onto interiors. Rooms are gloriously refurbished when reflections of objects outside their walls strangely intrude and superimpose themselves. A man returning home on a sunny day opens his door to see "red-gold sunlight" lying "in puddles across the floor" ("Interior" J). The warm splashes of color remind him of flowers that bloom late in the season, and the room seems suddenly filled with a deep yellow, orange, and red blossoming: "the drawing-room / seems to essentialize / asters, dahlias and golden-rod." The impression of flowers is augmented by that of fire, as "the colours of autumn / within four walls burn / more richly than maples." The observer feels as if he is being splendidly welcomed, imaginary asters "fanfaring his return" home to "this domestic fire / carried indoors from outside." His hearth has been "rekindled" by an optical fantasy. The site of daily domesticity has been cast, literally, in a new light, its human warmth and significance reinforced and illumined by this strewing of a floral tribute, this rich burning at his hearth. Elsewhere an interior is subjected to a more watery conjuring: shadows cast through windows by the moving branches of "tree limbs and the leaves out there" create the illusion of an underwater scene:

> The room is submerged under restless waters—
> the floating shadows of the birches
> swimming in sunlight through the sable shade
> where armchairs and a table
> have taken root within four walls:
>
> ("In the Room" VS)

The enclosed space of the room is opened up by these optical effects; it seems as unbounded as the natural submarine environment it mimics. "Distance has come indoors," and this disorienting reversal of land and water, interior and exterior, manifests power "to reclaim the angled confine for the season / dancing it back to space."

The frequency with which Tomlinson focuses on optical illusions originating in the interplay of sun and shade may recall for many readers the terms used by Plato in his famous allegory. The prisoners in Plato's cave mistook the shadows projected by firelight onto their cavern walls for real objects; thus they lived in a world of illusions that they failed to recognize as such. Tomlinson's poems, in contrast, invest the illusions born of shadows with a vitality fully equal to that of the phenomenal forms they so intriguingly misrepresent. He accepts with equanimity "the shadows and obscurity at the edge of the visual."[10] And while Plato posits an either-or situation in which his prisoners must commit themselves solely to truth or solely to illusion, Tomlinson urges readers toward a more all-embracing, multiform idea of truth, one that acknowledges the illuminating potential of all information derived from the senses.[11] Since the "shadows" that play such a prominent role in his poetry never exert a permanently deceiving effect, they enrich the observer's experience of the actual rather than threatening it. Thus the title Tomlinson chooses for one of his first collections of poetry, *Seeing Is Believing*, announces a theme that endures throughout his subsequent career. His enthusiastic receptiveness to optical illusion infuses a clichéd expression with new meaning. Not only should we refuse to trust in the existence or legitimacy of what we cannot "see," we should extend our trust to *all* we see, whether or not our perceptions prove to correspond fully with external reality. Perception *per se* is a gift, recharging daily existence with unanticipated sources of meditation and delight. "How much we bring to our moments of perception," Tomlinson exclaims; and "how much our moments of perception bring to us—awarenesses always extensible, always offering new facets."[12] The actual itself so often proves to be tinged with the miraculous that the "sheer impossibility" inherent in perceptual accidents simply offers an extra measure of largesse ("Tyrrenhean: From the Train" R). Watching a "cloud of gnats" on a December day, for example, Tomlinson marvels at the appearance of these tiny insects in winter: "One can scarcely make out what they are, and their winter dance seems such a weightless celebration of improbables (how did they escape last night's frost?—the birds of the day before?) that what one actually sees is more than the sight—an instance radiating unlooked-for instances, a swarm of unreasoning hopes suddenly and vulnerably brought into the open" ("The Insistence of Things" WI).

The sensory reality of such evocative "improbables" can assist us, moreover, in broadening our understanding of "the real":

> To enter the real,
> how far
> must we feel beyond
> the world in which we already are?
>
> It is all here
> but we are not. . . .
>
> ("Song" DW)

To fathom the "all" that really is "here," it is necessary to acknowledge that much supposedly ordinary perception augments hard data with imaginative projection. "It is the mind sees," Tomlinson reminds us: "But what it sees consists not solely of that by which it is confronted grasped in the light of that which it remembers. It sees possibility" ("Skullshapes" WW). Each time we confront visible signs of something not immediately present, e.g., "the track of the deer / That strayed last night into the garden," we in fact extend our "believing" to include unseen realities ("The Track of the Deer" J).[13] The animal that made the tracks is not now within range of vision, yet we assume its reality; the frost-rimmed hoof-marks bring us "the edge of all imaginings," a boundary demarcating different dimensions of perception. We do not question the flesh-and-blood tangibility of "the departed deer"; our perception of its tracks "glimmers with the presence / Of sensed, substantial, and yet absent things." We draw continuously on images "stored within the mind's bright satellite" to fill in sensory lacunae, simultaneously seeing and creating "a world imagined that is really there" ("Here and There" A).

Examples discussed earlier in chapter 2 illustrate how recollection of particular images permits collage-like construction of a "double scene," in which immediate sensory impressions are brought into sharp juxtaposition with those retrieved ("Letter to Uehata" A). In such instances, the actual assumes immediate mental adjacency with the remembered, as when Tomlinson's recollection of Japanese trees converges with the "wintry sinuousness" of English trees, images from "then" complicating his perception "now": "since I returned, the trees have a Japanese look." Such confrontation between perceptions originating in different times and places is possible, as Tomlinson points out, only because "the mind's embrace" contains a record of previous perceptual experiences ("A Sense of Distance" WW). These are subject to instantaneous recall; at any moment they may emerge, bidden or unbidden, in full vividness to enlarge the immediate with competing points of view. Clearly the co-existence of sensory experiences derived from different occasions, along with the manifold possibilities for juxtaposition and rearrangement these stored perceptions offer, vastly magnifies opportunities for border encounters of many kinds.[14] As a case in point, certainly Tomlinson's exploration of cultural and historical boundaries proves more complex and intriguing because of clashes, questions, and insights provoked by the convergence of remembered images with immediate sense impressions.

He reminds us regularly, too, that the planet we inhabit is in constant motion, rotating on its axis and orbiting around the sun. Perceptual experience of even the most "real" things fails to remain stable when the things themselves are "always moving, disintegrating, reforming," in a "world which is never quite *there* because light and time have changed it" ("Sight and Flight" NNY). The shadowplay in which so many illusions originate is an inevitable by-product of astronomical facts. Movement of tides and currents likewise animates the appearances around us, deranging our perception of even the most familiar phenomena: our senses confound us with reports of a world simultaneously "so real" and "surreal" ("Cronkhite Beach" F).[15] Pointing out flaws in our too-easy assumptions about the objective accuracy of everyday perceptions, Tomlinson offers further affirmation of the optical illusions exciting his attention, rejoicing in their marvellous revision of the ordinary. "What one actually sees is more than the sight" on so many occasions that the stunning suggestiveness of misapprehension "merely intensifies a daily experience" ("The Insistence of Things" WI, "Sight and Flight" NNY).

Taking this intensification process just one step further leads to the deliberate fabrications of human art. Living in a "so real," "surreal" world, a place subject to constant change, we are bound to think of the fantastical perceptions engendered by art as different only in degree, rather than in kind, from those occurring spontaneously. Apprehension, misapprehension, art: all three offer clues to a reality perpetually in process of redefining itself. Like Shakespeare's Prospero, Tomlinson indicates that the very conditions of earthly existence render the actual as "insubstantial" as products of artistic imagination:

> The cloud-capped towers, the gorgeous palaces,
> The solemn temples, the great globe itself,
> Yea, all which it inherit, shall dissolve,
> And, like this insubstantial pageant faded,
> Leave not a rack behind. . . .
>
> *(Tempest* 4.1.152–56)

Our most beautifully deliberate responses to elemental and organic activities, like our initial perceptions of them, prove no less and no more ephemeral than the manifestations on which they are based.

Tomlinson echoes the gist of Prospero's famous lines in a poem detailing the illusional effects of a "great cloud-barrier" in a sunset sky ("Poem" VS). Back-lit, the mounded clouds form a wholly imaginary landscape every bit as compelling as the "pageant" Shakespeare's protagonist devised to entertain Ferdinand and Miranda:

> A frontier to the land below, an illusion
>   That we live bounded by foot-hills,

> In touch with mountains soon to appear
> > Out of the hills themselves which go on growing
> Above us, cancelling the horizon here.

Magically emerging before the beholder's gaze, this mountainous Never-Never-Land *dissolves* at twilight, in synchrony with "the world's slow turning." While it lasts, however, the cloud-capped mirage asserts itself convincingly:

> And this illusion
> Holds us like a solid thing, as firm
> > As a poem in its imagining step by step
> A world into being that is not there—
> > Then is . . .

Claiming that optical illusion and literary artefact are equally potent ("imagining . . . a world into being"), and placing that claim in the context of cosmic flux, Tomlinson subtly reminds readers of Prospero's contention that art and reality are closely allied. Where Prospero emphasizes the "baseless" and "insubstantial" nature of both realms, however, Tomlinson underscores here the "firm" and "solid" power of all illusions, no matter what their source, to "hold" and intrigue us.[16] "Cancelling the horizon" of the commonplace, art kindles aspiration and enables us to move toward "high ground": it puts us "in touch with mountains soon to appear." Under the spell of the imaginary world art generates, "we, too, are within reach of summits."

"The artist lies / For the improvement of truth," he avers, adding: "believe him" ("A Meditation on John Constable" SIB). The intentional fabrication that is art provides us with perceptual options scarcely different from those we stumble upon every day in "this place of chiaroscuro" and evanescent appearances ("Mushrooms" S). Our assent to an artist's vision is "freely accorded" when that vision speaks to something deep within our own human nature, convincing us of its validity on some level other than the merely representational: "the illusion persuading us / That it exists as a human image" ("A Meditation on John Constable"). An image may be recognizably "human," in tune with some interior reality, even when it appears deficient in point-by-point fidelity to outward manifestations. As his friend Octavio Paz explains, Tomlinson celebrates the artistic imagination not principally as a force to "transform reality" but rather as one that can "make it more real."[17] The "hypotheses of fancy" may move us most effectually when their artifice is blatantly deliberate, for they "restore the world to us by denying its premises" ("Ceci n'est pas une Pipe" WW).

The opportunities for spectacle and reflection provided by deliberate artistic composition are happily expanded by the vagaries, large and small, stimulated on a regular basis by perceptual happenstance. A ferry crossing a lake is more intriguing, for instance, when observed "through the gaps in the foliage" of trees lining the shore because that accidental vantage point positions the moving boat in a delightfully disorienting context: "it takes / five seconds for a craft to sail through a cypress" ("Cypresses" J). Understanding the causes of such commonplace illusional experience in no way diminishes its wonderfully revitalizing effects. Describing how a rising crescent moon begins to "leap from side to side" of the roadway as his automobile cruises into the night, for instance, Tomlinson is "grateful for this bright companionship" ("The Journey" NNY). "Surprising" him again and again with its playful antics, the moon appears to hop, skip, and jump through the landscape: "unpredictably / Caught among the sticks of some right-hand tree / Or sailing left over roof and ridge." His enjoyment of the acrobatic show is untouched by his familiarity with the laws of physics that account for it: "explanations are less compelling" than the vivid immediacy of appearances, no matter now misleading he knows them to be.

Here, as always, "explanations" nonetheless play a distinct role in his appreciation of an unusual optical experience. Bestriding the boundary between illusion and reality, he invites us to yield to the compellingly peculiar effects of perceptual derangement without forfeiting our grip on the more ordinary arrangements these displace. New versions of the familiar prove amusing, "bracing," or inspiring, after all, chiefly by way of contrast ("Through Binoculars" N). The alternative perceptual events Tomlinson celebrates are valuable precisely because they *remain* alternatives, i.e., they offer us vacations from ordinary reality, not a permanent move away from it. In keeping with his predilection for contrapuntal movement and design, he takes readers back and forth between dichotomous perceptual experiences, revelling in the incongruities he discovers. He greets each new sensory adventure as an opportunity, valid in its own right, to reread the "shifting text" of reality ("Nature Poem" S).

"The Prisoner" illustrates with particular clarity how he positions himself and his readers precisely at the line dividing ordinary from extraordinary perception.

The Prisoner

This prismatic
green-glass
stopper
of a bottle
long destroyed
stands in the light
from our window where
it has taken up
the grey-white
shell shard
sharing the ledge
beside it: this,
which you might suppose
unchangeable and hard,
it transforms into
the image of a man who
sits there in a hat
—in this vitreous prison
a tight fit—
with one arm
(his left) bent
sideways to accommodate it
better: the top
of the inverted stopper
(now its base)
raises him up
in miniature majesty
on a sort of dais:
the awkward angularity
of the arm and the confinement
of the head confess
such a discomfort
and rigidity, it seems
as if this monarch of littleness
were only waiting
for someone to
remove the shard and thus
permit him to break out of his dream—

and this he does
the instant that I do.

(DW)

The contrast between actual and apparent objects of sight forms the crux of the reported experience. Tomlinson devotes the first twelve lines of the poem to explaining how he came to confuse a chunk of shell, observed through a faceted piece of colored glass, for a tiny man in a hat. The elaborate evocation of a miniature person cramped in a "vitreous prison" functions as contrast and alternative to the description of shell shard and wine stopper preceding it: it competes with that initial perception without extinguishing it. Syntax in the poem reinforces the idea that illusion assumes interest chiefly in juxtaposition with reality. Tomlinson packs the forty short lines of his poem into just one sentence; avoiding full stops by the generous use of colons, dashes, and parentheses, he contains two different perceptions of the objects before him in a single syntactic unit.

An understanding of the source of the illusion is important here if readers are to enjoy it, for the prisoner's predicament is torturous. Claustrophobically confined, with one arm unnaturally bent and pinioned, the tiny figure is fixed in a position of "discomfort / and rigidity." Having established the situation as make-believe, however, the poet is free to employ a light and witty approach instead of invoking the compassion and concern that otherwise would be required. The situation is fraught with paradox, moreover, for even in his apparent powerlessness the captive is described in regal terms. The button-like top of the upside-down wine stopper "raises him up / in miniature majesty / on a sort of dais," as if he were being honored rather than imprisoned. Completely filling the space into which he is crammed, he is "monarch of littleness." He enjoys enormous authority and status, ironically, in an extremely circumscribed situation. Both ruler and victim, he is hugely important—literally filling all the available space—and at the same time painfully impotent. His principal desire is to escape this environment which dominates him even as he dominates it, i.e., to "break out of his dream." The term "dream" reminds readers that both the prisoner and his predicament are unreal. An accident of lighting and perspective provides cues for what seems like the premise of a fairy tale: a Tom Thumb-like monarch uncomfortably trapped in the very kingdom he rules.

His release is secured by the perceiving human who exercises final dominance over this scene in which two different planes of reality converge. By lifting and removing the shell shard (a.k.a. tiny captive), the poet-observer empties the prison, destroys the illusion. He "permit[s]" the prisoner to "break out," an act of liberation emphasizing his own control over the situation. This act is possible only because he himself is not completely deceived by the optical illusion he is in the process of enjoying. He plays with it, allowing himself temporary immersion in its details, but his groundedness in an alternative perceptual reality enables him finally to move on. The poem therefore may be read as a subtle parable on the subject of perception.[18] In assenting to a particular vision of reality, one enjoys power within the territory defined by it; yet the essential limitations, or "littleness," of each such enclosed realm suggests its confining potential. Only by acknowledging other "kingdoms of possibilities" can one escape the prison-like narrowness inherent in any single point of view ("A Sense of Distance" WW).

Remaining receptive to various ways of seeing the world, alert to their causes and to their differences, allows Tomlinson to move freely back and forth between competing visions, to exercise choice and control. This flexible posture not only allows him to take full advantage of comical side effects in episodes of perceptual mischance, it enables him to engage in deliberate play. He himself is the source of certain intriguing illusions, as when he sets a saucer filled with water near his window, placing it with exact precision so as to reflect the rising moon shining into his kitchen. The poem's title, "Drawing Down the Moon," makes his intention plain: as the image of a new moon appears reflected on the surface of the water, it seems as if the poet actually has lured the moon into his own home, the way one might entice an insect with a dish of honey. The miniature crescent swims peacefully on his window sill, "a clear shard of newness," responsive to his desire to possess it (VS). Endymion-like, he is thrilled to have a moon of his very own, "a sleeping bride."

He is also well entertained by the reversals inherent in the situation he has created and now controls. Because the dish of water—a small, nearby object—now appears to contain the moon—a much larger and vastly more distant object—both seem dramatically changed in size and in position. The moon is now tiny and close at hand; the saucer, in contrast, has grown into an ocean: "it rocks with a tidal motion / as if that porcelain round / contained a small sea." Action is also reversed: ordinarily the moon creates the tides, but here the "tidal motion" of a dishful of water acts instead upon the moon, "throws into confusion / the image that it seizes / out of the sky." The now powerfully active dish of water shakes the moon into "pieces." Even the direction of gravitational force is reversed in the poem, the moon itself being *drawn down* to earth by the poet's magnetically attracting bait. In arranging this optical illusion for his own amazement, Tomlinson indicates that command of multiple perceptual alternatives is a source of power and delight. Like a benign wizard, he has demonstrated dominance over forces of nature; he has tamed an astronomical phenomenon.

On a mushroom-gathering expedition, confusing stones and dandelion puffs repeatedly for the elusive wild crop he seeks, he is moved to an elaborate and enthusiastic meditation on the subject of optical mistakes. Such sensory disorientation is salutary, he insists. By upsetting expectations and overturning preconceptions, deceptive appearances shake us out of lethargy and propel us into keenly heightened modes of awareness. "Played-with rather than deluded, waste / None of the sleights of seeing," he admonishes ("Mushrooms" S). Like a conjurer's tricks, such "sleights of seeing" are magically compelling and at the same time empirically explainable. Appreciating illusion without becoming permanently ensnared in it, we can be willing participants in sorcery rather than victims of it. We "may be taken in," but at the same time we are "taken beyond" familiar borders. Unthreatened by the spectre of competing perceptions in the multi-plied "weft of seeing," Tomlinson mines each for whatever kernel of enrichment it may contain. "Taste the sight / You gaze unsure of," he advises; "a resemblance, too, / Is real." The suggestive force of illusion leads him, paradoxically, "to a rind / That's true"; "for realer than a myth of clarities / Are the meanings that you read and are not there."

Accepting temporary sensory illusions whenever they occur, valuing them for the contrasting versions of reality they offer, and on occasion supplementing such accidents with deliberately contrived illusions of his own, Tomlinson models for readers an adventurous approach to perceptual experience. In the illimitable realm of the hypothetical, what seems obvious may prove mythical, and what is "not there" yield "meanings" irrefutably "real" ("Mushrooms"). "Spurred on by fantasy and reined in by reflection," Paz asserts, "Tomlinson's work submits to the double requirements of imagination and perception: one demands freedom and the other precision."[19] His poems guide readers with exactitude to the border line distinguishing alternative realities; poised there, he mines these variant versions of the real to the fullest extent, investigating each in itself as well as in relation to the other. His exploration of perceptual boundaries is accomplished with an elegant lightness of touch, a boundless capacity for make-believe, and a lavish appreciation of comic incongruity.[20] Seizing upon illusional experiences with unabating exhilaration, he demonstrates one of his principal strengths as a poet: a gift for conjoining play with high seriousness.

5
Graphic Framing

there, the whole, gigantic
aperture of the day
shuts down to a single
brilliant orifice . . .

A BORDER SURROUNDS THE REGION IT DELINEATES: IT IS AN OUTLINE, A rim. It separates, and it contains; defining edges, it provides edging. Tomlinson's poems call attention to this outlining property of borders in both human and natural environments. He observes, for example, "a wall / that enclosed from the neighbouring road / The silent community of graves," or an advancing evening suddenly fringed with color by the setting sun: "this green twilight has violet borders" ("The Churchyard Wall" SIB, "The Art of Poetry" N). "Contained space," he declares, "is wordlessly resonant," for it can "reconcile vacancy with its opposite" ("Oppositions" WW). Intriguingly, his interest in the phenomenon of framing concentrates with special frequency on gates, doors, windows, and similar apertures, i.e., spaces representing boundary breaks. Any gate-like opening offers the excitement—sometimes the danger—of exit and entry. As a route of access from one area to another, it threatens the containing function of a border by creating a breach in it: a "boundary wall . . . circles / And hides" what is within until "one discovers . . . the gate" ("The Ruin" SIB). Thus a curtain rustling in the breeze of an open window functions as "a fluctuating frontier" between "room" and "street," an incomplete and uneasily "shifting" barrier ("At Bob Lucid's Place" DW). A similar threat of incursion occurs in "Venice" when early morning shadows function as "doors," precisely delineated areas that seem to suggest the intrusion of night into the day now displacing it: "cut into by doors / The morning assumes night's burden" (N).

Paradoxically, any aperture fills the space it empties. A "defining window," for example, lends shape and identity to the "square of sky" it circumscribes ("Black Nude" PL). The "taut line" of an outside edge "contains" what it "surrounds": "the black outline separating brilliances / That would otherwise fuse" ("Dialogue" N). Shaped precisely by the broken edges of the border line it interrupts, a door or similar opening constitutes in itself a bounded enclosure, as a "tunnel of light" beneath a bridge, for example, is "contained by the reflected arc" of the structure forming it ("Venice" N). A pool of water glimpsed "through a rough window-slit" likewise completely "fills the aperture" that outlines it ("The Garden" A). "Doors," Tomlinson avers, "are both frame and monument" ("The Door" AS).

The peculiar ambiguity and mysterious promise of framed entryways assume centrality in many of Tomlinson's poems. Significantly, his work as a graphic artist allows him to explore this fascination in another medium as well. In the seventies, he became interested in decalcomania, a "surrealistic device" he describes at some length in "The Poet as Painter" (15): spreading an uneven coat of black pigment on a sheet of glossy white paper, he covers it with a second sheet, then lifts this off to make "random patterns" (15). He goes on to compose finished pictures by extending, modifying, and recombining these initial, arbitrarily formed patterns, using brush and hand as well as other tools (15–17). In creating a number of his compositions in the seventies, Tomlinson devised stencil-like "windows" which he moved over the decalcomania, selecting certain portions thus framed to scissor out and elaborate, usually in some form of collage, laying one framed shape beside or overlapping another. *In Black and White: The Graphics of Charles Tomlinson*, published in 1975, illustrates the range of finished designs he achieved using this method: *The Willendorf Grotto* and *Threatened Fruit*, for example, suggest the simultaneously precise and amorphous combinations to which it lends itself.[1] He drew his "windows" in imitation of the amorphic, irregular window shapes used by the Spanish architect Gaudi in the construction of Casa Batllo. "In those days he was obsessed by Gaudi," Tomlinson's friend, the critic Octavio Paz, reports. "He drew them [the dining-room windows in Casa Batllo] many times: what would happen if we could look out from these windows . . .?" As Paz explains, Tomlinson "fused" two different artistic modes and influences[2]; he employed Gaudi's arabesque window designs to "'react[] *with* and *against* the decalcomania.'"[3]

These scissored "windows" function like graphic counterparts of the doors, gates, slots, shafts, mirrors, and other framed passageways in Tomlinson's poems by outlining spontaneously occurring images, some of which he then selects for conscious artistic elaboration. Certainly the process of sliding paper windows over the randomly generated designs in his decalcomania—waiting for some piece of the whole to inspire him by virtue of this chance outlining—helps illumine his abiding interest as poet in the power of framing borders. Like his paper windows, the entryways in the poems frame portions of universe separate from the poet-viewer; he has not created the scenes described in the poems any more than, as a visual artist, he has dictated the forms into which the pigments of his decalcomania spread. Like the paper windows, too, each entryway attracting Tomlinson's notice becomes a mechanism of artistic choice, delimiting a piece of the world for poetic consideration. As graphic artist and as poet both, he utilizes frames to seize upon enticing sections of a larger whole. From the chaos of the world—or the decalcomania ("my chaos of crushed pigment floating in water")—he chooses fragments and then subjects them to transforming scrutiny (PP 19). Always he remains free to decide which of numerous framed images he will choose as the basis of picture or poem. In each instance his concern is the "observation of the fleeting moments of visual sensation," his object as artist "to catch this fleeting freshness and unite it to a stable form where others may share in it" (13).

Framing outlines assist Tomlinson in his quest to transcend "the merely personal" (PP 13). Guided by what he calls "an ethic distrustful of the drama of personality of which romantic art had made so much," he seeks to encounter "primal fullness [of being] on terms other than those we dictate" and "to break with preconceived images of the given" (14, 16). He therefore employs devices that enable him to "discover" rather than to "impose" meaning, explaining how seemingly fortuitous features of medium and technique, whether visual or verbal, lead him to "nutrifying" insights, in fact "towards the threshold of new perceptions" (15, 17, 16). He creates artefacts that are "the result of conscious and subconscious processes and of that strange, unifying moment of recognition when . . . what I'd found became what I'd chosen" (20). Looking at decalcomania through the arabesque shape of Gaudi's windows, like regarding a landscape through an open gate, Tomlinson simultaneously discovers and selects, achieving a workable balance between flux and form, between chance and choice. Thus he finds "*ouvertures*—openings through place into mystery."[4] In his ongoing search for such accidentally revelatory "openings," poems and graphics derived from framed views occupy a central place, illustrating some of his most deeply held philosophical and aesthetic concerns. Shaping our perception of particular portions of the universe, such outlining borders throw into relief the areas they define, enhancing the power of alien materials to move or amaze us.

The poems offer readers glimpses through windows, fissures, tunnels, arches, and similarly well defined openings, with effects at least as various as those he achieves in his graphic art.[5] Always they serve to set apart, to make special, to call attention, as, for instance, the human edging provided by the beggars just outside Mexican churches, "prologue and epilogue / to each gold interior," insistently highlights economic disparities and religious hypocrisies ("Los Pobrecitos" NNY). Whether it provokes celebration, disquiet, or amusement, each newly emerging, framed perception proves valuable, an unsought treasure unexpectedly presenting itself to conscious awareness:

> The dark of the window square might be
> A mineshaft of pure shadow, a way
> Through to the heart of the hill—the black
> Centre, if centre there were where
> Sight must travel such drops and intervals
>
> ("The View" WW)

These lines from "The View" highlight Tomlinson's tendency to conjoin potentially foreboding phenomena ("dark," "black," "pure shadow") with significant value: this is the darkness of a "*mine*shaft," a passageway to a rich lode at the "heart" and "centre" of things (emphasis added). In "Night-Piece: The Near and the Far," he employs another analogy drawn from mining to depict moonlight forcing a small, "fissured" opening through the layered darkness of a cloudy night, "prizing from black an ore of undertones" (SIB). He makes more elaborate use of mine imagery in the poem "By Night," when lights shining through farmhouse windows seem to "open three doors of fire" on the surface of a "swollen stream" below (VS). These portals into an illusory realm "might well be the entrance to some mine," a source of imaginable yet impalpable wealth. "How would you lift its liquid gold"? the poet demands of the reader. The rhetorical question suggests that these riches of "fire" or "gold" cannot be grasped or halted any more than can the "travelling" waters in which they appear to lie buried. The moving waters imitate the inexorable movement of time itself, for autumn rains have "freighted" the stream now flowing rapidly "towards what end / The winter's night awaits it with." The "doors of fire," or "strips / Of flame" attest to human occupation in an environment humans never fully master; they "inscribe our sign and presence here." Through these momentarily opened doorways, we catch a glimpse of the peculiarly human "gold" countless generations have sought to dip from the flux and flow of earthly existence.

His art, Tomlinson states, represents an attempt to discover "what lies behind or beneath" ordinary appearances, those "welcoming or threatening surfaces of the world" (PP 20). He traces his fascination with probing beneath the surface of things back to his boyhood experience of fishing. The fish in nearby marl pools and canals "helped bring back contemplation into lives":

The fishing-club, the Sunday matches, long hours watching the rufflings and changes of water, something both sane and mysterious came from all this. Why mysterious? Because the fisherman, if he is to be more than a random dabbler, must acquire an intuitive knowledge of the ways of fish and water, and within his stillness, at the centre of his capacity to wait and to contemplate, there is a sense that is ready to strike at the exact moment, that even knows, perhaps, how to lure into its own mental orbit creatures that he cannot even see under that surface on which his whole attention is concentrated. Piscator is an artist, as Walton knew. His discipline, looking out from himself but with his inner faculties deeply roused, might make a poet or painter of him if he had the latent powers within. (PP 10)

In his art, both literary and visual, he continues questing after illusive and "mysterious" presences lingering beneath the visible surfaces of the world, searching out the channels through which they may be glimpsed or intuited.

Not infrequently he points his readers toward passageways into primordial sources located deep within a core of earth or of self. "The Cavern," for instance, suggests a strong parallel between human and natural profundities. The poem juxtaposes the "mountain-interior" of a naturally formed cave against the equally "negative-dark mind" (AS). The cave seems almost alive with inchoate activity: the "pulse of the water-drop" creating "limestone" formations imitates the pulsation of a living heart; in the imagination of the poet-explorer, this "boneyard landscape grow[s] / into the identity of flesh." And because the "inhuman" shapes and chambers within the cave bear spooky resemblance to what lurks in the darkest depths of the subconscious, they "turn / human with . . . chill affinities." This "canyon within a mountain" is the exact counterpart of "the mind's / hollow." Hidden in "a deeper dark" of the cavern, moreover, arches and a "streaming buttress" suggest "the curtained sex" of "the self's unnameable and shaping home." Here is "fecund chaos" indeed. More obviously, even, than the murky waters below the surface of a "September Swamp," the bowels of the cavern are associated with id-like primacy of being.[6] A feature of the physical landscape—the mouth of a cavern—serves as a doorway into an abyss where untamed forces, both human and "inhuman," briefly make themselves manifest.[7]

"Focus," the fourth and last part of a sequence titled "In Winter Woods," highlights the sheer concentrated power of framed perception. One misty morning, "a burning / of verdure at the vapour's edge" begins to define a wooded hillside (AS). The eye then moves to a view outlined by "a black / cut block of fallen beech," which provides the "focus" promised by the poem's title:

> there, the whole, gigantic
> aperture of the day
> shuts down to a single
> brilliant orifice: a green
> glares up through this
> out of a dark of whiteness
> from the log—a moss
> that runs with the grain-mark, whirled
> like a river
> over a scape of rapids
> into a pool of mingling
> vortices. And the mind
> that swimmer, unabashed
> by season, encounters
> on entering, places
> as intimate as a fire's
> interior palaces: an Eden
> on whose emerald tinder,
> unblinded and unbounded
> from the dominance of white,
> the heart's eye enkindles.

By excluding so much from our view, a tightly circumscribed "aperture" becomes unexpectedly "gigantic" in its effects; it opens a path by closing things off, i.e., it "shuts down to a single / brilliant orifice." Strict boundaries paradoxically mediate "unbounded" sight and insight; they enable "the mind" to enter "an Eden" of inestimable value. Like the window-masks Tomlinson moves across his decalcomania, here a "single orifice" directs perception toward a wealth of mysterious images: "intimate," "interior," and appealing directly to "the heart's eye." The poem confronts the reader with a host of oppositions, all deriving from the special potency of framed vision.

Indeed, Tomlinson emphasizes in a variety of instances the paradoxical functioning of doorways: they promise and they prohibit, they hide and they reveal. Two poems that may be read as contrapuntal companion pieces, "The Gap" and "The Gate," approach aspects of such paradox by presenting playfully unusual situations. In "The Gap," Tomlinson muses on a "gateless gap," a breach in a wall that ought to be occupied by some sort of door but unaccountably is not (S). "As a confine gone," the empty space seems like "a saving grace," more alluring, perhaps, because all vestige of restraint is missing. The two severed edges of wall rise "to embrace absence, frame skies," a literally open-ended invitation to the beholder: "an image to be filled with the meaning / It doesn't yet have." This empty opening illustrates in exaggerated fashion the thrill of unknown and hence unmeasured potential that to some extent characterizes all entryways. At the same time, however, the missing door represents a boundary break, an "absence" of shape and definition, a leaching out of "meaning."

In "The Gate" Tomlinson meditates upon a diametrically different phenomenon—a gate standing in the middle of an "unfenced field" (F). Absurdly purposeless, this gate "teases the sight" as it sits there, "waiting for its fence" in order to accomplish its intended function. In this instance, "the mind demand[s] an enclosure that the eye / cannot supply it with"; the gate fills a gap that does not exist. The unenclosed field becomes "a place unspaced / And thus not quite there." Frustrated, the observer finds his glance drawn to the only outlined apertures available in this strange scene, those formed by the bars of the gate itself:

> The mocked mind,
> Busy with surroundings it can neither bound nor unbind,

>   Cedes to the eye the pleasure of passing
>   Where, between the gate's five bars,
>   Perpetual seawaves play of innumerable grasses.

The human eye is drawn inexorably even to such trivial bordering edges, which serve here to frame and hence highlight the humblest feature of the landscape: field-grasses moving in the breeze. The sight of a gate without a fence, like that of a fence without a gate, suggests to Tomlinson the significance of boundaries in the largest sense—of demarcations that shape identity and define relationships—and the potent ambiguity of doorlike phenomena that threaten to rend openings in them.

"Too little / has been said / of the door," Tomlinson avers in his poem of that title, for it is "full of the offer of space" (AS). It points toward both sides of a border, with "its one / face turned to the night's / downpour and its other / to the shift and glisten of firelight." The housedoor thus represents the meeting point between two different realms, the domestic and the wild. Hailing doors as "both frame and monument," Tomlinson continues in this poem to suggest the largest possible metaphoric meanings for them: "too little / has been said / of our coming through and leaving by them." Even the most concretely banal of doorways, he hints here, is tinged by the grand mystery of those ultimate passages, birth and death. In "The Picture of J.T. in a Prospect of Stone," he depicts his daughter poised "between / the stone lips / of a sheep-stile," the stile itself forming a dividing line between "village graves" and "village green" (PL). The child thus stands within a doorlike opening in a barrier representing the less palpable boundary line between her as yet unshaped future life—"her unmown green"—and her eventual death—"her doom (unknown)." Like the passageways in "The Door," this framed space interrupting a border marks the crossing point between two great unknowns.

In "The Shaft," Tomlinson takes readers to a similarly resonant point of entry, exploring the dark "passageway" of an abandoned mine (S). Piercing deep into the earth, it seems the quintessence of all burial chambers, imaginably even the route to a pre-Christian underworld. One almost expects to discover "pharaohs / Awaiting excavation" alongside the old mining gear. As foreboding as "a place of sacrifice," and inspiring "a vertigo that dropped through centuries," the further depths of this water-filled tunnel evoke ominous sensations: "the shaft was not a place to stare into / Or not for long." Reflections of daylight from the upper end flicker on the water surface:

> Doubled by water to a tremulous fire
> And signalling you back to the moist door
> Into whose darkness you had turned aside
> Out of the sun of an unfinished summer.

Clearly the shaft provides a route of access to darkly dangerous territory, associated with death itself. The poet heeds the "signalling" to turn back to the upper world of light and life (his own "unfinished summer"), but he is exhilarated, nonetheless, by this chance to venture a step or two across the threshold to subterranean realms. He depicts a similarly "dark" passageway in "Swallows" ("Portuguese Pieces" J). The birds are "messengers" between "day and night," he announces, "bringing news / from gods older than those / who pose in the gold interiors." Suddenly a swallow "disappear[s]," arrow-like, into a "dark slot" in the side of a building, flying through this aperture into an unseen, perhaps mystical, place where "older" gods still wield their powers.

In his poems, in fact, much as in his decalcomanic collages, Tomlinson typically takes his readers through passageways opening into regions that have something of the uncanny about them, e.g., a "keyhole door / Into darkness" leading to "a planned secretiveness" ("The Garden" A). The equivalent of "finger-tips in the paint," verbally rendered images "open into caves, burrows, waters, a world to be tracked, followed through."[8] In "The Discovery" he blends the eerie with the whimsical, describing a hike along the bed of a dried-up stream. "Deep between the high / tree-shut-in banks," the route the poet and his companions follow is "almost a tunnel" (DW). The drought has provided them with the unique opportunity to go where "no one had walked . . . before / nor could they." The narrowly enclosed path takes them to a world never before seen and never to be seen again, since "now the water reoccupies / the course we clambered." In the poem's final lines Tomlinson compares the "us" of the poem to space explorers: "if no one / followed us . . . then / we were the first and last men on the moon." Like Alice jumping down the rabbit hole into a weird new world, the hikers have walked through a temporarily opened passageway into an utterly novel environment, a place ordinarily not only unreachable, but nonexistent. In "The Garden," the poet and his companions similarly pass through a "subterranean door / Into an imaginary place that time / Turned real" (A).

In "At the Trade Center" Tomlinson creates a temporary, one-of-a-kind frame for Manhattan, modifying the panoramic view from the top of the World Trade Center by gazing at it through his own hand: "outstretched to touch and cover / The falling height beneath" (NNY). In so doing, he magnifies the illusion of control already created by height: the cityscape below appears to be literally within his grasp, miniaturized and comprehensible. "The Bridge is small from this new vantage," he remarks; "I spread my fingers / And the traffic runs between." He notes, in particular, how closely bounded by natural features this "hived" city really is:

> Rivers both sides of this island
> Tug the gaze askance from the grid of streets
> To the sea- and bird-ways, the expanse
> That drinks the reverberation of these energies.

So viewed, the encircling waters seem sufficiently extensive to contain the one-of-a-kind "energies" generated by the human population of a place rich in complexities and contradictions. The poet's Brobdingnagian—if not, indeed, godlike—sense of holding the hum of Manhattan "between the nakedness of fingers" quickly gives way to the realization that this act of framing is momentary: "What can a hand bring back into a view / No rule of thumb made possible?" New York City is a phenomenon evidently not explicable in terms of ordinary assumptions. Outlined by the poet's own "knuckled promontory of flesh," however, the city and all its baffling intricacies appear momentarily containable.

Mirrors, which strangely multiply and transform what they appear to contain, predictably and repeatedly attract Tomlinson's attention. Supplying highly unusual, framed glimpses of the actual, mirrors open into territory that is tantalizingly unreachable. Either deliberately or accidentally, and whatever its composition (e.g., glass, water), a mirroring surface replicates the visual reality it bounds and reflects, at the same time exaggerating, inverting, or otherwise distorting that reality: "a mirror lies, and / . . . may even lie with art" ("Reflections" SIB). "Its glinting bound" may offer accidental gifts of perception, "replenish the eye / with all that terrain / it cannot see," opening into suggestively *other* realms ("Legend" NNY). The surface of the reflecting glass or water functions, moreover, as a transparent boundary; offering a clear view of a place the observer cannot enter, it both opens and bars the way. As the numerous examples in chapter 4 sufficiently indicate, Tomlinson investigates the boundary between actual and illusional perception in a variety of contexts, always with marked exuberance. Reflected images constitute a large and important category of the optical distortions claiming his interest, and these assume especially concentrated potency when they are precisely bounded and enclosed.

In "Transaction at Mallards Pike," Tomlinson articulates appreciation for the curious reflections he descries on a small lake by turning once again to mining terminology (e.g., "ore," "black gold"), but he augments this substantially with religious imagery (J). He invests the ungraspable mystery of the world below the water's surface with a kind of sacredness:

Transaction at Mallards Pike
for Richard Verrall

> The trunks of the spruce at Mallards Pike
>   Float their reflections out across the lake
> Into its depths. This columned church,
>   This underwater shrine, sways in the wind;
> Its dark recession might well be a mine
>   Like those on either shore, but here
> It is the light transforms itself to ore
>   Not to be sold: the sliding darks
> Yield up no miner's harvest of black gold
>   To be weighed and traded afterwards.
> Even the swimmer through that foundered nave
>   Is robbed of the wealth of it we have
> In our dealings with a sun and surface that
>   Offers itself as mirror to the trees,
> Then jostles their rigid tallnesses to a play
>   Caught only here between the wood and light—
> Walkers on water dark alone can drown,
>   Weightlessly undulated between dawn and sundown.

The spruce trees surrounding the lake appear in reflection to resemble a "columned church" or "underwater shrine," and the interplay of "sun and surface" generates a "wealth" of "gold" more precious than any "miner's harvest." Its very lack of concreteness means this gift of perception cannot be "weighed" in ordinary terms, nor can it finally be "traded" or lost. Attempts to approach more closely to the "foundered nave," so plainly visible to the eye, would be futile: a "swimmer" seeking physical entry would of necessity be "robbed" of what the more distant observer so gratefully receives. For this revised version of reality is "caught only here," framed in space ("between the wood and light") and in time ("between dawn and sundown"). The spectacle of trees turned to "walkers on water," as "their rigid tallnesses" are "jostle[d]" by mirrored sunlight into the semblance of movement, precisely captures the mixture of reverence and playfulness with which Tomlinson regards this transitory phenomenon of sight, this *"ouverture"* into the unobtainable.

In "The Well" he contemplates once again the images of trees reflected in a body of water. In this instance, the foliage closely surrounding an old well serves to give a darker and thicker border to what he calls this "small, clear mirror" (R). As the water reflects the faces of those who gaze down into it, the trees are "framing the roundel that we make, / A circling frieze." Supplying form to the piece of world it selects, the reflection makes it special by throwing it into relief, in effect creating a temporary work of art. This "frieze" is all the more appealing because it is unstable, susceptible to seemingly infinite variation: letting down a line weighted with a stone to test the water's depth, observers watch their "images liquidly multiply, flow out / And past all bounds." Paradoxically, the tree-lined well acts as shaping boundary for what proves to be an *unbounded* variety of images.

Provoking a wide range of aesthetic, emotional, and philosophical responses, the extraordinary worlds apparently contained in mirrors compel attention and demand credence, however temporary. "The river's mirrorings remake a world," Tomlinson comments in "Below Tintern," and "that world seems true" (S). Despite its topsy-turvy layout (e.g., "that inverted sky"), such a reinvented reality is "set wide with invitation," and we contemplate with pleasure the possibility of crossing "those liquid thresholds."[9] Describing elsewhere the tiny mirrors created by water collected "in the boles of trees," Tomlinson imagines that every such "door of water" might permit him to "enter a world reverted, a catacomb / Of branching ways where the roots splay" ("At the Edge" F). Roots and branches become confused as directions reverse themselves: upper and lower regions appear to change places. A mysterious, labyrinthine world beckons. The hints offered by the tiny, "secreted / Water-holes" are confirmed a few lines later by the image of a nesting "hole" in a stream bank. The poet observes a tiny bird scurrying in and out of the mouth of this passageway "with such an energy of glancing lightness" it causes him to "measure all the force unspied / That stirred inside that bank." Reminiscent of Frost's "Spring Pools," Tomlinson's depiction of nature's "force" here is just as uncanny, although less threatening, than the earlier poet's. "The Way Through" strikes a more ominous note, as the reflection of sky in the water pooled inside a sea-cave "reads like a gap in the floor of rock / That you could fall through" (R). The mirroring effect of sky on water is so distorted by the cavern walls that a dramatically threatening "downward way" seems to open up: a "crevice that speaks of falling / . . . through a space that does not yet exist." The poet goes on to equate this apparently bottomless abyss with the end of the world ("as Dies Irae widens the last crevasse").

The ability of mirrors to display a reality beyond the familiar, "a space which does not yet exist," need not always prove portentous, however, as Tomlinson often reminds us. On occasion, a mirror's artful distortions move him to more lighthearted musings. When small pools of rainwater "fill[ ] all the streets / With mirrors," he notes happily how these "confront[ ] the city with itself in fragments" ("Parking Lot" A):

> PARKING reading as ARK reversed
>   (I took it for Russian). A slice of a building
> Has got in on the reflection of a car
>   Disintegrating and reassembling between raindrops:
> A piece of tree dances across the wrinkling image.
>   Parked, I see half a man
> Float by, and hear from the missing portion
>   A throat being cleared and then
> He walks away into his own entirety

The constant movement of objects in and across the glistening, irregularly shaped puddles makes for a kaleidoscopic effect, as bits of the scene re-order themselves to form a succession of absurdly incomplete and juxtaposed images. Much like the "appreciative maple" he observes soaking up the rainwater, Tomlinson, too, revels in the weather, enjoying the comedic novelty of these temporary miniature mirrors that have transformed an ordinary place into a carnival version of itself.

Another persistent, if apparently unlikely, framing device to be found in Tomlinson's poetry (one that almost threatens to rival his fascination with mirrors) is the automobile windshield. It serves the outlining function of openings such as doors, windows, or gates, and it possesses in addition the reflecting, distorting capacities of mirrors and bodies of water. Its distinguishing feature, however, is that of motion. Unlike a gate or a pond, a mirror or a doorway, the automobile windshield propels itself and its passengers through the landscape, presenting a series of continuously changing images. The windshield serves, moreover, as a unique "framing glass" for these images, slicing out for our inspection arbitrary segments of whatever is rushing past ("The Windshield" WW). Demonstrating obvious resemblance to the paper windows of Tomlinson's collage art, this mobile frame creates new and otherwise unobtainable visual effects, effects often tinged with provocative optical distortion. He celebrates in numerous poems the ability of automobile travel to offer novel and "nutrifying" views of the world (PP 17). "In driving, of course, you see things at a different speed and at a different angle from those which one's ancestors knew," he observes; "so there's fresh perception for you and a different way of looking at the landscape."[10]

There are intriguing parallels, as well as self-evident differences, between car windshields and the Gaudiesque windows Tomlinson utilizes in his decalcomania. Most obviously, the shape and size of Gaudi's windows are determined by aesthetic considerations as much as by practical issues of construction and intended use. The windshield in an automobile is designed along principles of aerodynamics, symmetry, and angularity, while Gaudi's windows assume a huge variety of asymmetrical, amoeboid shapes; their outlines appear organic rather than geometric. Such differences are tellingly counterbalanced by other factors, however. In both cases, a window provides sole visual access to a world otherwise hidden from the viewer. Discussing his graphics, Tomlinson describes his windows alternatively as "masks"; the scissored openings in a piece of paper serve as eyeholes through which the observer may glimpse only a small portion of paper-covered decalcomania. As masks, the windows thus become, as Paz points out, "objects which *conceal*" even as they "serve . . . to *reveal*."[11] Similarly, the automobile conceals from driver and passengers the world through which they are journeying except for the special and constricted view of it provided by the windows. Another intriguing commonality stems from Gaudi's achievement in the design of his windows, as in other architectural structures, of an effect of motion, of "undulating . . . rhythm."[12] "Sliding, rippling, dissolving, re-forming," Gaudi's fluid and fantastical lines suggest constant movement and metamorphosis, rather than stasis.[13] Such effects, the distinguishing mark of Gaudi's style, in some sense mimic the movement of a car through space and the resulting flow of images observed through its windows.

Fascinated by the fluid reframing of images the car windscreen accomplishes, Tomlinson attempts to articulate in his poems the evocative effects created by such rapid succession of captured (and sometimes reflected) images: "things always moving, disintegrating, re-forming" ("Sight and Flight" NNY). In "Carscape," for instance, he ponders how time seems to stand still and destinations indefinitely recede when he drives into a setting sun. "Mirrored / the rear window / holds a glowing / almost-gone-day," but as he drives toward the sunset "against its glare," the day seems magically to prolong itself (WrW). Watching the interplay of clouds and light, he sees "many vanishings / replenished," and in the last line of the poem he articulates the paradoxical visual effect at its most extreme: this scene of setting sun "could still be dawn." The forward progress of his vehicle through space makes time seem to halt, providing a distorted perception of ordinary temporal process. Similarly, a journey to Palermo at night appears to pull "a tunnel of trees," or "an asphalt waterway," around the moving vehicle ("Palermo" R). Once again an image seems to be indefinitely prolonged, "a discovery" that "the car-lights keep extending / Ahead of themselves." The "illusion" created by the moving eyehole of the windshield is more real to those inside the vehicle than is the actual "vista" outside it.

"Arizona Highway" comments on a related experience, this time as the poet approaches a sunrise: "we have driven into day" (AS). The opening lines draw on vocabulary familiar from Tomlinson's discussion of "window" and "mask" in connection with his decalcomanic collage-work:

> To become the face of space,
> snatching a flowing mask
> of emptiness
> from where the parallels meet.

Almost predatory, as if eager to consume the desert landscape before it, "the windshield drinks / the telegraphed desert miles." The poet-speaker declares himself to be "no more / than invaded transparency," so that it is he, as much as the windshield, who has *become* "the face of space." Assuming "glass identity," he in effect trades places with the personified windshield, now a "devouring and dusty eye." In this strange suspension of his human personality, the poet experiences "pure duration," for time, too, has been suspended by the sensation of moving toward images faster than they can recede before the car. Reality itself appears to be in flux, "all / transition, transformation." The steady flow of images projected by the moving vehicle creates a weirdly protean world in which place, time, window, and observer temporarily seem to interpenetrate.[14] Indeed, the central metaphor in the poem is one of ingestion and transformation. The car window and the human eye take in the desert sands but are simultaneously "invaded" by the scene they "devour." When the speaker wakes from a brief nap, he discovers fragments of the scene from outside the car—"fine-ground glass of the sand grains"—actually inside the vehicle, coating his hands and "burn[ing]" his "lips and tongue." Now he is literally eating the desert that his eye, assisted by the "snatching" windshield, has been absorbing, and the desert sand itself has been redefined as "glass" and thus linked to the mediating auto window. In this subtly wrought poem, "all" is indeed "transformation," as traveller, vehicle, and landscape come together, pressing against one another's boundaries in metaphors that suggest the heightened effect of mobile, framed perception on human imagination.

"Drive" offers another variation on the theme of "things . . . disintegrating, re-forming," as the poet this time contrasts a drive at dawn with the return journey through the same scene in full light of day. What he has seen on the initial trip is strangely obscured by brighter light and the about-face in direction of travel:

> First light strikes
> across a landmass
> daylight hides:
>
> (WrW)

Tomlinson is intrigued, even a trifle disconcerted, to notice how perceived reality appears not merely changed, but "undone," or dismantled, by shifts in lighting and perspective:

5: GRAPHIC FRAMING 141

> I return driving
> to the same view undone:
> the windscreen takes it in
> as a high and brilliant
> emptiness . . .

He then draws an analogy between "the lost / continent (it seems) / of day's beginnings" and human life. Caught up in the fullness of daily activities ("the cross- / tides of chaos"), we leave behind us an "infinity of unmarked / mornings" and "spaces unsounded." All too apt to "believe our eyes (our lies) / that there is nothing there / but what we see," we forget to acknowledge interior landscapes, or those passed through long ago, no longer visibly present to us but no less real for that. The poet concludes with a gentle admonition drawn from this round-trip journey and disappearing "view," hinting that we might translate our experience in the automobile to more intangible realms of perception. In our lives, as in our vehicles, much is hidden (or masked); what we see or comprehend from any single point of view, or point in time, is less than the whole of what is "there." Thus the accidental rearrangement of a view from a car creates one of the *"ouvertures"* Tomlinson so values—opening to insight transcending the ordinariness of the precipitating occasion.

Just as Tomlinson's paper windows permit him to find and create meaning in the larger chaos of his decalcomania, the car windshield discloses comprehensible portions of a much vaster whole. Driving through a March storm, the poet sees unexpected beauty in the "glittering reflections [of snow-clouds] over the windshield" ("The Windshield" WW). "Sailing through" the play of shadows on glass, the clouds "seem[] to be dancing," their movement exaggerated and aesthetically ordered by the distorting medium. Because the windshield provides an altered and limited view of the storm, "the force / contained by the framing glass," it offers unique possibilities for the appreciation of an otherwise overwhelming spectacle. "The random fierceness of season and day" has been rendered manageable, lovely, even measurable ("for sky is sky and no measure of itself"), "contained" and modified by the outlining, reflecting window. Here, as in several other poems, the car windshield emerges as perhaps a more potent viewing mechanism even than the paper windows of Tomlinson's graphics, for the windshield is more than an empty opening. A substance, albeit transparent, it can augment the scene it reveals with special effects created by the light thrown off its surface. Confronted under certain conditions with more than what the windshield outlines, the observer must reconcile what is seen *through* the glass with what is seen *on* the glass.

The poem "Night Ride" offers a particularly striking example of the interplay possible between framed views and framed reflections. In contrast to the bulk of Tomlinson's automobile poems, "Night Ride" voices complaints about urban commuter traffic and attendant irritations of crowded contemporary cities: "lives . . . cramped in beside / This swathe of roadway," "too many of us . . . edging behind each other" on the jammed thoroughfares (WI). Here Tomlinson appears to be disparaging the automobile as a symbol of urban ills rather than celebrating it as an instrument of extraordinary perception. Yet he has woven into his grim comments elaborate descriptions of the many "lamps" casting patterns across the evening commuter's horizon: windows "blaze," hearths "glimmer," and "scatterings" from roadside "sodium circuits" "drip pendants" of light over the dark contours of the city. Long lines of autos contribute to the dizzying display "with dipped beams down the shining wet." These "terrestrial galaxies," "fixed stars and moving," are the signal beacons of an all too imperfect human community, but Tomlinson's metaphors elevate them to astral beauty and significance. Even as he disapprovingly notes that "our lights seem more beautiful than our lives," he marvels at "the catseyes and glittering asterisks" bouncing off road surfaces and windshields. The gleaming show of lights observed on and through auto windows provides a surprising if insufficient compensation for harried commuters, a consolatory counterpoint to urban aggravations.[15]

Tomlinson's perhaps most stunning salute to the windshield as moving frame occurs in a poem called "The Arch." Driving toward a section of road lined on both sides by tall, leafy trees ("the windscreen frames the image"), the traveller perceives this corridor of trees as if it were an intact structure, "all apparent mass and solidity" (NNY). Once having entered the archway, however, he sees with surprise that it is not solid at all. Observed from within, it proves to be a veritable sieve, the foliage latticed with empty spaces, glimpses of open sky. Tomlinson describes this change in perception as if the arch were actually falling to pieces over the roof of the speeding car: "you swing in under and fragments / (Or so the glance would say) start / Falling away." The amazed observer finds himself "staring up into / A shattered canopy, a leaf-floor / Swaying apart." What the eye sees is a spectacular architectural collapse, followed in due course by an equally wondrous rebuilding: miraculously, "ledge on ledge of green masonry . . . / Flows back into place." Glancing back through the rear window, the observer watches the arch grow solid again, closing "finally round an immovable keystone." With its "eye for metamorphosis," the car has acted here as a catalyst for magic. Watching solid substance dissolve and reassemble before our eyes, we have participated in a kind of sorcery: the seemingly stable world, observed through the windows of a moving car, reveals an unsuspected plasticity.

In these poems featuring auto travel, windshields function very much like the window-masks in his graphics, serving as peepholes into a realm of mysterious images that appear to be always in flux, in the process of becoming. With its emphasis on instantaneous reframing, "The Arch," even more than the other automobile poems, shows traces, too, of Tomlinson's early enthusiasm for film, an interest he describes as both technical and philosophical.[16] "I was obsessed by cinema," he has said, particularly with its "fluidity of movement and clarity of image." He singles out Orson Welles for special admiration, mentioning "a stunning opening sequence" in *A Touch of Evil*, "an extended crane-shot that," appropriately enough, "shows a car journey across a Mexican town."[17] Although his initial ambition to succeed as a screen scriptwriter soon yielded to more enduring affinities for other genres and media, the ability of the car windshield to achieve effects very like those of a motion-picture camera lens allows Tomlinson to indulge his old "obsession" indirectly. Like a finished film, composed of individual "frames" edited and spliced, a moving car presents a series of images in such rapid succession that the beholder enjoys a seamlessly unrolling sequence of perceptions.

Thus a number of impulses converge in these automobile poems that take the eye on framed journeys through varied landscapes and weathers. The moving car serves the poet well as both subject and device, enabling him to articulate a host of favorite concerns. Recording and mediating encounters between the observing human consciousness and portions of an external reality, the windshield intensifies our experience of a world that appears to be perpetually in movement, in process.[18] At the same time, the windshield's shaping outline acts as a fixative mechanism in this flux; it defines an area and an angle of vision. The perceiving human may choose to elaborate, to meditate upon any of these arbitrarily defined views of the world, counterbalancing fortuity with deliberate intent. Finally, the perspectives afforded by a moving window sometimes induce intriguingly, marvelously inaccurate perceptions. Thus the special properties of the containing boundaries formed by automobile windows allow Tomlinson to explore contrapuntal relationships that preoccupy him in one form or another throughout his career, e.g., chaos and design, fact and illusion, discovery and invention, possession and dispossession. Treating a seemingly banal and uninspiring feature of contemporary life as a form of experiential art, he affirms distinctly modern aesthetic ideas. He translates into the medium of language methods and effects drawn from his graphic art, substituting for an eerie welter of pigment the equally evocative medley of forms in the real world, thus investing this particular group of framing windows with cinematic dynamism.

More marvelous even than mysterious doorways, travelling windows, and reflecting mirrors, however, are those regions in the mind itself that conjure up, and perhaps remold, distinct portions of the external world. Like a mirror, the mind reflects (and reflects upon) the actual; in its role as agent of fertile juxtaposition, it functions as a metaphoric doorway, providing access to treasures of memory and imagination. In the mind's own "kingdoms of possibilities," what is literally distant or past ("the door is shut") can be summoned to recollection with vivid immediacy, like a door "flung wide" ("A Sense of Distance" WW). Art, in particular, which is both a product of the imagination and a stimulus to it, frequently provides a framed route of entry from immediate and ordinary sources of awareness to those less commonly accessible. In an early poem, "Nine Variations on a Chinese Winter Setting," Tomlinson observes:

> The outline of the water-dragon
> Is not embroidered with so intricate a thread
> As that with which the flute
> Defines the tangible borders of a mood.

(N)

Key vocabulary here ("outline," "define," and "borders") faultlessly echoes that which he applies to much more literally conceived delineating edges in the physical universe. The music of the flute creates new boundaries—and hence new territory—in which the human consciousness can wander. In "Small Action Poem," Tomlinson likens the effect of music to a freshly discovered, newly opened passageway. The musician's physical manipulation of an instrument seems insufficient to account for the seemingly suprasensory results: "It is like / Chopin / shaking / music from the fingers" (AS). The listener has entered a place where, briefly, mere notes ("nothing but notes") perform "sorcery": "the door / is open now." In this poem an open door commemorates the ability of music to make us believe we have stepped across a threshold "to arrive / unexpectedly / at somewhere" in a world newly invented.

Tomlinson draws the visual arts into this same conceit. By "opening door on door / of space," for instance, a painting by Braque enables us "to enter space anew," in fact, "to enter *a new* space" ("The Miracle of the Bottle and the Fishes," emphasis added, R). Another poem, "On a Collage of Marie José Paz," pays tribute to the intriguing boundary-building and border-breaching characteristic of Tomlinson's own favorite genre of collage. He calls the picture itself a "house / of patches," and the house metaphor permits him very naturally to declare that one particular "scrap" composing it is "a window" (DW). This piece of the collage, a "landscape / photograph," seems window-like because the beholder sees it in two ways: once as itself—a photograph—and once as an element composing a section of tree in the collage. As a section of tree, it is in effect opaque, disappearing into the illusion of the tree-shape it helps to form; as a photograph depicting a panoramic view of another place, it appears to open a hole in the tree, offering a framed glimpse of a landscape mysteriously contained within. "Where / are we?" Tomlinson asks, bewildered by this double effect. We are "neither here nor there," but somewhere in imaginative space where two possibilities exist simultaneously: the everyday tree with its solid trunk, and the magical tree with its window-view into another world.

The collage artist thus has "cleared a space" in which the imagination can operate. Again, as in "The Discovery," readers experience the sensation of popping through an unexpected passageway into fantastically foreign territory, where anything may happen:

> By the stair of sight,
> from the side we cannot see,
> I climb down into it [the "window"],
> all at once free

A work of art here permits imaginative movement into a new dimension. The artist has created an "image that makes room for / entrance." For the beholder, the experience of entering proves liberating, yet Tomlinson follows up his declaration that he is "all at once free" of the constraints of the ordinary with the observation that this freedom occurs within strictly defined parameters:

> in this tiny confine
> I can compare
> only to the atmosphere we breathe
> in a poem's stanza—

Comparing the window-like "scrap" of collage to the stanza in a poem, he indirectly makes the case that, in all the arts, *form* functions like a door- or windowframe.

Without the boundaries provided by formal principles, whether dictated by medium or genre or other criteria, neither picture, nor poem, nor melody would possess the concentrated power to move us. Discrete units such as stanzas help forge patterns of meaning in otherwise "featureless," undifferentiated materials; they "contain" and hence they "compel" ("Hedgerows" NNY). The stanza serves Tomlinson as illustrative example again in "Movements," where the process of artistic creation takes place "in an interior" (and "before an audience of none"). Elements of the work-in-progress "will arise at the threshold of his mind," where inspiration and craft come together: "Stanza by stanza (room by room)," he proceeds "deeper in. Door / opens on door" (WrW). Taking us through the passageways of its own designs ever "deeper" into places we have not previously visited, art exhilarates us emotionally as well as intellectually.

The illuminating image of the window-in-a-tree in the poem "On a Collage of Marie José Paz" helps readers visualize with instant clarity exactly how a "tiny confine" can represent a place to be "free," i.e., to comprehend the mutually sustaining relationship between form and freedom. Tomlinson's preoccupation with doors and windows—with the boundaries, both literal and figurative, they break and make—persists throughout his career. He is "expert in dramatizing" the "excitements and perplexities" such apertures embody.[19] They concentrate and therefore heighten the already significant effects of "discontinuity, incalculableness, and often humor" resulting from juxtaposition, e.g., of different places, times, events, conditions, or perceptions.[20] These tightly bounded entryways are precious because they illumine territory radically alien, yet tantalizingly close at hand. Like the individual components of a collage, they are sharply defined and self-contained; the access they promise proves potent in its concentrated keenness.

6
Contiguity and Conjunction

a lingering / At the edge of time, a perfect neighbouring

POISED BETWEEN PRINCIPLES OF CONVERGENCE AND DIVERGENCE, PALpitant with the disparate energies flanking them, borders are places of "perpetual threshold" ("Departure" S). In separating, they connect; they provide rare meeting ground for oppositional entities and forces. Sites of truce, treaty, and negotiation (to use more of Tomlinson's favorite terms), shared borders make neighbors out of strangers, promoting alliance as well as conflict. The boundaries sectoring the landscape of his poetry enforce exclusion and cooperation, or comparison and contrast, with equal facility. Contiguity necessarily cuts two ways: the same tight edging that brings differences into relief also highlights similarities. Alongside jolting incongruities and illuminating dichotomies, readers encounter compelling correspondences, revelatory resemblances.

Numerous poems discover and probe correspondences linking a series of distinctly different realms. In "Picking Mushrooms by Moonlight," a sequence of resemblances spans enormous distances, literal and figurative, connecting the earth with the sky, the organic with the inorganic, the human with the nonhuman, the natural with the otherworldly:

Picking Mushrooms by Moonlight

Strange how these tiny moons across the meadows,
Wax with the moon itself out of the shadows.
Harvest is over, yet this scattered crop,
Solidifying moonlight, drop by drop,
Answers to the urging of that O,
And so do we, exclaiming as we go,

6: CONTIGUITY AND CONJUNCTION 149

> With rounded lips translating shape to sound,
> At finding so much treasure on the ground
> Marked out by light. We stoop and gather there
> These lunar fruits of the advancing year:
> So late in time, yet timely at this date,
> They show what forces linger and outwait
> Each change of season, rhyme made visible
> And felt on the fingertips at every pull.
>
> (DW)

For practical reasons the activity of mushroom gathering is pursued at night, under a full moon. Spotting the mushrooms evidently is easier in the dark, when the soft glow of moonshine causes their white caps to stand out, "marked out by light," against an otherwise dark background of vegetation. In the very first line, moreover, Tomlinson introduces the correspondence between mushroom and moon on which the whole poem hinges. Similarities in shape and color make the round disks in the meadow look like miniature versions of the bright satellite overhead: mushrooms are "tiny moons," "lunar fruits," or, more fancifully, drops of "solidifying moonlight." This likeness goes beyond mere appearance. In a cause-and-effect relationship, mushrooms "wax with the moon": not only do they become more easily discernible as moonbeams pick them "out of the shadows," they grow, as superstition has it, during the night in response to the moon's generative impulse. Springing up with magical swiftness, apparently from one day to the next, they enjoy a spooky reputation; while other plants are nurtured by the sun's warmth, they alone are regarded as products ("fruits") of the moon's cooler beams.

Moon and mushroom provide yet another example, then, of things that "complement[] / in opposition," the emphasis here falling on *complement*: a large, distant, inorganic object enters into mysterious conjunction with something small, nearby, and organic ("At Holwell Farm" SIB). The necessary, almost mystical connection between astronomical influence and vegetative growth extends itself into the human realm as well. The "O" representing the shape of both moon and mushroom is repeated in the "rounded lips" and cry (Oh!) of the exultant searchers. The circular "O" pattern joins the visual and the auditory in a sequence of multisensory apprehension that also includes the tactile, as the round shape of each mushroom is "felt on the fingertips at every pull." Even the sense of taste is included by implication in this sequence, since the human gatherers clearly intend to eat the "crop" they are in process of collecting.

Reference to "the advancing year" indicates that the ripening of the mushrooms occurs in early fall; "harvest is over." This wild crop distinguishes itself from ordinary products of human agriculture in its lateness, as well as in its supposedly "lunar" sources. The concluding lines of the poem return to the "strange" origin of mushrooms. Out of synchrony with normal developmental cycles, they are artefacts of special, possibly occult, "forces" that "linger and outwait," with seemingly deliberate intent, the "change of season." The poem thus illustrates a spectrum of correspondences embracing the natural, the human, and the supernatural. "Rhyme" is Tomlinson's chosen metaphor for the principle of cosmic congruence he celebrates in the poem. Resemblances based on the "O" shape create a chord-like, multidimensional progression of echoes: "rhyme made visible." The paradox inherent in the device of rhyme, which balances the certainties of design with the fortuitousness of chance, serves well to characterize a chain of likenesses reassuring in its repetitions, yet mysterious in its ultimate sources.[1] Tomlinson highlights the importance of rhyme as a metaphor here by choosing to write the poem in the form of a couplet sonnet. An exception in the canon of his work, it conforms with great fidelity to the requirements of this verse type. Metrically it maintains a loose but persuasive iambic pentameter; its rhyme scheme is based on end rhymes, mostly full, arranged in pairs. Some internal rhyming occurs, but this does not overwhelm the strong effect of the metrically regular, end-rhyming couplets. Indirectly, but irresistibly, the poem's formal features underscore the idea of echoing repetition which is also its topic and its theme. Characteristically, here, Tomlinson's own description of his approach to poetic form holds true: "technical features help to bring out the variety of what is for me one world."[2]

The image of the circle, or "O," linking moon, mushroom, and mouth (as well as sight, sound, touch, and taste) points to a view of the cosmos as a perfect, unifying whole. Employing this ancient symbol, Tomlinson reinforces the mental picture he puts forward in "Ode to Arnold Schoenberg" of an all-embracing "unity," within which a continuous process of dissolution and resolution is enacted (PL). His poems disclose "a world ungraspably various and yet made to cohere."[3] This larger arena of integration includes impulses antagonistic to harmony and consonance, e.g., "dissonance" and "disrupt[ion]," which undergo a "redefin[ing]" and a restoration. The unity that Tomlinson posits is no static perfection, obviously, but a multistranded, restless "whole in which / discontinuities are held."⁴ As the carefully selected examples of circularity in "Picking Mushrooms by Moonlight" indicate, both the cosmos itself and the human mind apprehending it exhibit this kind of dynamic containment of difference-in-sameness, sameness-in-difference: both seethe with disparate identities and colliding energies they encompass but never finally tame.

The history of the planet itself is a temporal sequence of discrete, often warring, forces. An archaeological dig discloses successive layering, artefacts of human occupancy and invasion interspersed with remains of evolving plant and animal life and evidence of geological upheaval: "history's particles refusing / both completion / and extinction" ("Near Corinium" S). Collectively, the individuated "particles" point to a larger, potentially discernible wholeness:

>   it is as though
>   this torn tapestry
>   faded calligraphy
>   were whole
>   if only one could adjust
>   one's eyes to them.

Images of "tapestry" and "calligraphy" suggest coherent designs, susceptible to human interpretation, but the use of the subjunctive mood in these lines—along with the adjectives "faded" and "torn"—places us at a "perpetual threshold" of comprehension ("Departure" S). Our faculties stretch to encompass a larger integration, engaged in a process that, like the spiraling cycles of history itself, can be neither completed nor ended.

The circle recurs as an image of completion and wholeness in many contexts in the poems, marking human-to-human connections as well as those linking disparate spheres (e.g., domesticated and wild, terrestrial and extraterrestrial). In the four-part poem "Winter Journey," for example, the poet focuses movingly on his temporary separation from a beloved domestic intimate. Addressing the absent one throughout, he follows in his imagination the journey he does not share, at the same time evoking the landscape of home ("the stream goes lapping . . . clear / Down all its course, renewing and re-rhymed") and recollecting past domestic catastrophes ("I thought back to our flood") (R). Suspended in a kind of personal limbo by an all-consuming absence, consciously "waiting," he conveys a poignant expectancy. Toward evening on the day of the much anticipated return, he lays the table "where, tonight, we eat," noting that the close of day will coincide with the restoration of domestic normalcy: "dwindling day / Must yield to the lights that beam you in / And the circle hurry to complete itself where you began." Natural and human cyclicity work in tandem here, the journeying person moving in apparent harmony with the journeying sun.[5]

Repeatedly Tomlinson insists that world and mind correspond: they constitute two fully valid, intersecting realities. The phenomenal world is primary, the *sine qua non* of our existence, but it is available to us only through the mediation of human senses and human consciousness. The universe within and the universe without are, necessarily, equally important to us, "for all ways begin, either from the eyes out / Or the eyes in" ("Movements" WrW). The mind discovers relationships (a likeness, say, between moon and mushroom) and the mouth gives voice to those discoveries: "word and world rhyme" ("Rhymes" S). Human experience is "linked in rhyme" to the nonhuman realm of "earth, water, time" ("To My Daughter" J). In the poem "Chance" Tomlinson highlights this connectedness by introducing a series of observed "resemblances," noticing how the "spume" of waves hitting rock looks like "driving snow," "foam-motes" take flight "like tiny birds," and "clicking pebbles" dragged forward by the tide sound like "chattering dice" (A):

>   What do they tell
>   These occurrences, these resemblances that speak to you
>   With no human voice? What they told then
>   Was that the energies pouring through space and time,
>   Spun into snow-lace, suspended into flight,
>   Had waited on our chance appearance here,
>   To take their measure, to re-murmur in human sounds
>   The nearing roar of this story of far beginnings
>   As it shapes out and resounds itself along the shore.

These lines affirm the importance of human consciousness and "human voice" powerfully. The emergence of our particular species may be accidental, yet the entire nonhuman universe appears to have "waited" with urgent anticipation for "our chance appearance" on the scene. Engaging our faculties to apprehend external phenomena, reframing these "in human sounds" and terms, we provide them with significance and context. The "resemblances" and relationships among things are real, but it is we who recognize, articulate, and preserve them.

The mind is itself a "bright satellite" equal to any circling the heavens ("Here and There" A).[6] Or, conversely, it is a worthy receptor for "the illumination [the moon] pours / Into the shadows and the watcher's mind" ("Variation" A). World and mind are like mirror images, reacting to the same set of variegated stimuli; "the mind / That floating thing" is the equivalent of a planet suspended in space ("Above the Rio Grande" A). And in composing a drawing or poem, the human artist in turn creates a "little universe" (PP 18). Tomlinson explains this two-way equivalence eloquently in a poem about an unusual work of art. Describing the scene depicted on an engraved glass goblet, he discusses the combined effects of curvature, lighting, and motion on a translucent medium: "at first sight / there is nothing to see" ("On a Glass Engraving by Peter David" DW). The beholder slowly differentiates "the stippled surface" from the "depth" of the engraved lines and begins then to discern shapes. Revolving on its base inside a lighted cabinet like a tiny planet, the goblet appears to be a primal "pool of origin" out of which "dark forms" of flora and fauna gradually "solidify." Experiencing this piece of art is like watching the creation of life out of primordial chaos; designs emerge from the "swirl" of a "vitreous / whirlpool." The poet concludes that the artist's vision "opens two ways—" i.e., inward and outward. His vision is equally congruent with world and with mind, for it re-creates and contains a universe, preserving and illuminating a "speckled" multiformity: "the world and the mind's eye / curving together / round this speckled frieze."

Delight in analogies, along with a propensity for discovering them, appears to be a peculiarly human attribute, one that may lead to inspiration and invention. In "Gutenberg and the Grapes," Tomlinson suggests how wine-makers' equipment and techniques provided stimulus for Johannes Gutenberg. "Watching them turn the screw / tighter, tighter" to force the grapes through "the press," he realized how this procedure might be transferable to a whole new process—book-making: "he knew at last / what it was / he was looking for" (J). In "The Vineyard Above the Sea" Tomlinson presents a more complicated chain of likenesses and cooperative interaction. The correspondences he identifies center around the wine for which the town of Corniglia,

Italy, is famous: "wine like daylight, tasting of the sea" (VS). Lifting a glass of it "towards the sun," the poet-speaker sees it in relationship to the "light" that helped to nurture the grapes and to the sea whose salty atmosphere imparts "asperity" to its flavor. Like the mushrooms that are compared to essence of moon ("solidifying moonlight, drop by drop"), the wine represents a translation of light and sea into a different medium.

Within the poet's lifted glass he also sees the reflected images, in miniature, of the whole surrounding locale: sea, cliffs, vineyards, town. "Catching" and holding these, the glass contains a whole landscape "essentialized." The temporary optical illusion reveals an only slightly exaggerated version of the truth, namely, that the wine represents a distillation of the various elements necessary to its production. A combination of effort is required to make it, farmers and vintners supplementing the natural sustenance provided by sun, rain, and soil. The poem further suggests a close conjunction between wild and domesticated portions of the scene by personifying natural elements. The walled cliffs supporting the vineyards, and separating them from the sea, look like a "rugged forehead"; the vines themselves are "cables" helpfully "hoisting a harvest to the summit." The town, known by what is "almost a woman's name," seems "maternal" in its relationship to the grape crop. It watches benignly over "a geology festooned, transformed" by human agriculture, the vines decorating it like garlands. The rocky shore seems to have been struggling toward exactly this cooperative endeavor; "through the centuries" it has "hunched a way / Towards these cube-crystals of the houses, / This saline precipice, this glass of light." The poem offers a toast to this conjoining of disparate energies, as the poet lifts the glass of wine in which they so happily culminate.

The poem affirms correspondences based upon rationally explicable mutual effort and influence, yet there is an element of mystery in the transmutation of daylight to wine, or "geology" to vineyard, that transcends logic. Even the most seemingly ordinary instance of congruence, or "rhyme," is energized in part by subrational connective forces, like the linking of words by virtue of phonetics rather than meaning.[7] Tinged with the suggestion of mystery and miracle, resemblances involve a temporary overlap or exchange of identity, apprehension of one thing as if it were something else. Moon and mushroom and mouth are all at once interchangeable, linked by the poet's recognition of the circular shape that makes them one. The discovery of analogies is therefore in itself a transformative event. Energized by the "perception of design and recurrent form in nature,"[8] Tomlinson's poems are filled with praise for what he variously dubs "alchemy," "transfiguration," "metamorphosis," or "transformation": as disparate phenomena conjoin, they bring us to the verge of "the circle that [we] seek," suggesting underlying oneness in a cosmos characterized by multiplicity ("Mushrooms" S).

In terms of perception, analogy is the flip side of anomaly, and Tomlinson's poems amply demonstrate how both may be associated with illusion. Frequently, as examples in chapter 4 indicate, he concentrates on disjunctive instances of misapprehension. He explores intriguing dichotomies, poignant as well as comical in their effects, based on frankly acknowledged perceptual mistakes: his house is not built in the boughs of a tree; the living room is not under water; the moon is not leapfrogging down the road; a shell shard is not a tiny man; a truck is not balancing on top of a bedroom bureau. Just as these incongruities delivered by misperception are characterized by magic, or wizardry, the apprehension of correspondences, however provisional or fictive, is resonant with transformational, seemingly transcendent energies. Michael Edwards points out that "one of the accompaniments of chance is similitude," arguing that in Tomlinson's non-Christian but reverent approach to seeing chance operates like "a kind of friendly providence."[9]

"The Metamorphosis" illustrates the transmogrifying effect of illusion based on resemblance: "bluebells come crowding a fellside / a stream once veined" (S). Nourished, apparently, by traces of sediment in the soil of the old streambed, bluebells now fill it with a blue iridescence, the dancing flower-heads imitating the movement of water as well as its color: "they flow through its bed, each rope / And rivulet, each tributary thread / found-out by flowers." Again the device of rhyme subtly reinforces connections; " 'each tributary thr*ead*' " of the old path . . . rhymes reminder of its former '*bed*.' "[10] The "imaginary water" collects in mirage-like "marshes and pools" in the valley below the fellside, changing grassy cliffs and fields into a persuasive waterscape:

> So that the mind, in salutory confusion,
> Surrendering up its powers to the illusion,
>   Could, swimming in metamorphoses, believe
> Water itself might move like a flowing of flowers.

Willingly "the mind" yields to "salutory confusion" in which a three-way process of correspondence and transformation occurs. First flowers are perceived as water, and then the resemblance is reversed: water is perceived as flower-like. This second image, of water moving "like a flowing of flowers," represents an even more wonderfully evocative transformation than the initial illusion of flowers-as-water. A third and final instance of correspondence is created by the poet's choice of the verb *swim*. Investigating a resemblance between flowers and water that works both ways, the mind itself now seems to be "swimming in metamorphoses," floating (and flowering) amid protean possibilities.

Tomlinson returns to the resemblance between blue flowers and water in "Bluebells," where he reports "seeing the purple tide / Overflow from the wood to meet us" (A). He reiterates in this poem that some indiscernible "nutriment of earth" is responsible for feeding and shaping the vast cluster of flowers. "If we could fly above them," he speculates, we could see that shape clearly and perhaps "read / The sprawled, imperial hieroglyph of this spread." Like a nineteenth-century Transcendentalist, he avers that elements in the natural world function as a kind of picture-writing, conveying meanings that our human faculties are poised on the brink of deciphering.[11] Just as this particular pattern of flower growth may reveal the course of a dried-up stream or the outline of a stand of dead and decomposed trees, all such spontaneously occurring hieroglyphs offer clues to connections, visible and invisible, among diverse phenomena, potential routes of communication between nature and mind. Tomlinson emphasizes the importance of a perceiving and decoding human presence in the closing lines of the poem, where he notes that the "bell-mouths" of the flowers are "silent." "It is only our words" that "colour" and give voice to their special qualities and often riddling implications.

In the course of the poem, the opening comparison between bluebells and water (that "purple tide") gives way to an elaborately playful military metaphor. Showing their "imperial" colors, the flowers "advance": "they / Swarm down the woodbank, a flower army." This comparison between flowers and an advancing troop of soldiers lends a forward-driving, stalwart character to the floral abundance. Tomlinson's metaphor takes on unexpected metaphysical overtones, moreover, when he declares that the horde of flowers resembles "the angelic orders . . . visible in time." The bluish-purple blossoms "glow" as if they were indeed the "iridescent shadow / Of such splendour." By the end of the poem the tangible, organic reality of wild flowers is resonant with implied connections to both human and supernatural domains. The bluebells are both "in time" and beyond it, natural and "angelic," ordinary and splendid, vegetative and sentient, "silent" and suggestive. Figurative language provides linguistic foundation for the transformative connections Tomlinson affirms; here as throughout his poetry he exploits metaphor, especially, to invoke contiguity and assert powerful resemblances.

He articulates an affinity with nineteenth-century American Transcendental philosophy, in particular its emphasis on organic correspondences, very explicitly in a poem inspired by Walt Whitman. Adopting his predecessor's title, "Crossing Brooklyn Ferry," he recreates the thematic core of Whitman's poem within a vastly contracted line span (nine lines in comparison with one hundred and thirty-two).[12] Immediately, in its opening statement, his poem begins to recast the connections, or crossings, that Whitman's poem proclaims:

Crossing Brooklyn Ferry

To cross a ferry that is no longer there,
The eye must pilot you to the farther shore:
It travels the distance instantaneously
And time also: the stakes that you can see
Raggedly jettying into nothingness
Are the ghosts of Whitman's ferry: their images
Crowding the enfilade of steel and stone
Have the whole East River to reflect upon
And the tall solidities it liquefies.

(NNY)

Just as the human sense of sight in effect overcomes the limitations of space by traversing huge distances "instantaneously," so the mind's eye, guided by memory and imagination, overcomes the limitations of reality itself, conjuring up for the beholder what "is no longer there." Tomlinson's "pilot[ing]" eye confirms Whitman's conviction that "it avails not, time nor place—distance avails not" (20).[13] Tomlinson claims participation in the connectedness Whitman hypothesizes between himself and posterity, those ferry passengers he pictures crossing "from shore to shore years hence" (5). Even though the ferry has ceased to exist, Tomlinson's powers of empathetic perception easily restore it in his imagination, enabling him to cross over in fulfillment of Whitman's prophecy. And although Whitman was mistaken in supposing that Brooklyn Ferry would be in operation "ever so many hundred years hence," he was right in principle: changes wrought by time *are* insignificant ("avail not"); indeed, external reality itself is insignificant compared with the creative potential of the human spirit (18). Virtually indestructible, this spirit survives even the death of individuals, connecting Walt Whitman here with Charles Tomlinson. Implicitly we, the readers of Tomlinson's poem, are included in this connection forged between the living and the dead.

One of Tomlinson's chief purposes is to assert that in some sense Whitman was right: "ghosts" of his ferry do remain. Men and women of a future generation stand where Whitman stood, see what he saw (with some help from the mind's eye), and think of him, witnessing the triumph of human imagination over physical limitations of time and space. Providing this sympathetic gloss on Whitman's Transcendental views, Tomlinson refrains from any direct assertion of belief in a pantheistically conceived "soul." Subtly he hints, nevertheless, that there are connections, connections a twentieth-century mind can appreciate, between different points in time, different points in space, and different dimensions of reality. Like Whitman, but without subscribing to Transcendentalism *per se*, we too can apprehend a relationship between the material and the immaterial. The final image in Tomlinson's poem is that of "tall solidities" which the East River "liquefies," an everyday illustration of how material objects may be translated from one dimension to another. His rephrasing of Whitman's casual observation concerning "the reflection of the summer sky in the water" causes a mundane phenomenon to seem suddenly miraculous (31): objects melt before the reader's eyes into another medium, the solid and the palpable becoming fluid and impalpable.

Tomlinson's "tall solidities" sound very like the "appearances" hailed in the conclusion of Whitman's poem, those "dumb, beautiful ministers" which "furnish [their] parts toward the soul" (120, 132). For Whitman, "appearances" represent the physical properties of matter, that "necessary film" that "continue[s] to envelop the soul" (121). In the final lines of his poem, he urges us to appreciate the ultimately spiritual essence which these "appearances" mediate. Not by denying the importance of material reality but by embracing it, he declares, do we realize its more than material significance. Tomlinson indirectly supports the union of matter and spirit represented by

Whitman's "dumb, beautiful ministers" with his image of "solidities" being "liquefie[d]." That transformation of the palpable into the impalpable is carried one step further by conspicuous wordplay in the next-to-last line of the poem. The "stakes . . . jettying into nothingness" which represent Whitman's lost ferry "have the whole East River to reflect upon." They enjoy opportunity to engage in two kinds of *reflection,* casting mirror images on the water's surface and at the same time contemplating their surroundings. In proposing this second, mental version of reflection, Tomlinson personifies material objects, endowing them with an actively meditative capacity. Standing as it does, at the end of a line, the phrase "reflect upon" commands strong emphasis, suggesting sympathy with fundamental Transcendental notions: perhaps there really is congruence between mental and material energies.

The participial use of the verb in Whitman's title helps make his point that the transit he depicts is ongoing, perpetual: we are all engaged in a continuous process of movement between the part and the whole, i.e., personal identity and the "float forever held in solution" (62). In fact, Whitman articulates a view of the cosmos very close to Tomlinson's: it is a "simple, compact, well-join'd scheme" which comprises, paradoxically, disparate elements, all "disintegrated yet part of the scheme" (7). There is movement, too, between present and future, or present and past, between life and death. In a more banal sense, we travel between land and water, city and country, one place and another, e.g., Brooklyn and Manhattan. To all the connections celebrated in Whitman's poem, Tomlinson adds one more, a connection unanticipated by his predecessor. He creates in his poem a viable link between an ostensibly outworn mode of thought, i.e., Transcendentalism, and the modern mind. He demonstrates philosophical and imaginative continuity between us and Walt Whitman, rephrasing Whitman's ideas and images in terms we are bound to find plausible.

In poem after poem Tomlinson uncovers analogies that serve, like Whitman's ferry, to link separate spheres. "Let there be treaties, bridges," he exhorts, "chords under the hands, to be spanned / Sustained" ("Against Extremity" WW). Important as signifiers of contiguity or concord, all three of these images—treaty, bridge, and chord—recur frequently.[14] They forge connections without blurring boundaries.[15] By means of either political negotiations, physical structures, or principles of musical harmony, they span distances, bringing disparate regions into communication and contact. Indeed, the poems themselves represent "Tomlinson's delicate negotiations with the world," as Edward Hirsch notes, for they mediate "interchange, balance."[16] The image of the chord implies a particularly subtle and intangible mode of conjoining. The simultaneous sounding of two or more discrete notes in a chord produces an effect of seamless harmony, preserving distinctions even as it integrates them into a larger coherence, "in a single element the chord of grace" ("At Wells: polyphony" PL). Like the chains of rhyme in his poems, chains of analogy form "bridges," or chordal progressions, spanning vast physical, emotional, and mental distances. Unlike bridge or treaty, a chord embodies the paradox of wordless communication, including all the impalpable influence and supersensible possibilities associated with music.[17] In this respect the chord is closely related to rhyme, another important image of connection in Tomlinson's work and one also based on sound. Like the distinct notes united in a chord, things joined by rhyme demonstrate "consonances unforeseen" by reason alone ("The Return" R). Hinting at "the immeasurable," both rhymes and chords contribute to an impalpable bridging; they discover inexplicable congruence linking "here with elsewhere" ("The Faring" S).

"In New Mexico" presents an initially disorienting progression of resemblances, one that appears to turn the world topsy-turvy. Clouds float across the sky like sailing vessels, "feathery proliferations of cloud-boats / Careless of anchorage" (A). This same "flotilla" casts its shadows onto the earth below, which appears to be a mirror image of the ocean-like sky above: "this dry sea-bed they pied with their shadows" (A). Earth and sky, land and sea, seem interchangeable; the beholder grows directionally confused, unable even to distinguish up from down. The very solidity of the earth appears to be undermined by the projection onto it of a vast activity originating above:

> By afternoon, scarcely the rocks held their own:
> The ground was no more than a screen
>   Onto which the heavens could project themselves
> And alter it at will. True,
>   You could pick up a stone and feel
> That was a tight world still, but the white
>   Seed of the cottonwood as the breeze that was shaping the cloud
> Took hold of the tree and shook it,
>   Was drifting across the sand like shreds of sky.

The poem records pervasive movement and metamorphosis; everything on earth is subject to alteration by "the heavens." The conclud-

6: CONTIGUITY AND CONJUNCTION   161

ing comparison of seedpod to cloud caps the beholder's growing recognition that the world is not altogether "tight"; identity is not fixed, but protean. In this final instance of transformative resemblance, the white fibres of cottonwood float past like small versions of the "feathery" clouds overhead: seedpods *become* "shreds of sky." The effect of this sequence of enigmatic analogies is disconcerting, yet gently exhilarating. Like a meditative fingering and refingering of notes in a chord, it represents a continual reshuffling of echoing energies.

"Above the Rio Grande," printed directly following "In New Mexico" in *Annunciations*, continues the exploration of destabilized, shifting identities. Principal elements in the scene are once again clouds, rocks, light, and shadow.

Above the Rio Grande
for Claude-Marie Senninger

The light, in its daylong play, refuses
    The mountains' certainty that they
Will never change—range on range of them
    In an illumination that looks like snow.
On this afternoon when the clouds are one impending grey
    Above the Rio Grande, the light will not obey
Either the clouds' or the rocks' command
    To keep its distance from them. It shifts and shows
Even the cloudshadows how to transform
    The very stones by opening over them
Dark wings that cradle and crease their solidity—
    As if to say: I gather up the rocks
Out of their world of things that are merely things,
    I call dark wings to be bearers of light
As they sail off the shapes they pall
    And, in their wake, leave this brightening snowfall
That melts and is renewed. Yet if the light
    Washes the rocks away, the rocks remain
To tell what it is, and only so
    Can they both flow and stay, and the mind
That floating thing, steady to know itself
    In all the exceedings of its certainty,
As here, beneath the expanses deepening
    Through the cloud-rock ranges of evening sky.

By changing the outward appearance of the mountains, hour by hour, sun and shadow in effect "transform" these exceedingly solid, seemingly unchangeable phenomena. Light "washes . . . away" rock, "melts" and "renew[s]" manifestations of its own making. More explicitly than in the poem immediately preceding it, with its quick reference to "the heavens," the "play" of sun and clouds overhead is associated here with transcendence. The image of cloudshadows as cradling wings evokes an all-encompassing, awe-inspiring power, something perhaps equivalent to the Holy Ghost in the guise of a dove. This winged presence speaks and acts with quasi-biblical authority, exercising powers of genesis and apocalypse. Though "dark," the wings paradoxically are "bearers of light," lending to the "world of things that are merely things" a significance that seems to transcend the material.

The poem presents a balancing of light with shadow, creation with destruction, "illumination" with resistance, the "world of things" with a world beyond them: forces of transfiguration (light) are countered by those of materialism (rock). Characterized by constant flux, the universe is a place in process, its various elements malleable but far from amorphous. Things "both flow and stay." Like the world itself, the "floating" mind can "steady to know itself" only in the context of that unceasing systole and diastole. Here Tomlinson links natural facts and human consciousness with something more ineffable, for which "light" is the symbol. Its transformative power discloses the underlying kinship of all that it touches, so that even the unyielding hardness of "rock" and the threadlike softness of "cloud" temporarily are conjoined in the "cloud-rock ranges of evening sky." The breath-taking progression of "linked analogies" in this poem might be understood and applauded by the likes of Whitman, Emerson, Thoreau, or Melville.[18]

Tomlinson exploits double meaning associated with the term "light" to underline the correspondence and all but divine equivalencies of world and mind. This is evident in "Above the Rio Grande" and even more apparent in "Trebiano." He devotes the third section of that three-part poem to description of sunlight fading at the approach of a fitful rainstorm. An elemental tug-of-war plays itself out: "the linear glint" of sunlight "goes out as the rain / Shadows it over," but rain nevertheless "yields for an instant to a far suggestion / Of sun" (VS). A balance of sorts is achieved, as the final lines of the poem disclose: "rain / Glitters and slides into gutters," but lingering glimmers of sunshine emit a "phosphorescence" that "enamels these now shimmering roofs." Sun and rain combine to glaze the housetops with a pearly sheen that owes the quality of its brightness equally to water and to light. The poet-speaker goes on to compare the unyielding efforts of the sun in this situation to human efforts to endure and know a nonhuman environment:

> We are that continuing race
> Defying the attempts of earth itself
> To have done and huddle us off it. We
> Persist like the returning light that, overcome,
> Reaches out to touch the surfaces it had lost,
> As if it were resurrected from under a sea

Like sunlight contending against the darkening effects of a storm, humanity continues to resist nature's threats and even to "touch" its otherness, i.e., to apprehend and perhaps influence it. The choice of the term *resurrect* to articulate the parallel successes of "returning light" and our "continuing race" infuses both natural and human activity with an aura of metaphysical potency. The equilibrium negotiated between light and darkness furthermore models that between nature and humanity.

Tomlinson's assertion of a vitally metamorphosing connectedness stops just short of unequivocal Pantheism, just as the "rhymes" and resemblances uncovered in his poems confound but never quite dissolve the boundaries of individual identity.[19] "One does not need to go beyond sense experience to some mythic union," he avers; "the 'I' can only be responsible in relationship and not by dissolving itself away into ecstasy or the Oversoul."[20] Rather than proclaiming an inherent divinity in things, he celebrates phenomena and processes in the external universe as worthy equivalents of the divine. "It seems to me that my poetry is religious," he has explained, "in the sense that I am awed by things that exceed my grasp and I am awed by the mystery of a universe that refuses to be tidied away."[21] Accordingly he draws on language and imagery from sacred tradition, investing flowers, reflections, sun, or clouds, for example, with qualities inspiring reverence and awe.[22] Bluebells are not in fact angels, any more than wing-shaped clouds are literally manifestations of the Holy Spirit, but, in certain moments at least, they possess a seemingly supra-ordinary power to move us. The poems return repeatedly to sunlight, especially, with its attendant shadowing activity, identifying it as a natural element of obviously central importance. "Light touches the sense awake, / First fiat crossing the aeons to an eye / That sees it is still good" ("At a Glance" NNY). In terms of human perception it is a first cause, an agent of creation, destruction, and transformation.[23] The physical effects of light are so powerful and so essential that they assume almost metaphysical importance. Enabling us to see faraway objects and vistas clearly, light vanquishes distance, causing "whole tracts and counties" to be "melted" away.

In the poem "Annunciation," each ray of light emerges as a "flashing wing," an "angel of appearances" that creates the world each day anew by rendering it visible (A). A "'grail of origin,'" sunlight lends "'shining dispensation'" to everyday objects, stimulating a "'domestic miracle'" in the poet's own kitchen. The most ordinary of environments is transfigured by this "solvent ray":

> Utensils caught a shine
> that could not be used, utility
> unsaid by this invasion
> from outer space, this gratuitous occasion
> of unchaptered gospel.

Imparting a "gratuitous" sheen to the mundane, sunlight inspires enormous thankfulness by offering unanticipated gifts; it elevates the ordinary to a new and extraordinary dimension of reality. The image of a "utility" that transcends usefulness, or of a kitchen "'cup'" literally "'spilling-over'" with gold-tinged rays of reflected light, points toward unlooked-for wonders in our daily environment: "'every day / is fortunate.'" The piling up of biblical references associates sunlight with supernatural glory, yet the poem resists anything like an explicitly Christian reading. Indeed, Tomlinson is attempting here, as he has stated, "to redefine Christian concepts, something I've been doing quietly for a long time."[24] This "annunciation" foretells an "'unaccountable birth'" that recurs on a regular basis: the natural phenomenon of sunlight gives life over and over to something equivalent to a deity.[25] The blessings praised here are not mentioned, moreover, in the Christian Bible; this is new, unwritten "gospel." There is subtle wit in the description of this amazing "'birth'" as an "invasion / from outer space"; the authority of the Bible suddenly blends with the comic sensationalism of tabloid journalism as the poet locates the origin of the sun's rays quite literally in "space."

Many poems elaborate on the image of the sun as author of miraculous "'birth'" and wondrous gifts; this natural phenomenon serves Tomlinson as an irresistible example of the transcendent potential in an all-too-often unexamined, under-appreciated physical environment. "At Huexotla" presents the transformational capacities of sunlight emphatically, juxtaposing natural and supernatural miracles. The poet-speaker discovers cages of songbirds "flanking the altar" in a church in Mexico (R). As sunlight pours in on the decorated church interior, metallic cage wires, and yellow bird plumage ("sun on the gold"), the birds burst into beautiful song. The light is the literal cause of the music, i.e., the birds sing by day and grow quiet in darkness; "only night would staunch" their singing. The biologically explicable, cause-and-effect relationship between sun and bird music nonetheless is described as "the alchemy of light transmuting / gold to song." Taking place at the church altar, this natural example of transmutation stands in implicit comparison and contrast with church sacraments (such as transubstantiation) also occurring at that site. The juxtaposition suggests that the sun is responsible for "alchemy" as much worthy of reverence or awe as that sponsored by religious institutions. All these examples show that Tomlinson does not seek to invest the sun or any other natural phenomenon with divinity in the normal understanding of that term. Like Wallace Stevens, he presents the sun, indeed, the whole of nature, "not as a god, but as a god might be."[26]

Consistently his poems proclaim the physical universe to be a place of inherent glory. Highlighted by his "calm and cherishing attention," as Calvin Bedient states, "the objects of this world suddenly stand forth as part of [a] beautiful mystery."[27] As he observes the white trail behind an airplane gradually "catching a glow of gold" in the afternoon sunshine, for example, Tomlinson wonders why humans would ask for anything more than such a sight, in and of itself ("For Want of Seraphim" VS):

> so why should heaven be poor
> for want of seraphim where this
> thin gold thread
> goes on unroving
> in mythless apotheosis
> above the dead and living?

In posing this rhetorical question, he expresses bafflement at the tendency implicit in most organized faiths to locate "apotheosis" elsewhere, to derive spiritual sustenance from "myth" rather than from the overwhelming beauty surrounding us: the "ungainsayableness that religion [once] knew about."[28] It is "we alone," he avers, who have "invented angels" ("Chronochromie" A). Yet nature is replete with equivalent wonders, including "other feathered things" that sing, namely, birds. Again he expresses frustration that humans would substitute "angels," with all the accompanying apparatus of doctrine and ritual, for the glorious plenitude of immediate reality. Exercising human intelligence and imagination as we listen to birdsong, "we alone" derive from this sensory experience something approaching a supersensible ecstasy. We "hear brink and beginning in their wordless words— / Hear space begetting time once more." Because the power to evoke awe, thankfulness, and reverence is immanent in things themselves, no additional inscribing of their value is necessary. A group of cypress trees reminds the poet momentarily of a "convocation of tall, thin clerics," complete with a pair of trees resembling "mother and child," but immediately he questions the tendency to embellish or interpret nature with icons implying an externally defined sacredness ("Cypresses" J).[29] Is the stand of trees really a "shrine," he asks, or rather a portion of the physical universe "needing no further miracle or shaping story / to be what it is?"

Discussing the influence of Ruskin on his thinking and writing in a 1995 interview, Tomlinson notes, "I try to bring the nineteenth-century Ruskin up to date, by subtracting his religious pieties from his phenomenology."[30] In the poem "Blaubeuren" he explains the results of this *subtraction* more elaborately, articulating a creed grounded in the intrinsic worth of natural phenomena and processes. The late afternoon sun, as it "blazes towards the death and resurrection / Of the year," provides impetus for his meditations (DW). The colors of the autumn foliage reflect the sun's "glow," and "the season climbs in conflagration." Reiterated fire imagery characterizes the impending close of the day, as well as of the seasonal cycle, reminding him of his own inevitable death. He seeks to articulate the value of human existence given the condition of inescapable mortality:

> To be outlived by this,
> By the recurrences and the generations, as today
> Has lived beyond the century of Dürer—

> His rocks stand jutting from the foliage here—
> Is to say: I have lived
> Between the red blaze and the white,
> I have taken the sacrament of the leaf
> That spells my death, and I have asked to be,
> Breathing it in at every pore of sense,
> Servant to all I see riding this wave
> Of fire and air—

In these lines he attributes a kind of holiness to every element of the natural world, discovering in its ephemeral beauty reason enough to live and rejoice. Having "taken the sacrament of the leaf," he accepts the finality of death, seizing the immediate opportunity to experience *this* world "with every pore of sense" and cherishing the natural blessing of its details for a necessarily limited span of time, "while the light still holds." Tomlinson's "reverence" consists, Denis Donoghue aptly states, in "acknowledging that we receive more than we can ever give, and that we make up the difference—if we do at all—by tact, in wonder, assent, and local recognitions."[31] One of the chief purposes Tomlinson accomplishes in his poems is the articulation of that wonder, along with a precise rendering of the local details inspiring it.

Probing the sensory fullness of the world he gratefully if briefly inhabits, he discovers connective links and transformational energies that hover on the verge of transcendence. His poems regularly bring readers to ultimate boundaries, i.e., those separating physical and metaphysical realities. The profound "sense of mystery in visual phenomena" he communicates is, as Ruth Grogan notes, "optical at first, then edging toward metaphysical."[32] His habit of employing rhetorical questions and the subjunctive mood when considering supernatural meanings, or invoking religious tradition, assists to position him precisely at that line of possibility. Repeatedly discovered parallels between activities in the sky and those on earth imply with particular force something like a supernaturalism latent in natural phenomena. The coolness of moonlight nurtures the fantastical growth of mushrooms; cloudshapes construct and reconstruct the appearance of earth's topography; sunlight irradiates and transmutes everything it touches, investing earthly objects with a glow of irrefutable preciousness. As part of the chain of resemblances joining the illimitability of space with the definitiveness of matter, starlight similarly is brought into close conjunction with things much closer at hand. "Scattered constellations of the gulls" serve, for example, as "messengers from that unending sea, the sky," ratifying a kinship between different realms that approaches singleness of identity ("The Faring" S). Sea and sky again appear to exchange positions, or identities, in "Night Fishers," where "a sky spread out beneath us, constellations / Swimming into view wherever fish / Lit up its dark with phosphor" (NNY).

In "Fireflies," pulsating lights put forth by insects are compared to the stars. Lit up from within by "the signal light of the firefly," the shape of a rose is outlined by "explosions" of "phosphorous," every petal and fold distinguishable in that glow (F). The flower represents a tightly enclosed universe whose pattern of construction has been rendered visible in all its marvelousness: "that close world lies / Pulsing within its halo, glows." This image causes the poet to look up and re-interpret "the whole of darkness" as "a forming rose." So regarded, the night assumes a more comprehensible, more architecturally complete design.[33] Illumined by the "swarming" and "teem[ing]" activity of "tiny stars," the sky appears to be an active and vital place, as if the "circulation" of heavenly bodies were speeded up to become perceptible to the human senses. Just as the insects' light clarifies the shape of the flower, so constellations of stars serve as "stitches of light that fleck and thread a sea" of sky, suggesting "shapes" even in the indefiniteness of space: "cosmos grows / Out of their circlings." No longer opaque, flat, and static, the night sky assumes "surfaces" and "discovered depths," all "filled by a flowering."

The power of the analogy moves in both directions: the ephemeral and mundane phenomenon of summer insect activity is linked with more enduring and important cosmic movement, and the impersonal, distant reality of stars is brought nearer, charged with organic life and purpose.[34] The analogy triggers a "flowering" of understanding, moreover, in the observing, interpreting human consciousness. In specifying a rose, when any variety of flower would fit the parallel drawn between insects and stars, Tomlinson exploits a host of long-standing associations. As an emblem of perfection, the rose lends the idea of nonpareil completeness to the cosmic design affirmed in the poem. The rose plays a significant role, moreover, in a variety of Christian legends, so that the transfiguring energies operating in the poem— particularly evident as tenor and vehicle change places in the central metaphor—assume a suggestively miraculous quality. Terminology and associations borrowed from orthodox religious tradition help him to make a case for the "apotheosis" he extols in the physical universe, its "mythless" but nonetheless "immeasurable" splendor ("For Want of Seraphim" VS, "The Faring" S). He infuses the here-and-now with ultimate, supernatural potency associated with concepts like grace, revelation, gospel, apocalypse, resurrection, sacrament, heaven, or Eden.[35] As his liberal use of metaphor drawn from ecclesiastical sources indicates, the "contraries / Of this place" we inhabit allow themselves to be defined principally through paradox: the poems rejoice in a sacredness liberated from doctrine, a "continuing revelation" that remains indeterminate, "never to be revealed" ("In Arden" S, "Movements" WrW).[36]

The sublime character of the correspondences Tomlinson discovers (cloud and cottonwood seed, flower and cosmos, insects and stars, sea and sky, wine and sunlight) is further underscored by the hints these offer of ultimate connectedness—a connectedness that persists even in the face of manifest multiformity. The chains of analogy everywhere discernible may be only segments of a still vaster, more all-encompassing sequence of contiguity. This possibility is articulated explicitly in "Night Ferry." Watching the rippling effect of striated clouds in a night sky, the poet perceives this as analogous to the "ripple" in the waters he is travelling through. "Where does the ripple in the sky begin?" he wonders ("Night Ferry" R). "You'd think the ripple on the water spread / Through rock and pine, vibrating overhead / In one continuous circling-out of power." The momentary resemblance between elemental activities below and above seems more than a curious or accidental mirroring: it points toward the possibility, though not the certainty, of an unbroken cycle of connected energy. The poem offers other, supporting instances of resemblance, e.g., wharf lights form a "tiny constellation," the waters a "net . . . cast around us," and the boat's lights become "dolphin schools / Of light." Punctuated by light, the darkness presents to the travellers on the boat an ongoing series of metamorphoses. Drawn closer together by interchange of identity and by the encircling darkness, individual phenomena threaten to merge, but never quite escape their boundaries:[37] "Little unseams dark pines from dark of sky." The speaker's final impression is that he stands at the fulcrum of a perfect balancing, or at the center of a completed circle: "And we hang in the balance of fathoms, chart and stars."

The plenitude of lines of potential connection is at times almost overwhelming. An overnight snowfall, for instance, effectively transforms an environment, blocking well-known routes of access and creating new ones, "openings / which yesterday were not there" ("Second Song" DW). Filling in the outlines of ancient Roman roads that crisscross the English countryside, the snow brings these into sharp relief, bewildering the observer with "directions where there were none," an emerging "infinity of ways." Contemplating the sudden multiplying of options that "only a little snow / has chalked in," we realize that the snow has merely highlighted "ways" already present but normally overlooked. The suspicion naturally arises that innumerable connecting routes lie neglected around us, waiting to be discovered and followed. It is "as if a whole landscape might be unrolled / out of the atmosphere," shaken magically from the sky like those Roman roads. This sense of latent, converging possibilities frustrates even as it exhilarates: "to see, is to feel at your back this domain of a circle whose power consists in evading and refusing to be completed by you" ("Tout Entouré de Mon Regard" WW).

World and mind "rhyme," but do not merge ("Rhymes" S). Following each distinct "thread / Through the labyrinth of appearances," the human mind engages with things "refusing to be one without resistance" ("Movements" WrW).[38] Emergent meanings form a "moving calligraphy," a continuously metamorphosing intelligibility that eludes definitive interpretation. There is "a music of constancy" discernible "behind / The wide promiscuity" of disparate things, a larger connectedness forged by "links of water." This image perfectly embodies the idea of uninterrupted contiguity and "seamless momentum," a palpable yet ungraspable conjunction. Indirectly, too, these "links of water" point subtly toward the vast network of streams, rivers, and oceans dispersing itself around the globe, including the two-way process of evaporation and precipitation operating between the earth and its atmosphere. The sheer size of this circumfluent system of waterways is sufficient to inspire awe of almost mythic proportions. As a continuous circuit, it furthermore illustrates Tomlinson's contention that "edges are centres"; from every and any point, "lines of force" radiate outward, and each of these, if followed, "nets you a universe" ("At the Edge" F).

Far from leading to parochial views, Tomlinson's interest in precisely delimiting boundaries opens up perspectives that prove richly diverse, dynamically inclusive. On the far side of every border line there is new territory to be explored, unanticipated philosophical, aesthetic, ideological, or moral implications to be sifted. We inhabit a world rife with dichotomies and dissonance but nonetheless irradiated by "rhymes / And repetitions" that suggest the possibility of a dynamic, labyrinthine connectedness ("Movements"). Just as the exterior landscape contains a record of its own geological and evolutionary history, including artefacts of human cultures and conflicts, the interior landscape of ideas, values, and emotions likewise proves complex and multiform. To understand any portion of the earth's human or prehuman history, to grasp any point of view, concept, or belief, requires examination of it in relationship to a much larger, gloriously unblended whole.

Notes

INTRODUCTION

1. In a review addressing Tomlinson's work prior to 1980, Valentine Cunningham explicitly mentions the poet's preoccupation with borders, observing that Tomlinson's poems "persistently inhabit thresholds, envisage fences, walls, treelines, frontiers." "Flowing Benedictions," *English* 28, no. 130 (1979): 88. Clearly Tomlinson's fascination with these and a host of similar boundary-defining features of the physical landscape has continued unabated in the ensuing twenty-plus years of his career.

2. Throughout this and all succeeding chapters, quotations from Tomlinson's poems published through 1985 are taken from the text of *The Collected Poems* (Rev. ed. Oxford: Oxford University Press, 1987). Quotations from poems published thereafter are taken from the collections in which they appeared: *The Return* (Oxford: Oxford University Press, 1987); *Annunciations* (Oxford: Oxford University Press, 1989); *The Door in the Wall* (Oxford: Oxford University Press, 1992); *Jubilation* (Oxford: Oxford University Press, 1995); *The Vineyard Above the Sea* (Manchester: Carcanet, 1999). For the sake of consistency, all poems are identified by title and the initials of the volume in which they first were collected: See List of Abbreviations.

3. Bruce Meyer, "A Human Balance: An Interview with Charles Tomlinson," *The Hudson Review* 43, no. 3 (1990): 441.

4. Richard Swigg, *Charles Tomlinson and the Objective Tradition* (Lewisburg, Pa.: Bucknell University Press, 1994), 237, 38.

5. "Perception and Self in Charles Tomlinson's Early Poetry," *Rocky Mountain Review of Language and Literature* 36 (1982): 95.

6. Tomlinson's insistence on preservation of the boundaries between self and other constitutes a distinguishing characteristic of his poetic stance and thus has drawn comment from many readers, in a variety of contexts. Edward Hirsch, for instance, praises Tomlinson's "healthy and sustained respect for the Other." "The Meditative Eye of Charles Tomlinson," *The Hollins Critic* 15, no. 2 (1978): 8. Denis Donoghue similarly notes that Tomlinson "goes down to rock bottom, to the relation between the individual consciousness and the Other." "The Proper Plenitude of Fact," in *The Ordinary Universe: Soundings in Modern Literature* (New York: Macmillan, 1968), 22. Michael Kirkham asserts that "the otherness of the outer world is always in Tomlinson's poetry a source of inner nourishment." "Philip Larkin and Charles Tomlinson: Realism and Art," in *The Present*, vol. 8 of *The New Pelican Guide to English Literature*, ed. Boris Ford (Harmondsworth: Penguin, 1983; reprint 1986), 308. Or, as Robert J. Stanton puts it, "to see possibility is to realize the reality of 'otherness.' Tomlinson denies personal interference in his work so to gain a realization of the full 'self' which is fulfilled by allowing the 'other' to flow freely

through his mind, untainted by his ego." "Charles Tomlinson and the Process of Defining Relationships," *North Dakota Quarterly* 45, no. 3 (1977): 50. Brian John remarks on the "acknowledgement of otherness" crucial to Tomlinson's philosophical and ethical perception. *The World as Event: The Poetry of Charles Tomlinson* (Montreal: McGill-Queen's University Press, 1989), 72. Tomlinson himself has spoken of his "distrust of the ego," his conviction that "you must respect what is other than you." Alan Ross and Charles Tomlinson, "Words and Water, an Interview," in *Charles Tomlinson: Man and Artist*, ed. Kathleen O'Gorman (Columbia: University of Missouri Press, 1988), 231.

7. Swigg, *Objective Tradition*, 236.

8. Michael Hennessey observes that Tomlinson characteristically "denies the expansive ego in favor of a containment of the self." "Perception and Self," 101. Denis Donoghue, too, discusses Tomlinson's commitment as poet-observer to a stance that embodies "reverence, propriety, a sense of limits, identity; it is pious, poetic, never predatory." "The Proper Plenitude of Fact," 23. Willard Spiegelman comes to similar conclusions, stating that Tomlinson "is a real believer in limits, caution, and the difficult necessity of proportion." "The Rituals of Perception," *Parnassus* 7 (1979): 153.

9. Brian John comments on the relationship to be found between boundaries in the physical landscape and those in the world of art: "Tomlinson's gaze is constantly being tugged askance, drawn along lines of vista, mapping with grids and shaping order through boundaries, whether the discipline of the stanza or of the rhyme or the building of a wall." *World as Event*, 39.

10. *Passionate Intellect: The Poetry of Charles Tomlinson* (Liverpool: Liverpool University Press, 1999), 42.

Chapter 1. Elemental Demarcation

1. Donald Davie notes, for example, "how ardently" Tomlinson "responds to landscapes and skyscapes, to a single tree or stand of trees, to the swell of a hillside, to the behavior of running water!" Foreword to *Charles Tomlinson: Man and Artist*, ed. Kathleen O'Gorman (Columbia: University of Missouri Press, 1988), 2. Michael Kirkham similarly points out the centrality in Tomlinson's poetry of "the phenomenal world, the reality of place, landscape, and weather." "An Agnostic's Grace," in *Man and Artist*, 155. Timothy Clark observes "Tomlinson's overall ecological mode of thought," the weight he places on "the complex relationships between organism and environment." *Charles Tomlinson* (Plymouth: Northcote House, 1999), 45.

2. "My subtitle is 'The Four Elements,'" he declares at the outset, organizing the opening portion of his essay around this topic and illustrating his comments with memories of the Midlands region of England where he spent his childhood (PP 10). And in the poem "Response to Hopkins" he offers powerful testimony to the ongoing imaginative and emotional centrality of the elements in his view of the world:

> What by my measure is the heaven of desire?
> This inconstant constancy—earth, water, fire.
>
> (DW)

3. Michael Kirkham, *Passionate Intellect: The Poetry of Charles Tomlinson* (Liverpool: Liverpool University Press, 1999), 193.

4. Bruce Meyer, "A Human Balance: An Interview with Charles Tomlinson," *The Hudson Review* 43, no. 3 (1990): 447, 446.

5. Discussing "At Holwell Farm," Brian John notes that "the season stands at a threshold, frontier, or vortex-point, capable of marrying the contrary states in a synthesis which sharpens one's awareness of all seasons, of the natural cyclism, and of time itself." *The World as Event: The Poetry of Charles Tomlinson* (Montreal: McGill-Queen's University Press, 1989), 26.

6. For a more fully developed discussion of this poem, including its relationship to Keats's ode "To Autumn," see Saunders, "Tomlinson's 'October' and Keats's 'To Autumn,'" *The Explicator* 58, no. 1 (1999): 55–57.

7. The allusion to Wallace Stevens's "Peter Quince at the Clavier" underlines the power of music to trigger feeling and to speak to the spirit. "So the selfsame sounds / On my spirit make a music, too," Quince asserts in the opening lines of the poem, and Tomlinson's borrowing in the phrasing of "those selfsame notes" lends extra force to the boundary-defining role he assigns music in this poem. *The Palm at the End of the Mind: Selected Poems and a Play*, ed. Holly Stevens (New York: Random, 1972), 8.

8. "Unclenching the Mind," in *Man and Artist*, 75–76.

9. Michael Edwards, "The Poetry of Charles Tomlinson," in *Man and Artist*, 146.

10. In his discussion of this poem, Sydney Lea offers the following observation: "The author treasures demarcation and—in every sense—cultivation; and yet I've said we must avoid applying simple dialectics to an artist so subtle. However ominous its presence, some ineffable otherness charges Tomlinson's imagination. . . . So 'The Peak' ends, its affection for human construct countered by an acknowledgement of possible sublimity." "To Use and Transform: Recent Poetry of Charles Tomlinson," *The Hudson Review* 46 (1994): 733.

11. "Civilization, in Tomlinson's conception," Michael Kirkham argues, "lacks health if it is not nature-centred; it presumes a negotiated alliance between the human and the non-human." *Passionate Intellect*, 201–2.

12. In his discussion of this poem, Michael Ponsford identifies the "empty triangle of land" as "a lost paradise," but goes on to complain of "the poet's tendency to idealize the landscape by denuding it of the human." "Charles Tomlinson's Motorway Poems," *Notes on Contemporary Literature* 17, no. 4 (1987): 4. Such a comment appears to give too little weight to the ecological concern in "From the Motorway." This particular piece of land is not altogether "empty," but rather filled with "the waste / They are dumping, truck by truck." Other poems provide ample evidence, moreover, of Tomlinson's ability to appreciate human presence in a landscape. See, for example, discussions of "The Peak" in chapter 1, or of "The Vineyard Above the Sea" in chapter 6.

13. Thomas H. Getz, "Charles Tomlinson's Manscapes," *Modern Poetry Studies* 11 (1983): 207. Brian John, too, comments on Tomlinson's many poems "directed against the blight of a landscape," his "constant campaign against mindless destruction and ugliness." *The World as Event*, 82. For further consideration of "disfigurement[s] of the landscape" presented in Tomlinson's poems—particularly the industrial Midlands of England, the "violated landscapes of his personal beginnings"—see "Manscapes 1958–1966" and "Manscapes 1969–1978," chapters 3 and 4 in Michael Kirkham's *Passionate Intellect*, 206, 203.

14. Michael Kirkham comments perceptively that encounters between man and nature in Tomlinson's poetry, even when the two are presented as antagonists, prove "energizing"; they produce "a tonic effect on the human constitution—clearing the mind, strengthening the will, quickening sense and feeling." *Passionate Intellect*, 86.

Chapter 2. Cultural and Historical Boundaries

1. Kathleen O'Gorman discusses the "tensions between a number of different elements" (e.g., political, theological, historical) embodied in this poem, noting that the rituals enacted in the dance and in the poem itself constitute a "compelling encounter, a profoundly evocative center of experience." O'Gorman argues, too, that the "suspended syntax," short lines, and generous deployment of colons, semicolons, and dashes help to facilitate forward movement in the poem. "Space, Time, and Ritual in Tomlinson's Poetry," in *Charles Tomlinson: Man and Artist*, ed. Kathleen O'Gorman (Columbia: University of Missouri Press, 1988), 101–2.

2. Michael Kirkham points out that "perspective deepens" when, as here, "a temporal dimension" is added: "The metaphor used by Tomlinson is that of widening circles. The first two circles are the 'near' of England and the 'far' of the American Southwest—which are at once different places and different times, a here-now and a there-then. The third and largest circle is the 'single sphere' of the containing mind. As the perspective deepens the circles widen, the self embracing more and more of an expanding world." *Passionate Intellect: The Poetry of Charles Tomlinson* (Liverpool: Liverpool University Press, 1999), 111.

3. "I always feel I rather left readers of that Macchu Picchu poem in the lurch and am nervous that I had not made it entirely clear that the entire thing is a skyscape filled with changes of clouds. I've never been to M.P., but my memory of photographs was suddenly jolted watching all this drama in the sky." Charles Tomlinson, Letter to the author, 19 July 1997.

4. *The Poems*, ed. Richard J. Finneran (New York: Macmillan, 1983), 193–94. For a more detailed discussion of the intertextual relationship between Tomlinson's poem and that of Yeats, including consideration of additional thematic and stylistic questions, see Saunders, "Text on Text: Charles Tomlinson and the Art of Sustained Allusion," *The Arkansas Quarterly* 2, no. 1 (1993): 30–41.

5. *Moby-Dick*, ed. Harrison Hayford and Hershel Parker (New York: Norton, 1967), 280.

6. Richard Swigg and Charles Tomlinson, "Tomlinson at Sixty," in *Man and Artist*, 225.

7. Ibid., 226.

8. Ibid., 229.

9. Michael Hennessey, "Chronology," in *Man and Artist*, 13–15.

10. Alan Ross and Charles Tomlinson, "Words and Water, an Interview," in *Man and Artist*, 30–31.

11. The unnamed critic is Kingsley Amis in *Poets of the 1950's* (1955). Richard Swigg, *Charles Tomlinson and the Objective Tradition* (Lewisburg, Pa.: Bucknell University Press, 1994), 214.

12. For useful discussions of the influence of American poetry and culture on Tomlinson's career, see the following: Harold Beaver, "Crossing Rebel Lines," Re-

view of *Some Americans: A Record* and *The Flood*, *Parnassus* 10 (1982): 117–24; Michel Delville, "The Civility of Relationships: Charles Tomlinson and the Conversion of American Modernism," *Symbiosis* 1, no. 1 (1997): 135–49; Michael Edwards, "Charles Tomlinson: Notes on Tradition and Impersonality," *Critical Quarterly* 15 (1973): 133–44; Dana Gioia, "Poetry Chronicle," *The Hudson Review* 34 (1981–82): 579–94; L. L. Lee, "Charles Tomlinson as American Un-American," *Contemporary Poetry: A Journal of Criticism* 2, no. 2 (1977): 11–15; Hearne Pardee, "A Distant Vision: Charles Tomlinson and American Art," *Partisan Review* 58 (1991): 554–62; Swigg, *Objective Tradition*; Richard Swigg, " 'Our Language Is Our Land': American Form, Spanish Translation, and English Speech in the Poetry of Charles Tomlinson," *Literary Imagination* 2, no. 1 (2000): 4–20; Alan Young, "Rooted Horizon: Charles Tomlinson and American Modernism," *Critical Quarterly* 24, no. 4 (1982): 67–73.

13. "Chronology," 13–14.

14. "Tomlinson at Sixty," 229; "Words and Water," 26.

15. Swigg, *Objective Tradition*, 13. Swigg's study provides the most thorough investigation available of Tomlinson's use of American sources (including Whitman, Williams, Eliot, Stevens, Moore, Auden). For detailed discussion of Tomlinson's adaptation of the Williams triad, see chapter 3.

16. Gioia, "Poetry Chronicle," 582.

17. "Words and Water," 23.

18. Jordi Doce explains Tomlinson's internationalism with special reference to Spanish and Latin American literatures and cultures: "His work shows us how local preoccupations may grow and diversify when mingled with a wide cultural knowledge and awareness. He has managed to create a bridge between two traditions that have persistently ignored each other." Doce further comments on the fine balance, or "clear definition," Tomlinson achieves between international and English influences: "by appropriating a foreign discourse," she observes, he "has created expression for his idea of Englishness and the English landscape." "Charles Tomlinson between Two Traditions," *Agenda* 33, no. 2 (1995): 94, 83, 77.

19. "Words and Water," 29.

20. Bruce Meyer, "A Human Balance: An Interview with Charles Tomlinson," *The Hudson Review* 43, no. 3 (1990): 443, 442.

21. "Tomlinson at Sixty," 223.

22. Claude Roy, foreword to *Renga: A Chain of Poems* (New York: Braziller, 1971), 8–9.

23. Michael Edwards, "Collaborations," in *Man and Artist*, 110.

24. Octavio Paz, introduction to *Renga: A Chain of Poems*, 25.

25. Roy, foreword to *Renga*, 13.

26. Paz, introduction to *Renga*, 17.

27. Ibid., 26.

28. Charles Tomlinson, "The Unison: A Retrospect," in *Renga: A Chain of Poems*, 35.

29. Edwards, "Collaborations," 111, 112.

30. As Dana Gioia observes, "he is a post-modernist *par excellence*—deeply conscious of the international modern tradition but still deeply himself." "Poetry Chronicle," 582.

31. Edwards, "Collaborations," 152.

32. Timothy Clark, *Charles Tomlinson* (Plymouth: Northcote House, 1999), 63.

CHAPTER 3. CONTRAPUNTAL DESIGNS

1. Michael Edwards, "The Poetry of Charles Tomlinson," in *Charles Tomlinson: Man and Artist*, ed. Kathleen O'Gorman (Columbia: University of Missouri Press, 1988), 148. Edwards points out that "the vision of antithesis informs the whole of Tomlinson's work and leads one into the core of his imagining," 146. Michael Kirkham likewise notes how "antitheses serve to identify the dialectic of Tomlinson's poetic thinking," i.e., "that complex dynamic poise—the protean form, the diversified unity, the shifting coherence—which repeatedly Tomlinson discovers in his experience and exemplifies in his art." *Passionate Intellect: The Poetry of Charles Tomlinson* (Liverpool: Liverpool University Press, 1999), 90. Throughout his study of Tomlinson's work, Kirkham emphasizes the "state of complementary opposition" persistently animating the poems: "contraries that are in fact complementarities in that they are mutually exclusive viewpoints which are yet both true," 134, 218.

2. Willard Spiegelman identifies "encounter" as "Tomlinson's major theme and strategy." "The Rituals of Perception," *Parnassus* 7 (1979): 162. Michael Kirkham, too, addresses the importance of the terms "meeting" and "encounter" in his study of the poems: see *Passionate Intellect*, 77–91. "Encounters between opposites are the rule, not the exception, in Tomlinson's poetry," he asserts; poems tend to move toward that "moment" when "contraries commune," 62–63, 75.

3. Analyzing Tomlinson's adaptation of Williams's three-ply line, Richard Swigg notes how well "the mobile-like flotation of lines—the ever-changing balance of lengthy segment with smaller—" serves Tomlinson's passion for "keen balancing." *Charles Tomlinson and the Objective Tradition* (Lewisburg, Pa.: Bucknell University Press; London: Associated University Presses, 1994), 105. For further discussion of the triadic line in his work, see Paul Mariani, "Tomlinson's Use of the Williams Triad," in *Man and Artist*.

4. Richard Swigg and Charles Tomlinson, "Tomlinson at Sixty," in *Man and Artist*, 230.

5. In Tomlinson's vision, Richard Swigg argues, "a sense of balance and stability is worth nothing unless earned out of the subverting and the disintegrative." *Objective Tradition*, 195. Michael Kirkham comments on this "double focus in Tomlinson's poetry"—"upon the thing itself and the whole of which it is a part or sign." *Passionate Intellect*, 219.

6. In J. E. Chamberlain's phrasing, Tomlinson's poems "celebrate an interdependence" that constitutes "an uneasy truce, a treaty that will surely be broken." Recording "marriages of opposites," the poems are "structured by the most compelling of antiphonies." "Unclenching the Mind," in *Man and Artist*, 86, 87. Or, as Denis Donoghue puts it, "the poems try to make marriages out of divorces." "The Proper Plenitude of Fact," in *The Ordinary Universe: Soundings in Modern Literature* (New York: Macmillan, 1968), 24–25.

7. "Its origin is curious," Tomlinson reports of this poem. The idea for its unusual structure occurred to him while he was engaged in a translation project. Noticing how Paz "joined disparate segments" of *Blanco* paratactically, he "conceived the idea of doing this syntactically." Letter to the author, 14 February 1994.

8. Tomlinson's instructions to the reader, printed beneath the text of the poem, read as follows: "A reading should include (a) the italicized lines, (b) the unitalicized, (c) the whole as printed" (WW).

9. Swigg, *Objective Tradition*, 146. He adds: "His was to be an art not of re-

ceived frameworks but of new instancings: a poetry in which encounter and incident become central, in which relations with people, place, nature, and objects need different kinds of poetic form to suit the individual fact of each occasion," 23.

10. Bruce Meyer, "A Human Balance: An Interview with Charles Tomlinson," *The Hudson Review* 43, no. 3 (1990): 448.

11. Sydney Lea, "To Use and Transform: Recent Poetry of Charles Tomlinson," *The Hudson Review* 46 (1994): 732.

12. In addition to "Like Greek Prose" (VS) and "The Chances of Rhyme" (WW), see, for instance, "Movements" (WrW), "Hill Walk" (WI), "Rhymes" (S), "The Faring" (S), "Embassy" (S), "In Arden" (S), "The Return" (R), "Winter Journey" (R), "Harvest" (A), "Picking Mushrooms by Moonlight" (DW), "To My Daughter" (J), "Against Travel" (J).

13. Working deftly with innumerable "variants of sound," Tomlinson notes with regret that, "more and more," even sophisticated readers fail to hear rhymes "unless they pop up at the end of lines & certainly not the slant variety." Letter to the author, 30 December 2001.

14. As Donald Wesling points out, Tomlinson's poem appears to have been inspired at least in part by a comment of Baudelaire's concerning "les hasards de la rime" from "Le Soleil." *The Chances of Rhyme: Device and Modernity* (Berkeley and Los Angeles: University of California Press, 1980), 130.

15. Ibid., 132.

16. "Charles Tomlinson and the Process of Defining Relationships," *North Dakota Quarterly* 45, no. 3 (1977): 49.

17. Willard Spiegelman discusses the connective effect of rhyme in conjunction with that of other devices: "Rhymes, found or invented, cement the things of the world. Pairings of all sorts . . . make for civil and reciprocal relationships. . . . metaphor is like rhyme, a way of detecting or designing a relationship." "The Rituals of Perception," 158.

18. "Quirky juxtaposition," as J. E. Chamberlain indicates, is central to Tomlinson's poetic stance: "Impressions and expressions, mirrorings and makings, desires and regrets, questions and answers—these are the complementary items, and they each map the locus of a point; where they intersect is where the poem finds its center." "Unclenching the Mind," 74, 80.

19. Reginald Gibbons, "'With So Exact a Care,'" *Agenda* 16, no. 2 (1978): 57; Brian John, *The World as Event: The Poetry of Charles Tomlinson* (Montreal: McGill-Queen's University Press, 1989), 79.

20. Michael Kirkham points to yet another dimension of contrast set up in the poem. "Not until the end of the poem are the human figures in the landscape precisely identified: 'The title, without disapprobation, says *Merchants*.' Crossers of boundaries, intermediaries between distinct but complementary interests, agents of interchange—merchants are named by the painter and, with a challenging emphasis, by the poet as worthy representatives of humanity in its self-defining enterprise of civilization." *Passionate Intellect*, 85.

21. Norbert Lynton, *The Story of Modern Art* (Englewood Cliffs, N.J.: Prentice-Hall, 1990), 75.

22. Ibid., 74.

23. For wide-ranging discussion of Blake's influence on Tomlinson, see Richard Swigg's "Contraries and Relations," chapter 5 in *Charles Tomlinson and the Objective Tradition*, 146–55. In the course of his analysis Swigg refers to an early poem

that Tomlinson chose never to reprint—"Peace Between Us, William Blake," which alludes specifically to Blake's lamb-tiger dichotomy (153–54).

24. "The Tyger," 1793, reprinted in *English Romantic Writers*, ed. David Perkins (New York: Harcourt, 1967), 59.

25. Brian John emphasizes this point. In Tomlinson's poetic universe, "definition is subject to redefinition . . . with new perspectives and vistas, with increased awareness and perpetual reassessment." John further argues that "to know the world as event is to participate in dynamic interchange with the world; in order for that interchange to reveal the real, it requires constant appraisal and the exercise of judgment." Throughout his career Tomlinson is concerned with "that definition which becomes possible only through the tension of dialectical opposites." *World as Event*, 28, 29, 42.

26. Tomlinson's dynamic approach to perception and assessment is noted by Richard Swigg, who identifies in the poems "a judicious play of mind that constantly reassesses the changing relationships between self and world." *Objective Tradition*, 15. Reginald Gibbons praises "the tense musculature" of Tomlinson's poems, "a balancing of opposing forces and impulses which refuses to simplify any event, object, or person into a static repose, but which insists on that uncertainty of counterpoised tensions." This sense of "taut oppositions" is, Gibbons states, Tomlinson's "poetic signature." "With So Exact a Care," 56, 52.

27. Calvin Bedient characterizes the "inclusive reciprocity" of Tomlinson's poetics as follows: "the true grace of any and every relationship is neither a giving nor a receiving, but an interchange and balance of the two." "Charles Tomlinson," in *Eight Contemporary Poets* (London: Oxford University Press, 1975), 19.

Chapter 4. Perceptual Boundaries

1. Optical illusion forms an important subcategory of Tomlinson's ongoing and passionate interest in perception *per se*. Although few critical comments on his poetry concern themselves specifically or in detail with his persistent delight in *mis*apprehension, a large number address the general topic of perception, with emphasis on the optical. See, for instance, the following: Merle E. Brown, "Intuition vs. Perception: On Charles Tomlinson's 'Under the Moon's Reign,'" in *Double Lyric: Divisiveness and Communal Creativity in Recent English Poetry* (New York: Columbia University Press, 1980); J. E. Chamberlain, "Unclenching the Mind," in *Charles Tomlinson: Man and Artist*, ed. Kathleen O'Gorman (Columbia: University of Missouri Press, 1988); Denis Donoghue, "The Proper Plenitude of Fact," in *The Ordinary Universe: Soundings in Modern Literature* (New York: Macmillan, 1968); Michael Edwards, "Charles Tomlinson's Seeing and Believing," in *Poetry and Possibility* (Basingstoke: Macmillan, 1988); Reginald Gibbons, "'With So Exact a Care,'" *Agenda* 16, no. 2 (1978): 52–58; Julian Gitzen, "Charles Tomlinson and the Plenitude of Fact," *Critical Quarterly* 13 (1971): 355–62; Ruth Grogan, "Tomlinson, Ruskin, and Language Skepticism," *Essays in Literature* 17, no. 1 (1990): 30–42; J. Keith Hardie, "Charles Tomlinson and the Language of Silence," *Boundary 2* 15, no. 1–2 (1986/1987): 211–34; Michael Hennessey, "Perception and Self in Charles Tomlinson's Early Poetry," *Rocky Mountain Review of Language and Literature* 36 (1982): 95–102; Edward Hirsch, "The Meditative Eye of Charles Tomlinson," *The Hollins Critic* 15, no. 2 (1978): 1–12; Edward Hirsch, "'Out There

Is the World': The Visual Imperative in the Poetry of George Oppen and Charles Tomlinson," in *George Oppen: Man and Poet*, ed. Burton Hatlen (Orono, Maine: National Poetry Foundation, 1981); Michael Kirkham, "An Ethic of Perception," in *Passionate Intellect: The Poetry of Charles Tomlinson* (Liverpool: Liverpool University Press, 1999); Michael Kirkham, "Philip Larkin and Charles Tomlinson: Realism and Art," in *The Present*, vol. 8 of *The New Pelican Guide to English Literature*, ed. Boris Ford (Harmondsworth: Penguin, 1983; reprint 1986); Edward Lobb, "Charles Tomlinson: The Dimensions of a World," *Cambridge Quarterly* 16, no. 2 (1987): 162–68; Octavio Paz, "The Graphics of Charles Tomlinson," in *In Black and White: The Graphics of Charles Tomlinson* (Cheadle: Carcanet, 1976); Monroe K. Spears, "Shapes and Surfaces: David Jones, with a Glance at Charles Tomlinson," *Contemporary Literature* 12 (1971): 402–19; Willard Spiegelman, "The Rituals of Perception," *Parnassus* 7 (1979): 151–64; Robert J. Stanton, "Charles Tomlinson and the Process of Defining Relationships," *North Dakota Quarterly* 45, no. 3 (1977): 47–60; Evan Watkins, "Charles Tomlinson: The Poetry of Experience," in *The Critical Act: Criticism and Community* (New Haven: Yale University Press, 1978); A. Kingsley Weatherhead, "Charles Tomlinson," in *The British Dissonance: Essays on Ten Contemporary Poets* (Columbia: University of Missouri Press, 1983); Donald Wesling, "An Avant-Garde Careful and Bold," in "Fifteen Ways of Looking at a Tomlinson," in *PN Review* 5, no. 1 (1977): 43–45.

2. Jed Rasula and Mike Erwin, "An Interview with Charles Tomlinson," *Contemporary Literature* 16, no. 4 (1975): 406–7.

3. Julian Gitzen addresses Tomlinson's exploration of "visual problems" and the trustworthiness of the senses in "Charles Tomlinson and the Plenitude of Fact," 359.

4. "Tomlinson has always worked to incorporate in one vision the near and the far, the data of sense experience and the 'something else' ("Canal" PL 6–7) of imagination; repeatedly his poems explore outward from the known to the edges of the known and just beyond." Kirkham, *Passionate Intellect*, 220.

5. Rainer Lengeler points out the heart of the poet's happy misperception: a "holism" capped by the final image of "'the encircling trees' as integration motif." "Charles Tomlinson: An Eden in Arden," in *Poetry in the British Isles: Non-Metropolitan Perspectives*, ed. Hans-Werner Ludwig and Lothar Fietz (Cardiff: University of Wales Press, 1995), 214.

6. In his discussion of this poem, Richard Swigg comments: "By not taking the counterfeit image as literal, one has the freedom to admit inside that '*street*' the 'tree' that ineradicably grows there—like a fact of human desire whose sought branching and interknitting cannot make one ignore other facts, but which partners and opens out their darkness." *Charles Tomlinson and the Objective Tradition* (Lewisburg, Pa.: Bucknell University Press, 1994), 92.

7. "Rooted in experience of a vividly physical world," Brian John points out, "Tomlinson's perspectives, landscapes, objects, or mental processes are never ends in themselves"; rather, "the experiences he charts possess ultimately a moral and social significance." *The World as Event: The Poetry of Charles Tomlinson* (Montreal: McGill-Queen's University Press, 1989), 72.

8. Robert Pinksy notes that Tomlinson presents "involuntary perception" as the source of "something similar to a work of art." *The Situation of Poetry: Contemporary Poetry and Its Traditions* (Princeton: Princeton University Press, 1976), 91.

9. "Tomlinson, Ruskin, and Moore: Facts and Fir Trees," *Twentieth Century Literature* 35, no. 2 (1989): 187.

10. Ibid., 193.

11. See J. Keith Hardie's "Charles Tomlinson and the Language of Silence" for a detailed discussion of Tomlinson's interest in phenomenology, in particular his indebtedness to the philosopher Maurice Merleau-Ponty. Of special relevance is his affirmation of Merleau-Ponty's argument that "significance resides wholly in perception," and hence his tendency to "treat perception as the source of all knowledge," 218, 213.

12. Rasula and Erwin, "Interview with Charles Tomlinson," 408.

13. As Michael Kirkham states, "the mind brings to the instant of vision the contents of memory," adding to this the "play of imagination," so that "the mind sees facts and possibilities" equally. *Passionate Intellect*, 29, 30.

14. "A perception never occurs in a vacuum; the self experiencing that perception is able, through analysis and memory, to establish associations among particular perceptions." John, *World as Event*, 16.

15. Robert J. Stanton takes up this point, stating: "The ability to gather information with the senses is not enough to explain the fullness of any object, because the object is intrinsically related to other objects and to a substanceless world beyond itself. An object is extended and moves in the existence of Time." "Charles Tomlinson and the Process of Defining Relationships," 56.

16. The allusion to *The Tempest* is subtly rendered but represents "a very conscious intention" on Tomlinson's part. "I thought the passage was so familiar I didn't bother to annotate it!" Letter to the author, 30 December 2001.

17. Paz, "The Graphics of Charles Tomlinson," 14.

18. In "The Golden Flowerpot" E. T. A. Hoffmann portrays his protagonist imprisoned at a moment of crisis in a small glass container. This claustrophobic durance represents artistic, spiritual, and emotional paralysis. It seems likely that Tomlinson intends his poem as a gloss on that well-known episode in Hoffmann's story.

19. Paz, "The Graphics of Charles Tomlinson," 14–15.

20. "Irony and celebration ride together," as Michael Kirkham confirms, in Tomlinson's presentation of disparities "between fact and appearance, thing and image, reality and imagination." "An Agnostic's Grace," in *Man and Artist*, 179, 178.

Chapter 5. Graphic Framing

1. Reproduced in *In Black and White: The Graphics of Charles Tomlinson* (Cheadle: Carcanet, 1976), 29, 50.

2. Octavio Paz, "The Graphics of Charles Tomlinson," in *In Black and White*, 12.

3. Charles Tomlinson, quoted in Paz, "The Graphics of Charles Tomlinson," 13.

4. Alan Ross and Charles Tomlinson, "Words and Water, an Interview," in *Charles Tomlinson: Man and Artist*, ed. Kathleen O'Gorman (Columbia: University of Missouri Press, 1988), 35.

5. J. E. Chamberlain comments briefly on Tomlinson's recurrent interest in doors and windows, "favorite conjurings" that mark moments of suspended awareness. He observes, too, that the doors and windows in Tomlinson's poetry are remi-

niscent of the window-masks in his decalcomanic painting. "Unclenching the Mind," in *Man and Artist*, 89, 90.

6. Noting the many "tunnels, shafts, wells" in Tomlinson's poetry, Michael Kirkham identifies these as "images for the self's entry into further lengths and breadths of vision." "Philip Larkin and Charles Tomlinson: Realism and Art," in *The Present* (Harmondsworth: Penguin, 1983), 310.

7. Ruth Grogan offers a provocative analysis of the sometimes "menacing . . . presences" evident in Tomlinson's work, including consideration of possibly "antithetical" impulses distinguishing the paintings from the poems. "Language and Graphics," in *Man and Artist*, 192, 186.

8. Charles Tomlinson, "To Begin: Notes on Graphics," in *In Black and White*, 20.

9. Michael Edwards discusses "the appeal and the meaning of reflections" in Tomlinson's poetry, concentrating on "Below Tintern." He demonstrates that reflections frequently provide "hints of renewal," and that they allow scope for antiphonal activity between self and world: "the mind resembles reflections, and . . . by reflecting on objects and also reflecting them, it reconstitutes them in a possible world." "Charles Tomlinson's Seeing and Believing," in *Poetry and Possibility* (Basingstoke: Macmillan, 1988), 159, 160.

10. Bruce Meyer, "A Human Balance: An Interview with Charles Tomlinson," *The Hudson Review* 43, no. 3 (1990): 439.

11. "The Graphics of Charles Tomlinson," 13.

12. César Martinell, *Gaudi: His Life, His Theories, His Work*, trans. Judith Rohrer, ed. George R. Collins (Cambridge: MIT Press, 1975), 383.

13. *Shock of the New*, no. 5 of "The Threshold of Liberty," writ. Robert Hughes (New York, Time-Life, 1980).

14. As Michael Kirkham points out, Tomlinson's interest in "the meeting between self and not-self" predicates "a relationship . . . of interpenetration, not a Whitmanesque merging." "Realism and Art," 296.

15. The allusion in line twelve to Thoreau's *Walden* underlines the contrast Tomlinson draws between this impressive spectacle and its dismaying source. Portraying White Pond and Walden as "great crystals on the surface of the earth, Lakes of Light," Thoreau declares them to be "more beautiful than our lives." "Pure" and "contain[ing] no muck," these naturally lovely and precious phenomena rebuke a host of human failings, materialism in particular. *Walden*, 199. Tomlinson echoes Thoreau's description of an illumination "more beautiful than our lives," but where Thoreau's "lights" are reflected from wonderfully clear water surfaces, the lights Tomlinson observes emanate from crowded buildings, roadlamps, and automobiles—the very ills his poem castigates. Ultimately, as the graceful nod to Thoreau suggests, what Tomlinson sees shining forth on that British roadway is the Western community's collective rejection of the simple, natural values the earlier writer espoused. While Thoreau's praise of nature's power to inspire the human spirit is straightforward and fervent, Tomlinson's tribute to aesthetically pleasing side effects of urban sprawl rings with disgruntled irony.

16. Richard Swigg and Charles Tomlinson, "Tomlinson at Sixty," in *Man and Artist*, 227–28.

17. Ibid., 227.

18. "The physical world" in Tomlinson's poetry, as Michael Edwards states,

"contains thresholds. They are the entry to the reflected world [as in "Below Tintern"], and they also offer to usher one into the world's possibility, into its change." "Charles Tomlinson's Seeing and Believing," 164.

19. Valentine Cunningham, "Flowing Benedictions," in *English* 28, no. 130 (1979): 95. Calvin Bedient also notes the liberating possibilities Tomlinson associates with framing borders: "they are the limits of a vase or a window, not of a prison." "Charles Tomlinson," in *Eight Contemporary Poets* (London: Oxford University Press, 1975), 5.

20. Ruth Grogan, "Tomlinson, Ruskin, and Moore: Facts and Fir Trees," *Twentieth Century Literature* 35, no. 2 (1989): 191.

CHAPTER 6. CONTIGUITY AND CONJUNCTION

1. The "illumination of self through rhyme or 'neighbouring,'" as Brian John remarks, depends in Tomlinson's poetry upon the conjunction "of choice and chance." *The World as Event: The Poetry of Charles Tomlinson* (Montreal: McGill-Queen's University Press, 1989), 89.

2. Jordi Doce, "The Poet of the Eye: Charles Tomlinson Interviewed by Jordi Doce," *Agenda* 33, no. 2 (1995): 28.

3. Michael Kirkham, "Philip Larkin and Charles Tomlinson: Realism and Art," in *The Present* (Harmondsworth: Penguin, 1983), 305.

4. Michel Delville comments in a similar vein that "Tomlinson's quest for definition, unity and harmony within the fragmented and the dissonant also finds expression in his 'Ode to Arnold Schoenberg.'" "The Civility of Relationships: Charles Tomlinson and the Conversion of American Modernism," *Symbiosis* 1, no. 1 (1997): 140.

5. Brian John discusses this poem in considerable detail, pointing out that "the external world of sun, day, twilight, nighttime" appears to participate "sympathetically with the poet in enabling his wife's safe return." *World as Event*, 78. Michael Kirkham also offers an in-depth analysis of the "circular plot" of this "love poem." *Passionate Intellect: The Poetry of Charles Tomlinson* (Liverpool: Liverpool University Press, 1999), 298. (See 297–305 for full discussion of the poem.)

6. The poems offer what Michael Edwards names "a vivid Blakean celebration of the mind and its own 'sun,' its grasp, beyond presented facts, of 'all the kingdoms of possibilities.'" "The Poetry of Charles Tomlinson," in *Charles Tomlinson: Man and Artist*, ed. Kathleen O'Gorman (Columbia: University of Missouri Press, 1988), 145.

7. "Rhyme in Tomlinson's symbolism hinting as much at a hidden consonance as at fortuity, chance," Rainer Lengeler explains. "Charles Tomlinson: An Eden in Arden," in *Poetry in the British Isles: Non-Metropolitan Perspectives*, ed. Hans-Werner Ludwig and Lothar Fietz (Cardiff: University of Wales Press, 1995), 226.

8. Ruth Grogan, "Tomlinson, Ruskin, and Moore: Facts and Fir Trees," *Twentieth Century Literature* 35, no. 2 (1989): 193.

9. "Charles Tomlinson's Seeing and Believing," in *Poetry and Possibility* (Basingstoke: Macmillan, 1988), 158.

10. Richard Swigg, in *Charles Tomlinson and the Objective Tradition* (Lewisburg, Pa.: Bucknell University Press, 1994), 143.

11. John T. Irwin examines American Renaissance writers' metaphoric refer-

ences to hieroglyphical emblems in the context of nineteenth-century Egyptology, providing abundant historical and cultural background, in his 1980 book *American Hieroglyphics: The Symbol of the Egyptian Hieroglyphics in the American Renaissance* (New Haven: Yale University Press, 1980).

12. For discussion of the relationship between Tomlinson's poem and Whitman's in the context of literary allusion and imitation, see Saunders, "Text on Text: Charles Tomlinson and the Art of Sustained Allusion," *The Arkansas Quarterly* 2, no. 1 (1993): 33–35.

13. Citations are to line numbers in the 1891–92 edition, reprinted in *Leaves of Grass*, ed. Sculley Bradley and Harold W. Blodgett (New York: New York University Press, 1965), 159–65.

14. An important aspect of Michael Kirkham's purposes in *Passionate Intellect* is to investigate Tomlinson's work as "a poetry of negotiations; it is full of metaphors that imply a negotiated association or partnership—pacts, truces, treaties, leases—a vocabulary which, used equally for historical and perceptual phenomena, implies the whole civilizing enterprise of man." *Passionate Intellect*, 188.

15. Denis Donoghue writes appreciatively of the relationship between Tomlinson's "sense of limits" and his highly developed "reverence" toward the universe of forces and things outside the self: Tomlinson's attitude is "at once intelligible, reverent, and dynamic." "In the Scene of Being," *The Hudson Review* 14 (1961): 238.

16. "The Meditative Eye of Charles Tomlinson," *The Hollins Critic* 15, no. 2 (1978): 8.

17. Poems relying explicitly on the image of the musical chord include, for instance, "At Wells: polyphony" (PL), "The Impalpabilities" (PL), "Small Action Poem" (AS), "Against Extremity" (WW), "Of Beginning Light" (WrW), "Movements" (WrW), "In Arden" (S), "The Near and the Far" (F), "Programme Note" (F).

18. Ahab's fervent comment in "The Sphynx," for example, could serve as a quite accurate description of the chains of correspondence in Tomlinson's poems: "'O Nature, and O soul of man! how far beyond all utterance are your linked analogies! not the smallest atom stirs or lives in matter, but has its cunning duplicate in mind.'" Herman Melville, *Moby-Dick*, ed. Harrison Hayford and Hershel Parker (New York: Norton, 1967), 264.

19. "Like Stevens and others before him, Tomlinson is fascinated by the theme of transformation and metamorphosis. His fascination follows naturally from his view of the world—as a world which changes constantly, according to both the shifting light and the subjective perceiver," Brian John observes. He adds, moreover, that Tomlinson's "metamorphoses remain anchored firmly within time and resist transcendence." *World as Event*, 58, 60.

20. *Some Americans: A Personal Record* (Berkeley and Los Angeles: University of California Press, 1981), 9. In discussing his revulsion from any "surrender of self" in a "communion with impersonal forces," Tomlinson specifically mentions Emerson, indicating that such "striving back into original Oneness" is to him both antipathetic and false. *Some Americans*, 7–8.

21. Richard Swigg and Charles Tomlinson, "Tomlinson at Sixty," in *Man and Artist*, 232.

22. Michael Edwards argues that Tomlinson's preoccupation with perception is essentially religious, albeit non-Christian: "He sees the mysterious in the factual,"

and "a clear sighting of what is there, of what occurs, [can be] a form of worship." "Charles Tomlinson's Seeing and Believing," in *Poetry and Possibility* (Basingstoke: Macmillan, 1988), 163, 168. Edwards further explains that Tomlinson "draws back from transcendence . . . for the sake of discovering the world as a kind of permanent possibility of becoming, a continuous creation," 167–68.

23. "Everywhere in Tomlinson's art," Michael Kirkham asserts, "light, changing appearance, transfiguring fact, points to other possibilities than those realized, to other extensions of the real." *Passionate Intellect*, 251.

24. "Tomlinson at Sixty," 232.

25. As J. E. Chamberlain notes, "his poems, both early and late, offer to hold us in their spell, to keep us from conclusion, to create in us an evangelical patience for some revelation that, when it comes, will be more a suspicion than a certainty; and when it is gone, it will leave conviction without proof." "Unclenching the Mind," in *Man and Artist*, 80.

26. "Sunday Morning," in *The Palm at the End of the Mind: Selected Poems and a Play*, ed. Holly Stevens (New York: Random, 1972), 7.

27. "Charles Tomlinson," in *Eight Contemporary Poets* (London: Oxford University Press, 1975), 7.

28. "Tomlinson at Sixty," 232.

29. In chapter 5, "A Saving Grace," Michael Kirkham discusses Tomlinson's evocation of "sacramental language" and "the Christian associations of certain keywords in his poetic vocabulary." *Passionate Intellect*, 230.

30. "Charles Tomlinson Interviewed by Jordi Doce," 25.

31. "In the Scene of Being," 239. Richard Swigg, too, speaks of Tomlinson's "non-Christian yet religious impulse" as a kind of "wakened alertness." *Objective Tradition*, 78. And Michael Kirkham discusses in this context how "the act of discovering" in Tomlinson's poetry "is a kind of wakening or regeneration" and hence "wakens us, the onlookers, to new life." "An Agnostic's Grace," in *Man and Artist*, 157.

32. "Tomlinson, Ruskin, and Moore: Facts and Fir Trees," 193.

33. Donald Wesling argues that Tomlinson "sees reality in architectural terms, as an array of completed structures: skulls, bridges, texts"; thus the poems compel readers to regard individual segments of those structures in "taut contexts." "An Avant-Garde Careful and Bold," in "Fifteen Ways of Looking at a Tomlinson," *PN Review* 5, no. 1 (1977): 45. As Rainer Lengeler demonstrates, "signs of a holistic ideal are ubiquitous" in Tomlinson's poetry in general, and in "Fireflies" "subtly penetrating"—"shaping the poetical vision and structure." "An Eden in Arden," 215.

34. Formal elements contribute to Tomlinson's exploration of analogy in this poem, as Michael Kirkham points out: "the crisscross of outer and inner rhymes . . . add[s] a riddling confusion to the interplay between the real and the possible; the boundaries disappear between what is there and not there ('glows or goes'), between the solidity of 'rose' and the conjectural existence of 'suppose.'" "An Agnostic's Grace," in *Man and Artist*, 174.

35. Eden recurs as a favorite image throughout the body of Tomlinson's work, and he has discussed its essentially non-Christian but nonetheless religious evocations for him in "The Poet as Painter" as well as in interviews. Michael Kirkham provides a detailed investigation of the Eden motif in chapters 1 and 6 of *Passionate Intellect*, as well as in "An Agnostic's Grace." Useful comments on this topic may

also be found in the following: Michael Edwards, "Charles Tomlinson's Seeing and Believing"; Brian John, chapter 4 in *World as Event;* Michael Ponsford, "'To Wish Back Eden': The Community Theme in Charles Tomlinson's Verse," *The Midwest Quarterly* 30 (1989): 346–60; Willard Spiegelman, "The Rituals of Perception," *Parnassus* 7 (1979): 151–64; Joel F. Wilcox, "Tomlinson and the British Tradition," in *Man and Artist*.

36. As Edward Lobb observes, Tomlinson is "fundamentally a religious writer" in that he is "concerned with the shape and meaning of the world as a whole." His poetry "reveals the splendour of ordinary things." "By looking at things as honestly and intently as he does," moreover, "he restores their freshness and individuality; they become spiritual." "Charles Tomlinson: The Dimensions of a World." *Cambridge Quarterly* 16, no. 2 (1987): 166, 167.

37. Richard Swigg discusses Tomlinson's search for "the terms on which unfanciful wholeness might reemerge here and now," concluding that "it is the practical means that occupy him: the moment-by-moment way, without grand leaps, by which the consciousness finds a path through resistance and enters into a greater, branching whole." *Objective Tradition*, 119, 237.

38. As Brian John notes, "the thread and related imagery are more obviously visual expressions of Tomlinson's attempt to capture the dynamic and labyrinthine nature of experience." *World as Event*, 16.

Works Cited

Beaver, Harold. "Crossing Rebel Lines." Review of *Some Americans: A Record* and *The Flood*. *Parnassus* 10 (1982): 117–24.

Bedient, Calvin. "Charles Tomlinson." In *Eight Contemporary Poets*. London: Oxford University Press, 1975.

Blake, William. 1793. "The Tyger." In *English Romantic Writers*. Ed. David Perkins. New York: Harcourt, 1967.

Brown, Merle E. "Intuition vs. Perception: On Charles Tomlinson's 'Under the Moon's Reign.'" In *Double Lyric: Divisiveness and Communal Creativity in Recent English Poetry*. New York: Columbia University Press, 1980. First published in *Journal of Aesthetics and Art Criticism* 37 (1979): 277–93.

Chamberlain, J. E. "Unclenching the Mind." In *Charles Tomlinson: Man and Artist*. Ed. Kathleen O'Gorman. Columbia: University of Missouri Press, 1988.

Clark, Timothy. *Charles Tomlinson*. Plymouth: Northcote House in association with the British Council, 1999.

Cunningham, Valentine. "Flowing Benedictions." Review of *Selected Poems* and *The Shaft*. *English* 28, no. 130 (1979): 88–95.

Davie, Donald. Foreword to *Charles Tomlinson: Man and Artist*. Ed. Kathleen O'Gorman. Columbia: University of Missouri Press, 1988.

Delville, Michel. "The Civility of Relationships: Charles Tomlinson and the Conversion of American Modernism." *Symbiosis* 1, no. 1 (1997): 135–49.

Doce, Jordi. "Charles Tomlinson between Two Traditions." *Agenda* 33, no. 2 (1995): 72–96.

———. "The Poet of the Eye: Charles Tomlinson Interviewed by Jordi Doce." *Agenda* 33, no. 2 (1995): 22–30.

Donoghue, Denis. "In the Scene of Being." *The Hudson Review* 14 (1961): 232–46.

———. "The Proper Plenitude of Fact." In *The Ordinary Universe: Soundings in Modern Literature*. New York: Macmillan, 1968.

Edwards, Michael. "Charles Tomlinson: Notes on Tradition and Impersonality." *Critical Quarterly* 15 (1973): 133–44.

———. "Charles Tomlinson's Seeing and Believing." In *Poetry and Possibility*. Basingstoke: Macmillan, 1988.

———. "Collaborations." In *Charles Tomlinson: Man and Artist*. Ed. Kathleen O'Gorman. Columbia: University of Missouri Press, 1988. A version was first published as "Renga, Translation, and Eliot's Ghost" in *PN Review* 16, no. 7 (1980): 24–28.

———. "The Poetry of Charles Tomlinson." In *Charles Tomlinson: Man and Artist*.

Ed. Kathleen O'Gorman. Columbia: University of Missouri Press, 1988. First published in *Agenda* 9, no. 2–3 (1971): 127–41.

Getz, Thomas H. "Charles Tomlinson's Manscapes." *Modern Poetry Studies* 11 (1983): 207–18.

Gibbons, Reginald. "'With So Exact a Care.'" Review of *The Shaft*. *Agenda* 16, no. 2 (1978): 52–58.

Gioia, Dana. "Poetry Chronicle." *The Hudson Review* 34 (1981–82): 579–94.

Gitzen, Julian. "Charles Tomlinson and the Plenitude of Fact." *Critical Quarterly* 13 (1971): 355–62.

Grogan, Ruth. "Language and Graphics." In *Charles Tomlinson: Man and Artist*. Ed. Kathleen O'Gorman. Columbia: University of Missouri Press, 1988. First published as "Charles Tomlinson: Poet as Painter" in *Critical Quarterly* 19 (1977): 71–77.

———. "Tomlinson, Ruskin, and Language Skepticism." *Essays in Literature* 17, no. 1 (1990): 30–42.

———. "Tomlinson, Ruskin, and Moore: Facts and Fir Trees." *Twentieth Century Literature* 35, no. 2 (1989): 183–94.

Hardie, J. Keith. "Charles Tomlinson and the Language of Silence." *Boundary 2* 15, no. 1–2 (1986/1987): 211–34.

Hennessey, Michael. "Chronology." In *Charles Tomlinson: Man and Artist*. Ed. Kathleen O'Gorman. Columbia: University of Missouri Press, 1988.

———. "Perception and Self in Charles Tomlinson's Early Poetry." *Rocky Mountain Review of Language and Literature* 36 (1982): 95–102.

Hirsch, Edward. "The Meditative Eye of Charles Tomlinson." *The Hollins Critic* 15, no. 2 (1978): 1–12.

———. "'Out There Is the World': The Visual Imperative in the Poetry of George Oppen and Charles Tomlinson." In *George Oppen: Man and Poet*. Ed. Burton Hatlen. Orono, Maine: National Poetry Foundation, 1981.

Irwin, John T. *American Hieroglyphics: The Symbol of the Egyptian Hieroglyphics in the American Renaissance*. New Haven: Yale University Press, 1980.

John, Brian. *The World as Event: The Poetry of Charles Tomlinson*. Montreal: McGill-Queen's University Press, 1989.

Kirkham, Michael. "An Agnostic's Grace." In *Charles Tomlinson: Man and Artist*. Ed. Kathleen O'Gorman. Columbia: University of Missouri Press, 1988. First published in part in *PN Review* 12, no. 2 (1985): 25–26.

———. *Passionate Intellect: The Poetry of Charles Tomlinson*. Liverpool: Liverpool University Press, 1999.

———. "Philip Larkin and Charles Tomlinson: Realism and Art." In *The Present*. Vol. 8 of *The New Pelican Guide to English Literature*. Ed. Boris Ford. Harmondsworth: Penguin, 1983; reprint 1986.

Lea, Sydney. "To Use and Transform: Recent Poetry of Charles Tomlinson." *The Hudson Review* 46 (1994): 731–40.

Lee, L. L. "Charles Tomlinson as American Un-American." *Contemporary Poetry: A Journal of Criticism* 2, no. 2 (1977): 11–15.

Lengeler, Rainer. "Charles Tomlinson: An Eden in Arden." In *Poetry in the British*

Isles: Non-Metropolitan Perspectives. Ed. Hans-Werner Ludwig and Lothar Fietz. Cardiff: University of Wales Press, 1995.

Levi, Peter. In "Fifteen Ways of Looking at a Tomlinson." *PN Review* 5, no. 1 (1977): 40.

Lobb, Edward. "Charles Tomlinson: The Dimensions of a World." Review of *Collected Poems. Cambridge Quarterly* 16, no. 2 (1987): 162–68.

Lynton, Norbert. *The Story of Modern Art.* Englewood Cliffs, N.J.: Prentice-Hall, 1990.

Mariani, Paul. "Tomlinson's Use of the Williams Triad." In *Charles Tomlinson: Man and Artist.* Ed. Kathleen O'Gorman. Columbia: University of Missouri Press, 1988. First published in part in *Contemporary Literature* 18 (1977): 405–15.

Martinell, César. *Gaudi: His Life, His Theories, His Work.* Trans. Judith Rohrer. Ed. George R. Collins. Cambridge: MIT Press, 1975.

Melville, Herman. 1851. *Moby-Dick.* Ed. Harrison Hayford and Hershel Parker. New York: Norton, 1967.

Meyer, Bruce. "A Human Balance: An Interview with Charles Tomlinson." *The Hudson Review* 43, no. 3 (1990): 437–48.

O'Gorman, Kathleen, ed., *Charles Tomlinson: Man and Artist.* Columbia: University of Missouri Press, 1988.

———. "Space, Time, and Ritual in Tomlinson's Poetry." In *Charles Tomlinson: Man and Artist.* Ed. Kathleen O'Gorman. Columbia: University of Missouri Press, 1988. First published in *Sagetrieb* 2, no. 2 (1983): 85–98.

Pardee, Hearne. "A Distant Vision: Charles Tomlinson and American Art." *Partisan Review* 58 (1991): 554–62.

Paz, Octavio. "The Graphics of Charles Tomlinson." In *In Black and White: The Graphics of Charles Tomlinson.* Cheadle: Carcanet, 1976.

———. Introduction to *Renga: A Chain of Poems.* New York: Braziller, 1971.

Paz, Octavio, Jacques Roubaud, Edoardo Sanguineti, and Charles Tomlinson. *Renga: A Chain of Poems.* New York: Braziller, 1971.

Pinsky, Robert. *The Situation of Poetry: Contemporary Poetry and Its Traditions.* Princeton: Princeton University Press, 1976.

Ponsford, Michael. "Charles Tomlinson's Motorway Poems." *Notes on Contemporary Literature* 17, no. 4 (1987): 4–5.

———. "'To Wish Back Eden': The Community Theme in Charles Tomlinson's Verse." *The Midwest Quarterly* 30 (1989): 346–60.

Rasula, Jed, and Mike Erwin. "An Interview with Charles Tomlinson." *Contemporary Literature* 16, no. 4 (1975): 405–16.

Ross, Alan, and Charles Tomlinson. "Words and Water, an Interview." In *Charles Tomlinson: Man and Artist.* Ed. Kathleen O'Gorman. Columbia: University of Missouri Press, 1988. First published in *London Magazine* n.s. 20 (1981): 22–39.

Roy, Claude. Foreword to *Renga: A Chain of Poems.* New York: Braziller, 1971.

Saunders, Judith P. "Charles Tomlinson and the Automobile: Shifting Perspectives and a Moving Frame." *Sagetrieb* 14, no. 3 (1995): 107–18.

———. "Text on Text: Charles Tomlinson and the Art of Sustained Allusion." *The Arkansas Quarterly* 2, no. 1 (1993): 30–41.

———. "Tomlinson's 'October' and Keats's 'To Autumn.'" *The Explicator* 58, no. 1 (1999): 55–57.

Shakespeare, William. c. 1611. *The Tempest*. In *Shakespeare: The Complete Works*. Ed. G. B. Harrison. New York: Harcourt, 1952.

Shock of the New. No. 5 of "The Threshold of Liberty." Writ. Robert Hughes. New York: Time-Life, 1980.

Spears, Monroe K. "Shapes and Surfaces: David Jones, with a Glance at Charles Tomlinson." *Contemporary Literature* 12 (1971): 402–19.

Spiegelman, Willard. "The Rituals of Perception." Review of *Selected Poems 1951–1974* and *The Shaft*, by Charles Tomlinson. *Parnassus* 7 (1979): 151–64.

Stanton, Robert J. "Charles Tomlinson and the Process of Defining Relationships." *North Dakota Quarterly* 45, no. 3 (1977): 47–60.

Stevens, Wallace. 1923. "Peter Quince at the Clavier." In *The Palm at the End of the Mind: Selected Poems and a Play*. Ed. Holly Stevens. New York: Random, 1972.

———. "Sunday Morning." 1923. In *The Palm at the End of the Mind: Selected Poems and a Play*. Ed. Holly Stevens. New York: Random, 1972.

Swigg, Richard. *Charles Tomlinson and the Objective Tradition*. Lewisburg, Pa.: Bucknell University Press, 1994.

———. "'Our Language Is Our Land': American Form, Spanish Translation, and English Speech in the Poetry of Charles Tomlinson." *Literary Imagination* 2, no. 1 (2000): 4–20.

Swigg, Richard, and Charles Tomlinson. "Tomlinson at Sixty." In *Charles Tomlinson: Man and Artist*. Ed. Kathleen O'Gorman. Columbia: University of Missouri Press, 1988.

Thoreau, Henry D. 1854. *Walden*. Ed. J. Lyndon Shanley. Princeton: Princeton University Press, 1971.

Tomlinson, Charles. *Annunciations*. Oxford: Oxford University Press, 1989.

———. *The Collected Poems*. Rev. ed. Oxford: Oxford University Press, 1987.

———. *The Door in the Wall*. Oxford: Oxford University Press, 1992.

———. *Eden: Graphics and Poetry*. Bristol: Redcliffe, 1985.

———. *In Black and White: The Graphics of Charles Tomlinson*. Cheadle: Carcanet, 1976.

———. *Jubilation*. Oxford: Oxford University Press, 1995.

———. Letter to the author. 2 February 1994.

———. Letter to the author. 19 July 1997.

———. Letter to the author. 30 December 2001.

———. "The Poet as Painter." In *Eden: Graphics and Poetry*. Bristol: Redcliffe, 1985. First published in *Essays by Divers Hands: Innovation in Contemporary Literature*. n.s. 9. Ed. Vincent Cronin, FRSL. Woodbridge: Boydell, 1979.

———. *The Return*. Oxford: Oxford University Press, 1987.

———. *Some Americans: A Personal Record*. Berkeley and Los Angeles: University of California Press, 1981.

———. "To Begin: Notes on Graphics." In *In Black and White: The Graphics of Charles Tomlinson*. Cheadle: Carcanet, 1976.

———. "The Unison: A Retrospect." In *Renga: A Chain of Poems*. New York: Braziller, 1971.

———. *The Vineyard Above the Sea*. Manchester: Carcanet, 1999.

———. *William Carlos Williams: A Critical Anthology*. Harmondsworth: Penguin, 1972.

———. *William Carlos Williams: Selected Poems*. Harmondsworth: Penguin, 1976.

Watkins, Evan. "Charles Tomlinson: The Poetry of Experience." In *The Critical Act: Criticism and Community*. New Haven: Yale University Press, 1978.

Weatherhead, A. Kingsley. "Charles Tomlinson." In *The British Dissonance: Essays on Ten Contemporary Poets*. Columbia: University of Missouri Press, 1983.

Wesling, Donald. "An Avant-Garde Careful and Bold." In "Fifteen Ways of Looking at a Tomlinson." *PN Review* 5, no. 1 (1977): 43–45.

———. *The Chances of Rhyme: Device and Modernity*. Berkeley and Los Angeles: University of California Press, 1980.

———. "Process and Closure in Tomlinson's Prose Poems." In *Charles Tomlinson: Man and Artist*. Ed. Kathleen O'Gorman. Columbia: University of Missouri Press, 1988.

Whitman, Walt. "Crossing Brooklyn Ferry." 1891–92. Reprinted in *Leaves of Grass*. Ed. Sculley Bradley and Harold W. Blodgett. New York: New York University Press, 1965. New York: Norton, 1975.

Wilcox, Joel F. "Tomlinson and the British Tradition." In *Charles Tomlinson: Man and Artist*. Ed. Kathleen O'Gorman. Columbia: University of Missouri Press, 1988.

Yeats, W. B. "Sailing to Byzantium." *The Poems*. Ed. Richard J. Finneran. New York: Macmillan, 1983.

Young, Alan. "Rooted Horizon: Charles Tomlinson and American Modernism." *Critical Quarterly* 24, no. 4 (1982): 67–73.

General Index

Citation of the context in which a note reference occurs is given in parentheses.

Allegro, L' (Milton), 58
Amis, Kingsley, 175n. 11 (60)

Baudelaire, Charles Pierre: *Le Soleil*, 178n. 14 (86)
Bertolani, Pablo, 59–60
Blake, James W.: *The Sidewalks of New York*, 58
Blake, William: *The Tyger*, 96–97, 183n. 6 (153)

Catullus, 89
Cervantes, Miguel de: *Don Quixote*, 92
chord, 159–60, 161
Coleridge, Samuel Taylor: *Kubla Khan*, 100
Creeley, Robert, 61
Crossing Brooklyn Ferry (Whitman), 157–59
cubism, 109

Davie, Donald, 60, 173n. 1 (19)
decalcomania, 126–28, 131, 138, 139, 141, 143
Duncan, Robert, 61

Eden, 131, 169
Eliot, T. S.: *The Waste Land*, 64–65
Emerson, Ralph Waldo, 162, 184n. 20 (163)
Endymion, 122
enjambment (line breaks), 47, 48, 75, 84, 105

Freudian theory: id/ego/superego, 22–23, 130
Frost, Robert: *Spring Pools*, 137

Gaudi, Antoni, 126, 127, 138, 139
Golden Flowerpot, The (Hoffmann), 181n. 18 (122)
Gulliver's Travels (Swift), 91

hieroglyphs, 156
Hoffmann, E. T. A.: *The Golden Flowerpot*, 181n. 18 (122)
Hopkins, Gerard Manley, 173n. 2

Keats, John: *Ode on a Grecian Urn*, 113; *To Autumn*, 174n. 6 (28)
Kenner, Hugh, 61
Kubla Khan (Coleridge), 100

Line Breaks (enjambment), 47, 48, 75, 84, 105

Machado, Antonio, 62
Melville, Herman: *Moby-Dick*, 59, 184n. 18 (162)
Merleau-Ponty, Maurice, 181n. 11 (114)
Milton, John: *L'Allegro*, 58
Moby-Dick (Melville), 59, 184n. 18 (162)
Mondrian, Piet, 94–95, 100
Moore, Marianne, 61, 62

Ode on a Grecian Urn (Keats), 113
O'Keeffe, Georgia, 61, 62
Oppen, George, 60, 61, 62
Ovid, 62

Paz, Octavio: comments on Tomlinson's graphics, 118–19, 126, 138; comments on Tomlinson's poetry, 123; friendship with Tomlinson, 67; influ-

ence on Tomlinson, 60, 177n. 7 (80); translation and collaboration with Tomlinson: 62, 63, 64; *Airborn / Hijos del Aire*, 64; *Renga: A Chain of Poems*, 63, 64
Peter Quince at the Clavier (Stevens), 174n. 7 (29)
Plato, 114
Pound, Ezra, 62; *Cantos*, 64

rhyme, 22, 47, 65, 66, 70, 83–89, 94–95, 150, 152–53, 154, 155, 160, 170, 185n. 34 (169)
Rilke, Rainer Maria, 66
Roubaud, Jaques: *Renga: A Chain of Poems*, 63
Roy, Claude: *Renga: A Chain of Poems*, 176n. 22 (63), 176n. 25 (64)
Ruskin, John, 166

Sailing to Byzantium (Yeats), 57–59
Sancho Panza (Cervantes), 92
Sanguineti, Edoardo: *Renga: A Chain of Poems*, 63
Schoenberg, Arnold, 78
Shakespeare, William: *The Tempest*, 117–18
Shelley, Percy Bysshe, 62
Soleil, Le (Baudelaire), 178n. 14 (86)
sonnet, 63–64, 82
Spring Pools (Frost), 137
stanza, 17–18, 47, 70, 83, 146
Stevens, Wallace, 61, 62, 184n. 19 (163); *Peter Quince at the Clavier*, 174n. 7 (29); *Sunday Morning*, 165
Sunday Morning (Stevens), 165
Swift, Jonathan: *Gulliver's Travels*, 91

Tempest, The (Shakespeare), 117–18
Thoreau, Henry David, 162; *Walden*, 182n. 15 (142)
To Autumn (Keats), 174 n. 6 (28)
Tomlinson, Charles: foreign languages, 62–63, 64–67; interest in film, 143–44; international reputation, 61, 176n. 18 (62); translation projects, 62–63, 64; travel and residence abroad, 59–62, 67–68, 175n. 12 (61). Works: *Airborn / Hijos del Aire*, 64, 82; *Annunciations*, 161; *The Door in the Wall*, 67; *In Black and White: The Graphics of Charles Tomlinson*, 126, 182n. 8 (133); *Notes from New York*, 60–61; *The Poet as Painter*, 19, 87–88, 88–89, 126, 127, 129, 138, 153; *Renga: A Chain of Poems*, 63–64, 68, 82; *The Return*, 61; *Seeing is Believing*, 102, 114; *Some Americans: A Personal Record*, 62, 184n. 20 (163); *William Carlos Williams: A Critical Anthology*, 62; *William Carlos Williams: Selected Poems*, 61. See also Index of Poems by Charles Tomlinson
Touch of Evil, A (Welles), 143
Transcendentalism, 156, 157–59, 162; Oversoul, 163
triadic line, 78, 83
Tyger, The (Blake), 96–97, 183n. 6 (153)

Ungaretti, Giuseppe, 62

Vallejo, César, 62
Van Gogh, Vincent, 100

Wagner, Richard, 65–66
Walden (Thoreau), 182n. 15 (142)
Waste Land, The (Eliot), 64–65
Webern, Anton von, 78
Welles, Orson: *A Touch of Evil*, 143
Whitman, Walt, 61, 162, 182n. 14 (140); *Crossing Brooklyn Ferry*, 157–59
Williams, William Carlos, 61, 62
Winters, Ivor, 61

Yeats, William Butler: *Sailing to Byzantium*, 57–59

Zukovsky, Louis, 61

Index of Poems by Charles Tomlinson

"Above the Rio Grande," 153, 161–62
"After a Death," 19, 23, 28–29
"Against Extremity," 159, 184 n. 17 (160)
"Against Travel," 178 n. 12 (86)
"Along the Mohawk," 42–43, 52
"All Afternoon," 110
"Annunciation," 164
"Arch, The," 142–43
"Arizona Highway," 139–40
"Art of Poetry, The," 20, 125
"At a Glance," 23, 163–64
"At Barstow," 65–66
"At Bob Lucid's Place," 125
"At Delft," 30
"At Hanratty's," 53–54
"At Holwell Farm," 72–73, 90, 149, 174 n. 5 (28)
"At Huexotla," 165
"At the Autumn Equinox," 32–33
"At the Edge," 16, 24, 53, 136–37, 170
"At the Hill Fort," 29
"At the Trade Center," 60, 134
"At Trotsky's House," 61
"At Wells: polyphony," 160
"Atlantic, The," 20, 71
"Autumn," 20, 97

"Before the Concert," 112–13
"Below Tintern," 136
"Black Brook," 111
"Black Nude," 24, 126
"Blade, The," 26–28
"Blaubeuren," 166–67
"Bluebells," 156–57
"Bootblack, The," 50–51
"By Night," 128–29
"Byzantium," 56–59

"Carscape," 139
"Casarola," 19, 35

"Cavern, The," 129–30
"Ceci n'est pas une Pipe," 119
"Chance," 70, 152–53
"Chances of Rhyme, The," 74, 86–89
"Chestnut Avenue: at Alton House, The," 71
"Chronochromie," 166
"Churchyard Wall, The," 125
"Civilities of Lamplight," 30
"Cloud Change," 19, 98–99
"Comedy," 99–100, 103
"Consolations for Double Bass," 90–92
"Constitution Day," 50
"Cronkhite Beach," 72, 117
"Crossing Aguadilla," 54
"Crossing Brooklyn Ferry," 157–59
"Crossing the Moor," 74
"Cycle, The," 29–30
"Cypresses," 119, 166

"December," 20
"Death in the Desert, A," 29
"Departure," 148, 151
"Dialogue," 80, 126
"Discovery, The," 75, 133, 145
"Door, The," 126, 132
"Drawing Down the Moon," 122–23
"Drive," 140–41

"Embassy," 178 n. 12 (86)

"Far Point," 38–40
"Faring, The," 160, 168, 169, 178 n. 12 (86)
"February," 89
"Fiascherino," 77, 79
"Fire," 25, 73
"Fireflies," 168
"Flood, The," 23

INDEX OF POEMS BY CHARLES TOMLINSON

"Focus" (part IV from "In Winter Woods"), 130–31
"For Want of Seraphim," 165–66, 168–69
"Fountain," 102
"Fox Gallery, The," 30–31
"Foxes' Moon," 31–32
"From Porlock," 100
"From the Motorway," 37–38

"Gap, The," 131
"Garden, The," 126, 133–34
"Gate, The," 131–32
"Geese Going South," 33
"Glacier, The" 19
"Gutenberg and the Grapes," 153

"Harvest," 28, 178n. 12 (86)
"Hawks," 72
"The Hawthorn in Trent Vale," 36–37
"Head Hewn with an Axe," 24–25
"Hedgerows," 17, 41, 146
"Here and There," 56, 116, 153
"Hero Sandwiches," 61
"Hill Walk," 72, 178n. 12 (86)
"History of a House," 73
"History of a Malady," 89–90
"Hyphens," 104–5

"Icos," 20
"Images of Pefection," 28
"Impalpabilities, The," 97, 184n. 17 (160)
"In a Cambridge Garden," 67–68
"In Abruzzo," 19, 60
"In April," 28, 72
"In Arden," 72, 169, 178n. 12 (86), 184n. 17 (160)
"In March," 19, 26, 27, 28
"In Michoacán," 46–47, 83, 92–93
"In New Mexico," 160–61
"In the Balance," 72
"In the Emperor's Garden," 47–48
"In the Estuary," 77
"In the Room," 114
"In the Ward," 106–7
"In Winter Woods" (IV, "Focus"), 130–31
"Insistence of Things, The," 115, 117

"Interior," 113–14
"Into Distance," 70

"Jemez," 43–44
"Journey, The," 119

"Lament for Doormen," 60–61
"Legend," 19, 134
"Letter from Costa Brava," 72
"Letter to Uehata," 55, 116
"Like Greek Prose," 83–84, 89
"Lines," 71
"Listening to Leaves," 28, 79
"Logic," 79, 98
"Los Pobrecitos," 49–50, 84–86, 89, 92, 128

"Macchu Picchu," 56, 75
"MacKinnon's Boat," 21, 77–78
"Marine," 21
"Matachines, The" 51–52
"Meditation on John Constable, A," 118
"Mediterranean, The" 52–53
"Metamorphosis, The," 155–56
"Miracle of the Bottle and the Fishes, The," 145
"Mirror in the Roadway, The," 110–11
"Morning Moon, The," 107–8
"Morwenna's Cliff," 19, 20, 61, 77
"Movements," 79, 146, 152, 169, 170–71, 178n. 12 (86), 184n. 17 (160)
"Misprint," 75
"Mushrooms," 117, 123, 155
"Music and the Poet's Cat," 29

"9 A.M.," 111–12
"Nature Poem," 80, 119
"Near and the Far, The," 184n. 17 (160)
"Near Bickering," 19
"Near Corinium," 42, 151
"Near Hartland," 61
"Netherlands," 60, 94–95
"Night Ferry," 169
"Night Fishers," 168
"Night-Piece: The Near and the Far," 128
"Night Ride," 142
"Night Transfigured," 103

"Nine Variations on a Chinese Winter Setting," 144

"October," 28
"Ode to Arnold Schoenberg," 78–79, 83
"Of Beginning Light," 184 n. 17 (160)
"On a Collage of Marie José Paz," 145–46
"On a Glass Engraving by Peter David," 153
"On a Landscape by Li Ch'eng," 93–94
"On Madison," 51, 60
"On the Dunes," 72
"On the Principle of Blowclocks," 80–82, 90
"Oppositions," 73, 125
"Orion Over Farne," 72

"Palermo," 139
"Paris in Sixty-Nine," 60
"Parking Lot," 111, 137–38
"Peace Between Us, William Blake," 178–79 n. 23 (96)
"Peak, The," 33–34
"Perfection, The," 97
"Picking Mushrooms by Moonlight," 148–51, 154, 178 n. 12 (86)
"Picture of J. T. in a Prospect of Stone, The," 132
"Poem," 117
"Poem for my Father," 41–42, 61
"Porto Venere," 21
"Portuguese Pieces," 60; IV, "Swallows," 133
"Prisoner, The," 119–22
"Process, A," 71–72
"Programme Note," 184 n. 17 (160)

"Reeds," 20
"Reflections," 29, 134
"Response to Hopkins," 173 n. 2
"Return, The," 20, 70, 160, 178 n. 12 (86)
"Rhymes," 152, 170, 178 n. 12 (86)
"Roman Fugue," 89
"Rua do Carrical," 44–45
"Ruin, The," 125

"San Fruttuoso," 21
"San Juan," 54

"Sea Change," 97–98
"Second Song," 169–70
"Sense of Distance, A" 55, 116, 122, 144
"September Swamp," 21–23
"Shaft, The," 132–33
"Shadow, The," 25–26
"Shorelines," 77
"Sight and Flight," 24, 116, 117, 139
"Skullshapes," 115
"Small Action Poem," 144–45, 184 n. 17 (160)
"Snow Fences, The," 29
"Song," 115
"Stair, The," 112, 113
"Steel," 21
"Stone Walls: at Chew Magna," 24
"Suggestions for the Improvement of a Sunset," 23–24
"Swallows" (IV from "Portuguese Pieces"), 133
"Swimming Chenango lake," 76

"Tax Inspector, The," 66
"Teotihuacán," 45–46
"Through Binoculars," 103–4, 119
"Tiger Skull," 95–97
"To Ivor Gurney," 61
"To Modulate," 113
"To My Daughter," 68, 152, 178 n. 12 (86)
"Tout Entouré de Mon Regard," 170
"The Track of the Deer," 116
"Transaction at Mallards Pike," 135–36
"Trebiano," 35, 162–63
"Tree, The," 105–6
"Tree House, The," 113
"Trees, The," 23–24
"Tübingen," 60
"Two Views of Two Ghost Towns," 35–36
"Tyrrenhean: From the train," 107, 115

"Up at La Serra," 72
"Upstate," 28, 34–35, 41

"Valle de Oaxaco," 61
"Van Gogh," 100

"Varenna," 28
"Variant on a Scrap of Conversation," 108–9
"Variation," 153
"Venice," 125, 126
"View, The," 128
"Vineyard Above the Sea, The," 153–55

"Way of a World, The," 97
"Way Through, The," 137
"Weather Report," 37

"Weeper in Jalisco," 48–49
"Well, The," 136
"White Van, The," 104
"Windshield, The," 138, 141–42
"Winter Encounters," 70
"Winter Journey," 151–52, 178n. 12 (86)
"Winter-Piece," 20
"Words for the Madrigalist," 79–80, 83
"Writing on Sand," 36, 72

"Zipangu," 60